ANABAPTISM IN TYROL
FAITHFUL RESILIENCE THROUGH PERSECUTION
(1526-1626)

JOHANN LOSERTH

Translated by
H. HUGO BRINKMANN
Edited by
JONATHAN R. SEILING

ISBN: 978-0-9880993-5-7

A translation by Hugo Brinkmann of the two volumes by Johann Loserth: "Der Anabaptismus in Tirol: Von seinen Anfängen bis zum Tode Jakob Huters (1526–1536)," *Archiv für österreichische Geschichte* 78, 1892, 427–604; "Der Anabaptismus in Tirol: Vom Jahre 1536 bis zu seinem Erlöschen," *Archiv für österreichische Geschichte* 79, 1893, 127–276.

Emmy Barth Maendel, archivist and research scholar at Foxhill Bruderhof Community made available for publication the draft translation by Hugo Brinkmann, which he had completed prior to his death in 2011. Jonathan Seiling reviewed and revised the translation, with assistance from Zoe Suderman.

Cover graphic design by Imran Alizada.

Copyright © 2022 Gelassenheit Publications, Ltd.

73 Dufferin Street, St Catharines, Ohni:kara, Ontario, L2R 1Z9 Canada

All rights reserved.

No part of this book may be reproduced in any form or by any electronic or mechanical means, including information storage and retrieval systems, without written permission from the publisher, except for the use of brief quotations in a book review.

Die gmain, die christlich muetter,
die hat vil sön verlorn
bis auf den Jacob Huetter,
den hat Gott auserkorn.

The church, the Christian Mother,
so many sons has lost,
among them Jakob Hutter,
whom God himself did choose.

    Song by Jörg Bruckmaier

CONTENTS

Foreword   vii
Preface   xi

ITS BEGINNINGS TO THE DEATH OF HUTTER, 1526-36

1. Jakob Strauss and Urbanus Rhegius in Hall   3
2. The Rise of Anabaptism in Tyrol   18
3. Inroads and State Counter-Measures   29
4. North and South of the Brenner Pass   37
5. Hutter and Persecution in Tyrol, 1529-30   47
6. The Principal Mandate of May 12, 1532   62
7. "Hutterian Brethren" in Moravia   81
8. The Trial of the Wolkenstein Family, 1534   90
9. Persecution in Moravia   102
10. Persecution in Austria and Beyond in 1535   107
11. Hutter's Trial and Execution   115

FROM HUTTER'S DEATH TO EXTINCTION, 1536-1626

1. Post-Hutter: Offrus Griesinger, 1536-1538   127
2. Innsbruck Regional Government, 1539-1545   157
3. Hans Mändl's Activity and Trial, 1548-1561   179
4. Hansl Kräl's Election, 1561-1578   197
5. Anabaptists in the Bregenz Forest   206
6. Anabaptists in Tyrol, 1579-1599   212
7. Extinction of Tyrolean Anabaptism, 1600-1626   225

Notes   229
Index   263

FOREWORD

The following study is prominent among the early works on Anabaptism by the renowned historian, Johann Loserth (1846-1936). *Anabaptism in Tyrol* was first published in German as two separate volumes: In 1892, the first volume appeared in the *Archiv für österreichische Geschichte* with the subtitle, "From its Beginnings until the Death of Jakob Hutter (1526-1536)." In 1893, the same year Loserth became a professor of history at the University of Graz, Austria, the second volume appeared in the same journal with the subtitle, "From 1536 until Its Extinction." The sources he included in the appendices of both volumes, which have been omitted here, further enriched these groundbreaking studies.

As a combined two-volume study covering one century of the rise and demise of Anabaptism in Tyrol it is unfortunate that it waited 130 years to be published in English. Written in a journalistic style, Loserth assembles the massive trove of archival sources collected by the Austrian jurist and scholar, Dr. Josef R. von Beck (1815-1887), a debt which Loserth acknowledges on the title page of both volumes. While working as a judge in Bratislava in the 1850s, Beck began copying documents related to the history of Anabaptism which he found in archives throughout the Austro-Hungarian Empire. Included and preserved in

Beck's collection were also the writings by Anabaptists (and Hutterites in particular), which were confiscated and then stored in state archives. After the death of Beck, Loserth inherited his archival holdings, enabling him to undertake a series of wide-ranging studies based on these rare documentary sources; Loserth states in the preface that he made use of 1,317 documents on Tyrol from Beck's collection in preparing this study. Today the vast holdings of the "Beck collection" are made available at the state archives in Brno, Moravia in Czechia.

Born in Moravia, Johann Loserth was a Catholic who initially specialized in late medieval theology, earning his doctorate on the writings of John Wyclif and their impact on Jan Hus and the Hussite movement in Bohemia. This research incidentally led him to uncover several previously unknown Anabaptist communities in Austro-Hungary, which fuelled his scholarship for decades. He soon became a giant in the growing field of Anabaptist studies by standing on the shoulders of Josef von Beck's archival collection, also exploring beyond the extent of Beck's research.

Although Loserth already produced one article on Anabaptism in Moravia in 1884,[1] it was largely due to the Beck collection that he was able to publish a series of influential historical studies between 1891-1895, ranging from key leaders like Hubmaier, Blaurock and Hutter, covering large geographic regions of Tyrol, Bohemia, Hungary, Carinthia and smaller locales like Steiermark.[2] Until the end of his career he continued to edit sources and publish studies which profoundly shaped the general study of Anabaptism for the next century, including his work on Pilgram Marpeck.[3]

The value of *Anabaptism in Tyrol* is not primarily found in Loserth's own brief summaries of persons, places and events, but equally if not more so, in his inclusion of copious sources that were otherwise inaccessible, as he explains in the preface. Many archival sources Loserth quotes within the pages of this book are made available here in English for the first time in the nearly five centuries since they were penned.

Given Josef von Beck's legal profession, his interest in the juridical processes leading to the condemnation and execution of Anabaptists, the Beck Collection offers a wide-ranging and detailed conception of how Tyrol and Moravia applied the respective "anti-Anabaptist" imperial mandates. For this reason, persecution of Anabaptists is clarified throughout these two volumes extensively; for Tyrol, it is a topic of particular relevance within the scope of the trans-continental Anabaptist movements. If one compares the numbers of executions of Anabaptists in the first years of the mandates (pre-1530) and the numbers following 1530, Tyrol appears to have a disproportionately high rate of execution.[4] The decades of renewed and redesigned mandates against the Anabaptists, and their enforcement through acts of torture and execution, demonstrate both the tenacity of Anabaptists and the trenchant determination by the state to eradicate them from Tyrol. Beck paid particularly close attention to the lives and fates of Hutterite leaders and Loserth makes occasional mention of Protestants or "pre-Protestant" radicals in Tyrol and elsewhere, while describing vivacious Anabaptists and their virulent oppressors in stark contrast.[5]

The reader is presented therefore, with sources from the perspectives of both the state apparatus and Anabaptists themselves, including those non-Anabaptists who sympathized with their plight during the worst years of persecution. Loserth's discerning view of the imperial government's role in the decades of political turmoil—the various phases of the Reformations in Europe—also convey his empathy for the Moravian lords who struggled to maintain autonomy and resist encroachment by the Habsburgs. His source base included copious volumes of testimonies from Anabaptists and official government correspondence, particularly in Tyrol.[6]

For this reason it seemed fitting to replace the two, lengthy subtitles of the original publications with a few words that best describe what Loserth and Beck seemed inclined to highlight: the faithful resilience of the Anabaptist communities that originated in Tyrol and their experience through one century of persecution.

A few notes on the translator's approach may be warranted:

The translator has inserted some references to the English translation of the *Geschichtsbucher*, referring to the 1987 edition of *The Chron-*

icle of the Hutterian Brethren, volume 1. This edition is currently being updated and prepared for a re-issue, but until the new edition appears it seemed worthwhile to preserve the translator's insertion of the page numbers to the 1987 edition.

Names of people and places, which are sometimes provided in Italian and German, have largely been reproduced as Loserth stated them (for example, see the multiple spellings of Onofrius Griesinger), and in the endnotes the references appear as Loserth stated them ('Pressburg' instead of Bratislava); sometimes these proper nouns derive from historical sources in which orthography differs from modern spelling. However, in the case of Jakob Hutter, we have opted the common English usage of "Hutter" instead of "Huetter" or "Huter" as one usually finds in German.

Jonathan Seiling
    St Catharines, Ontario
    April 28, 2022, updated November 17, 2022

PREFACE

Among the unpublished papers Court Counsellor Dr. Josef von Beck has bequeathed to me for literary use there are *inter alia* numerous documents as well as extracts from such, correspondences etc. totalling 1,317 documents in 29 fascicles, which contain materials of importance for the history of the Anabaptists in Tyrol. Over a number of years Court Counsellor v. Beck had been collecting them in the imperial and royal house, court, and state archives, the archives of the imperial and royal ministries of finance, of culture and education as well as the archives of Brünn, Graz, Linz, Salzburg, Innsbruck, Brixen (Bressanone), Schaffhausen, Basel, Zurich, Munich, Nuremberg, and Augsburg, finally also in the libraries of Pressburg, Gran, and Pest. The most productive archives for the history of the Anabaptists in the alpine districts of Upper Austria are the Regents' Archives (*Statthalterarchiv*) at Innsbruck, which accordingly were also the most eagerly researched by J. v. Beck. Of the more important documents, he either made copied or requested them to be made in whole, while obtaining excerpts from others.

In its current state, this collection provides a graphic picture of the origin, the gradual expansion, and the suppression of Anabaptism in Tyrol during the course of a whole century (1526-1626), which was fraught with all kinds of difficulties. Of special interest is that section of the Tyrolean Anabaptist movement up to the death of Jakob Hutter, and it is that period that will be portrayed in the following pages.

As part of this section we not only present the materials just mentioned but also two sketches for a biography of Jakob Hutter—one of them brief, the other more extensive—which, though in no way ready for the press, nevertheless throw light on the way J. v. Beck intended the subject to be presented. True, neither was the whole of the material the author had gathered used for these sketches nor do they treat the subject in a clearly organized manner. Hence that situation required, to begin with, an integration and corresponding revision of Beck's presentation; for some individual chapters it demanded a total reworking of the subject.

With Hutter's death the Anabaptist movement in Tyrol had passed its climax, but also during the following decades it still presents a wealth of remarkable phenomena, which are due to be presented in a second and concluding treatise. For this period (1537 to 1626), too, J. v. Beck's literary bequest contains copious material he had gathered.

As regards the individual chapters of the following treatise, the first one has been kept shorter than the rest in view of the available pertinent works on the subject by Schönherr, Ruf, Waldner, and others.

[Omitted here is Loserth's description of the contents of the appendices, which included reproductions of archival sources that have not been included in this edition.]

Czernowitz, September 30, 1891.

J. Loserth

[Note: Loserth only prepared a preface for the first volume of *Anabaptism in Tyrol*, while the second volume contained no preface.]

Professor Dr. Johann Loserth (1846-1936)

ITS BEGINNINGS TO THE DEATH OF HUTTER, 1526-36

1
JAKOB STRAUSS AND URBANUS RHEGIUS IN HALL

PROTESTANT STIRRINGS IN TYROL: 1520-1525

ANABAPTISM SHARES with Protestantism the soil on which it grew. Just as in Switzerland and in Germany so in Tyrol, too, it appeared as the later-born offspring of the Reformation. According to the testimony of Heinrich Bullinger, it was the "Evangelicals" who prepared the ground for it in peasant huts and mining shafts, in the houses of burghers and the castles of noblemen.[1] From the teaching of the new "unfettered Gospel" all the malcontents in the country expected their spiritual and material well-being, hence the encouragement the evangelicals were being given everywhere, this in addition to the weakness of the clergy and the perplexities of a nonplussed and inactive regional administration, which only pulled itself together in the wake of the peasant revolt.

In defiance of the ruling prince's mandates,[2] a lot of Lutheran writings had been brought in and spread about by the many miners attracted by the rich ores of the Falkenstein, the Pfunderer Mountain, and other mining shafts, as well as by traveling merchants and bookkeepers, vagrants and mercenaries. These in turn drew in their wake all sorts of unsettled adventurers, who had become unfaithful to the established church and pretended to be missionaries of the unadulterated word of God, which was alleged to have been obscured and "fettered" until then. It may be true that some individuals meant it seriously, but there were many that only wanted to cause a great stir and be provided with bread and a job, and the more zealously such people railed in front of a crowd against the existing order, always eager for exciting novelties against the church and its institutions, the more popular they became.

An emissary of the new gospel, a certain Konrad from Swabia, in 1520-1521 was in this manner, moving about in the area of Meran, Brixen, and Sterzing. In 1521 a similar mission was carried out in the Inn valley by a former cleric from Berchtesgaden, Dr. Jakob Strauss.[3] At the invitation of the Schwaz ore miners he preached open-air sermons at Schwaz, which were well attended but did not breathe the gentleness of Christian love nor obedience to the authorities.[4] Having handed the preaching at Schwaz over to two monks from Berchtesgaden[5] Strauss moved in 1521 to Hall, where to begin with, he gave Latin lectures to the clergy about the Gospel of Matthew. "They accorded him great honor and came to know him as able and erudite."[6] A little later he started preaching in the Salvator's Church of the women's cloister in Hall, and when this church became too small for the increasing crowds, he switched to the pulpit of the parish church of St. Nicholas, with the consent of the parish priest Dr. Stephan Seligmann and of the town magistrate. In good weather he would preach in the town park or in the upper square. As Schweyger's *Chronicle* relates, he "possessed an excellent elocution and greatly pleased the common people with his preaching, but he heatedly attacked the clergy—bishops, priests, monks, and nuns—, criticizing and condemning their spiritual condition, bringing to light their abuses and inveighing against them. In part he also rejected ceremonies and church customs."

When summoned to Brixen by the bishop on account of these excesses, Strauss failed to appear and left it to the town council and the parishioners to defend him. These tried to justify him before the bishop and the government but without success. Nevertheless the "honorable council" kept its protective hand over him even then and had him accompanied and guarded by a number of armed citizens. On

Estomihi Sunday (March 2) when, after his sermon, Strauss refused "with heated words" to obey a renewed summons by the bishop, his escort chased away the two episcopal messengers and pursued them right to the house of the Lord.[7] This resulted in a serious riot, which was only calmed by some "good words" on the part of the two burgomasters Fuchsmagen and Waltenhofer. The council promised the emissaries that they would handle the preacher's case themselves and would send the bishop a message. After Strauss had submitted to the council a written statement in his defense, the council sent to Brixen an account "of Dr. Jakob's origin, bearing, and character and of how he conducted himself when preaching" and requested that he be left unhindered, as "his sermons were considered evangelical and just." The deputation left Hall on March 13, but does not seem to have achieved its objective, for it now turned to the government in Innsbruck with the request that the preacher be left unmolested.

The government asked the bishop not to press the matter, as things could be expected to gradually improve of their own accord, and the bishop refrained indeed from taking immediate action, following the emperor's direction to proceed in these matters in accordance with the advice of the Innsbruck government; he added, though, that he found it very hard to allow such a false teacher to preach. Strauss could now go on with his Lenten sermons and was guarded by the people and the town council against possible attacks.[8] Soon afterwards the bishop again asked the Innsbruck authorities to see to it that Strauss be sent away from Hall or be taken to Brixen to answer the charges against him.

This missive, too, remained unsuccessful. The bishop therefore sent three monitory letters to the parish priest Angerer in Innsbruck with the request to have one affixed to the parish church in Hall, the second one in Taur, and the third in Innsbruck. Even before this could be done, the government on April 22 reminded the Hall town council of the Edict of Worms and of the imperial mandate to do away with any Lutheran writing and false doctrine and ordered them to immediately get rid of that doctor Strauss as a "dangerous false teacher and rebel" and to do this secretly so as not to cause any disturbance among the people.

The Hall town council did make another attempt to let the government see the preacher in a more favorable light, but the bishop had already placed the matter before the metropolitan and the emperor. Now Strauss himself was summoned to appear before the government and the council was asked to send him out of the country.

On *Misericordia* Sunday (May 4) Strauss preached his farewell sermon in front of a large crowd of people from both town and countryside. "He informed them of his being torn away and mightily stirred up most of them—some to sadness and tears, some to wrath, some to disrespect and rebelliousness toward the priesthood. The following week, after a festive meal in his honor he left secretly, accompanied by two citizens, and took the nearest road toward Saxony."

From Haslach, Strauss addressed to the "honorable, dear lords and friends at Hall" a memorandum entitled "A brief Christian instruction on the false brotherhoods."[9] From there he moved on to Kemberg, a small town near Wittenberg. On August 4, he completed the sermon entitled: "A sensible and comforting teaching about St. Paul's phrase, that a man should examine himself first, and then eat the bread and drink from the cup (1 Cor 11:28); given at Hall in the Inn valley by Dr. Jakob Strauss in MDXXII. Buy and read it; it will please you."[10] The preface is dated August 4.

Strauss notes that he wrote out this sermon at the request of, and as a favor to, the whole parish and neighborhood at Hall. It was put into print when Strauss already was a cleric in Eisenach.[11] The treatise is mainly directed against abuses of confession and of the Lord's Supper and contains blistering invective against the Franciscans in Hall. He calls them seducers of the people, stone-blind and unlearned, who have never yet properly understood and preached one single word. The same violent tone is found also in other writings he sent from Eisenach in 1523, once more to his dear friends in Hall.[12]

Strauss, by the way, was also very dissatisfied with the Wittenberg reformation, commenting "if all the Lutherans want is to vex people, it would have been better if they had left it alone."[13]

The common people in Hall were so zealous in spreading their departed preacher's writings that they incurred the government's censure as follows: "Even though His Serene Highness has in his patrimonial dominions issued strict orders against the innovations and teachings of Luther, we hear nevertheless that in Hall Lutheran books and treatises are being publicly offered for sale and purchased." The town council is earnestly exhorted to act in accordance with the mandates issued.[14]

In place of Dr. Jakob Strauss the town council of Hall appointed Dr. Urbanus Rhegius and presented him to the bishop. All the Schweyger *Chronicle* has to tell about this "excellent and most erudite man" is that he was a preacher in Hall for "about two years," until the bishop and the reigning prince forbade him to remain there because of his preaching and he secretly escaped to Augsburg.

By the time he appeared in Hall, Urbanus Rhegius had already had quite an eventful past.[15] When Bishop Christoph of Stadion in 1520, appointed him at [the court preacher Dr. Johann] Fabri's recommendation, as cathedral preacher in Augsburg 1520, he proved a zealous champion of the new doctrine, and after arriving in Hall in September 1522, he was active there in the same spirit as his predecessor Strauss. As his sermons demonstrate, he inveighed particularly against indulgence peddlers and the evil of maintaining courtesans, against kermesses (church dedications) and holidays, against the pomp and images in churches, against fraternities and the use of the Latin language in church services, against the cult of Mary, the adoration of saints, against ordinations, offerings, and the saying of Mass.

When summoned to Brixen to answer charges, he refused to go there unless granted safe-conduct. This being denied at the government's advice,[16] Brixen asked the Innsbruck regents to have Rhegius sent away from Hall, lest the Lutheran doctrine continue to spread in Hall and the whole Inn valley.[17] The government replied that Rhegius was indeed in Hall but recently had preached neither publicly nor in secret, and given that His Serene Highness on a recent visit to Hall[18] had personally concerned himself with the aforementioned doctor's affairs, it would be inopportune to now proceed against the latter with arrest and imprisonment, "lest our action be contrary to the Prince's." As regards his altercations in Hall, Rhegius wrote to his friend Wolfgang Rychard[19] that the (Brixen) bishop had attempted to win him over first with flattery and then by threats, and when this proved unsuccessful, the bishop had incited the prince's wrath against him by calumny so that he could not feel safe throughout the summer. That is why had gone to Augsburg, where he had originally wanted to remain till the prince's rage had cooled down. On his then return to Hall the bishop had laid an ambush for him and with the prince's support, had made every attempt to chase him away from Hall. With the consent of the Hall citizenry (Rhegius went on to say) he had then returned to his hometown and was there waiting for the Hall citizens to bring his case to a successful conclusion in Nuremberg, where they were now resolutely representing it through Fabri. Rhegius would then return to Hall, where his mother was keeping house for him. If his case were to take an unfavorable turn, he would return to Augsburg, where a position was being held open for him—not that of a barber, but one with no ties attached, where he would not have to be afraid of some pseudo-bishop or similar person.[20]

In a booklet published in 1527, Rhegius writes [to the Hall citizens] about the same subject as follows:[21] "When I learned some years ago that God had also let light shine forth out of darkness for you and had put into your hearts something of the brightness of truth, I thanked God and besought him to bring to a conclusion what he had begun in you. But when I received the call to come to you and preach the Gospel, from that very hour Satan rose up against me and had me gain a reputation for preaching a new doctrine and for guiding the people away from the path of the established faith. That was the reason for my parting from you: I wanted to evade the envy. I was hoping that the truth would still find a place and be listened to. You should know that I preached among you nothing but the age-old Christian faith, as it has come down to us from Christ himself and the apostles."

While still at Hall, Rhegius had the following writings published:

1. *On Perfection and Fruit of Christ's Passion*, proclaimed by Dr. Urbanus Rhegius, preacher at Hall in the Inn valley, 1522.[22]
2. *A Sermon on Church Dedications*, preached at Hall in the Inn valley, 1522.[23]

3. *Sermon about the Third Commandment: How a Christian Ought to Celebrate, with an Indication of Various Abuses*, Preached at Hall in the Inn valley 1522.[24]
4. *About Repentance, Confession, Atonement: A Resolution*, Preached at Hall in the Inn valley by Urbanus Rhegius, 1523.[25]

In the sermon on church dedications, Rhegius laments the magnificent buildings: "Churches are now being built like great, vainglorious, imperial palaces: brightly lit, sumptuously overloaded with gold, silver, and precious stones, with costly paintings, gilded tablets, flags, mass vestments, chalices, crosses, organs, and such things. At the same time, though, people's hearts are sooty, desolate, dark; faith is feeble, love is cold, and hope wavering." He claims that there are useless fraternities, which would do better to let their money help the poor; that wooden idols are placed at the church doors and festooned with indulgences, that attempts are made to overcome the Turks by means of spears, halberds, and muskets and to thus bring them to faith. Faith, however, (maintains Rhegius) entered the world without any secular compulsion, solely through the apostles' preaching; hence even today "there is no other way to make Christians." "The devil," he says, "looks forward more gleefully to one single church dedication than to a thousand Good Fridays." "Here the church authorities ought to be very much on guard; with the shepherd asleep, though, who is going to ward off the wolf?"

The sermon on the third commandment is directed against the excessive number of church holidays: "Some blind shepherds cherish a lot of holidays as conducive to their own advantage. When the big bells sound forth, the peasants come running to see if something new has turned up, and if there is a relic of some kind left in the sacristy, it is brought forth and placed on the altar there to act as decoy for the gold-hungry priest. 'Fork over your money, you peasant!' the golden idols are shouting." "You people do love to see a lot of holidays, even though they are naught but sheer blasphemy! There are all too many red-letter days in the calendar but very few Christian sabbaths." "People go to church without knowing what it is all about. There is singing and reading in Latin, nothing of which is understandable to commoners. Preaching is done in the afternoon, when the belly is swollen with food and drink, the brain is addled, and the eyes are heavy with sleep. That's how we sit in church—just like monkeys. If you want to be a Christian, you have got to hear the Gospel—not only the rule of St. Francis or St. Dominic!"

Dr. Urbanus Rhegius' hopes of being able to remain at his post in Hall remained unfulfilled. As early as December 12, 1522, the bishop of Brixen (Bressanone) wrote to the bishop of Trent at Nuremberg that with Doctor Urbanus still in Hall and, although not preaching, "hatching a lot of bad conspirations," he (the bishop of Trent) should make an effort to have his stay in Hall ended by a mandate of the ruling prince.[26] The favor extended to Rhegius by the evangelically minded town councillors Rehlinger, Langenmantel, Welser, and Gösser in Augsburg opened to him the parish of St. Anna there. The fact that while Rhegius was still in Hall, several nuns of the Martin's Cloister there took off their habit, followed him to Augsburg, and got married there[27] shows that the seed scattered by Rhegius and his predecessor [Jakob Strauss] had fallen on receptive soil. On December 16, 1523, the government informs the burgomeister's office at Schwaz that "according to a reliable report a preacher of the order of barefooted monks at Schwaz had preached in an improper and seditious way from that monastery's pulpit."[28] On April 22, 1524, the government writes to Hildebrand von Spaur and Hans Zott that contrary to the prohibition issued, Lutheran books and tractates are on sale at the market place in Hall. "The burgomaster and council ought to be spoken to about this," so that such buying and selling be stopped, the transgressors be punished and the merchandise be confiscated.[29] In the area of Innichen and at Villgraten such tractates were being distributed by canon Mathias Messerschmied of Innichen, for which reason he was arrested and taken to Brixen. On November 26, 1524, the burgomaster, the councillors and jurors of Brixen asked the government to have the prisoner set free, but were told that their request could not be granted.[30] It was only after the canon had promised to mend his ways that he was released. He then fled to Switzerland.

In Stams, too, an obvious predilection for novel ways was to be felt.

On May 16, 1524, the Innsbruck authorities note that a run-away monk had recently turned up at Stams and had been arrested. The Stams subjects, though, had served notice that "if their monk was not released by Whitsun, they would intend to take direct action," whereupon the administrator released the monk.[31] Five days later the bailiwick of Bludenz and Sonnenberg is notified that Lutz Matl had recently, through sermons he had preached in the church of St. John at Stams, sacrilegiously "misled the common people through Lutheran doctrines." Matl is said to hail from the domain of Sonnenberg. Order is given to arrest him right away and to have this reported without delay.[32] A few days later the primissarius (*Frühmesser*) of Breitenwang, who "had been presumed to preach the Lutheran sect" was imprisoned in the Ehrenberg Castle and handed over to the bishop of Augsburg.[33] On June 6, 1524, the government orders the mining magistrate at Schwaz to "refuse the request of the two monks presently roaming around in Hall, who there have doffed their habit, walking about in secular garb, asking for a mining job."[34] Two days later Archduke Ferdinand newly enjoins upon the government a punctilious carrying out of the decrees issued against Lutheran doctrines, so that "the Christian order be upheld." On June 17, 1524, the district-and-mining magistrate at Rattenberg is instructed to render all necessary assistance to the administrator at Kropfberg, who has the imprisoned parish priest Eustachius under his guard, in case the subjects in the Ziller valley, acting in line with the resolution adopted at a popular assembly, might want to set that preacher free by force.[35] In the case of the primissarius at Reutte Hans Lederer, Jörg Paumann, and Hans Pögli are summoned to appear on the Thursday before the day of Mary Magdalene (July 21) before the regents and court counsellors at Innsbruck to answer charges.[36] This case, too, had most likely to do with the spread of Lutheran doctrines.

On July 5, 1524, new ordinances were sent to Schwaz regarding the attitude to be taken towards the monk, "who on market days had recently been preaching in a garden outside the town of Hall and who had been a worker at the Erb adit (gallery) of the Falkenstein mine." The selling of Lutheran books and tracts is once again ordered stopped.[37] On the following day the Innsbruck government writes to the judge at Rattenberg: it had been learned that there was a Lutheran priest at Hart in the Ziller valley, who on the pulpit as well as in the tavern there preaches against the order of the holy Christian church and berates the bishops and prelates. As regards the priest Eustachius, who during the past Lent had been preaching at Paumkirchen, the judge should come to an agreement with the Kropfberg administrator. "If that preacher is not called Eustachius, the judge should let him go free but should keep him under secret surveillance."[38] A report by the court counsellor of July 7, 1524, to His Serene Highness the Prince refers to the situation in the Stams monastery.[39] It relates that "there is a lay priest in Stams who in his sermons spouts the teaching of Luther" and that "some monks in that monastery adhere to that priest and soil themselves with the Lutheran sect." On hearing that, the court counsellor, jointly with the provost of the Brixen cathedral, had sent a commission to Stams to investigate the situation. That commission, consisting of some of the top authorities in the principality—the Innsbruck court counsellor and the provost of the Brixen cathedral (the latter having been appointed by the Brixen bishop to head the delegation)—was to "inquire after Lutheran books." The emissaries searched the cells and, with the exception of two or three, found in each one a lot of Lutheran books and tracts. These were taken away by the commissioners. There were six monks in the convent that "professed the Lutheran faith." In spite of all attempts to dissuade them, they held to their opinion that Luther has not yet been proved wrong and that they had found in his writings nothing but what is contained in the Gospel.

The peasants from the neighborhood, whom the lay priest had informed of what was going on, came to the monks' assistance and demanded that the seized books be returned to the lay priest and that the latter not be sent away[40] but be permitted to continue preaching the Gospel. In the end the commission was forced to lay the whole matter before the Innsbruck authorities. The judge in Stams was instructed to either "extract a promise" from the lay priest or to arrest him and keep him imprisoned until further orders. Five of the monks left the monastery; after five days, though, they voluntarily presented themselves to the authorities and only requested that they not be compelled to abjure their faith. The court counsellor was to immediately subject the Stams monastery to a "reformation," i.e. internal order was to be tightened and the brothers be placed under strict discipline. However, the chaos and confusion during the succeeding years make this highly unlikely.

There are also lively complaints about the new teachings gaining ground in Brixen and surroundings, in Bruneck and Taufers. A contemporary voice testifies that in that same year (1524) in Bruneck and Taufers, too, a "strange rumor" arose concerning "renouncers of the faith" and Lutheran-minded people, and that these caused a lot of trouble and distress.[41]

On August 10, 1524, the court counsellor writes as follows to the bailiff at Bregenz, who shortly before had reported that the Bludenz people were in part convinced Lutherans: As regards the priest Matten, who had presumed to cast off the order of the Christian church, he was to be arrested.[42] Eight days later the judge at Imst was ordered to arrest a man named Hans Singer, who in the church at Arzl on past Assumption Day (August 15) had presumed to bid the preacher in the pulpit to be silent and had spoken sacrilegiously against honoring the Mother of God.[43] This brought forth on September 1, 1524, a lengthy mandate of Ferdinand I to all his subjects in the upper Austrian areas. Among other things it says: "By way of implementing the Edict of Worms and the resolutions of the two imperial diets at Nuremberg in 1523 and 1524, as regards doing away with Luther's doctrine and all the evils resulting from it, we have recently in Regensburg agreed with several secular and spiritual princes to accept and uphold the edict [of Worms] as well as the mandates and resolutions, and not to tolerate that the Gospel be interpreted wrongly, with the result that Christian tradition and customs be obstructed. Nor do we want to tolerate in our lands any apostate members of religious orders, both male and female, nor any priests that want to embrace marriage. Being aware that the damned and seductive doctrines and shameless writings are mainly spread by the print shops, we decree that in future nobody is to dare print a book or picture unless this has previously been carefully examined and licensed for printing."[44] This mandate was also published everywhere in Tyrol, but even during the very next weeks we hear of trials there in matters of faith. On October 3, 1524, the Innsbruck authorities write as follows to judge Linhard Nortzen at Rattenberg and similarly also to Rudolf Fuchs: "It has come to our knowledge that in Rattenberg a schoolmaster, who is not even a priest, dares to preach Lutheran stuff from the pulpit." The schoolmaster was summoned to Innsbruck for a hearing on November 23.[45] On October 12, 1524, there is a report about Lutheran preachers doing their nefarious work at Stein[46] and three days later the bishop of Brixen is sent a written request to hold off with the publication of the mandates "concerning the spiritual reformation[47] including the Lutheran sect, unless already carried out." In Kufstein, too, the new spirit was astir: on October 27, the authorities order Sir Martin Paumgarten and Captain Fuchs of Fuchsperg to see to it that the chaplain of a Kufstein charitable foundation, who "adheres to the new teaching and preaches against the customs of the established church, who spouts his doctrines and articles in pubs and other places, and leads a disgusting life, enters no churches," be banished from the country and replaced by a suitable priest.[48]

Complaints keep coming in about Lutheran books being on sale all over the county of Tyrol, in defiance of all imperial edicts and of the Regensburg mandate.[49] Bozen is specifically mentioned[50] as a place where these writings are publicly offered for sale, the new teaching being brought in by merchants. As we learn from Dr. Beatus Widmann's report of July 3, 1525, to the bishop of Trent, a preacher named Stephan, formerly an Augustinian in "Rotenburg" had turned away from the traditional doctrine and is said to have become a preacher in Innsbruck. He is said to have digressed from the old-established teaching and to have preached "against the fasts and related prayers, against the church and spiritual obedience."[51] There is also talk of a meeting at "Abson" in favor of the new direction. Toward the end of the year 1524, we hear Archduke Ferdinand's loud lament at the "Lutheran sect's" gaining more and more ground in Tyrol every day. He complains about the clergy's tolerating that from the pulpits there is preaching against God, against the customs of the church and its authorities and that libelous writings are being circulated.[52] On January 15, 1525, he orders the Lutheran-minded preachers in Rattenberg and Kitzbühel removed.[53] In a letter of March 2, 1525, to the Innsbruck authorities the archduke approves of the banishment of the married preachers in Kufstein and Rattenberg.[54] "They should in no way be tolerated in the country. For though we have given permission for the holy Gospel to be proclaimed, it is not our opinion that this is to be done by married priests or other unsuitable persons."

On April 4, 1526, Emperor Charles V writes from Seville to the Tyrolean authorities that "it indeed surprises me how your and other regional authorities are said to have presumed, under the guise of the holy Gospel, and as though called for by it, to repeatedly ask our brother that permission be given for the seductive teaching of Luther to be preached in the lands in question." His Imperial Majesty—he says—would have expected his and his brother's mandates and orders to be accorded greater respect.[55]

Pope Clement VII's bull (May 28, 1525) to the bishop of Trent contains the complaint that in Germany and especially in the town and diocese of Trent parish priests, their *locum tenentes*, and other clergymen proclaim the iniquitous teaching of Luther, the breeding ground of all other kinds of heresy, refractoriness, and rebellion, that they publicly enter into marriage and other illicit liaisons, no longer say mass, administer communion in both kinds to people that have not been to confessional, and all in all hold forth about the clergy in a most disgraceful way. The bishop is ordered to search out and interrogate priests, vicars, and monks of that ilk and to have the recalcitrant ones handed over for appropriate punishment.[56]

From the town of Speier Ferdinand I wrote that "in defiance of the issued mandates a runaway monk had made his way to Sterzing, taken a wife there and committed many improper actions by his Lutheran teachings and sermons."[57] An order is accordingly issued to have the monk expelled from the country, seeing that military forces are still around there. On December 4, 1526, the government in Upper Austria informs the Cardinal in Salzburg that "Wolfgang Ochsenhauser, a priest who had been the Paumgartner chaplain in Kufstein, is presently staying at Hopfgarten with another priest by the name of Adam, he, too, a Lutheran and adherent of the new doctrine." Ochsenhauser is reported to have in a most unpriestly manner let his tonsure be overgrown by hair, to be traveling about carrying a musket, and to have started a lot of rebellion and other evils in Kufstein; it is requested that he be pursued and rendered harmless.[58]

Not only the clergy, but also laymen—ore miners, court clerks, students and others—take it upon themselves to preach the new gospel. At Brixen a tailor from Nieder-Vientl made himself heard in that way, and his action landed him in the tower.[59] On all sides the flames of enthusiasm for the new teaching were flaring upwards. The main center of those opposing the old churchly ways was the brotherhood at Schwaz with its many miners. When the reformation was put into practice in St. Gall, Appenzell and Grisons, numerous preachers arrived from those republics, crisscrossed the country in both secular and spiritual garb and would, in return for remuneration or food for the journey, hold forth wherever folk were ready to listen to them. And they were eagerly listened to, for they would tell the people things they could understand and were pleased to hear. For example, a certain Swiss man was preaching in Luther's ideas in Meran.[60]

The fact that the new teaching did not take a wider and deeper hold was due less to the governmental authorities, who were often exhorted by the reigning prince to show greater zeal, and were due to that prince's prudence and actions. Then, too, the anti-Catholic current abroad in the land had its force at least partially broken by many people's dislike of a teaching that, according to the prevailing opinion, had caused the peasants' rebellion with its horrors. In particular the "quiet and truly devout folk" in the land would have nothing to do with that teaching. It was in consequence of that growing reaction that the preacher whom Gaismair had brought to Brixen in July 1525, and who, according to the report of the cathedral provost had preached "nothing but rebellion and revolt," and who by other reports is reputed to have "preached a lot of heretical Lutheran doctrines in Brixen and the nearby villages as well as later at Sterzing and Meran," was (on August 21 1525) placed on the list of those who were to be either arrested or expelled from the country.

It would be excessive to pursue the trails of all these preachers active in the Tyrol; only one of them merits special consideration, at any rate on account of his renown: Karlstadt. This man, after in the summer of 1525, playing his part among burghers and peasants at and around Rothenburg on the Tauber and suffering hardships of many kinds, evaded the aftermath of the peasants' revolt by making his way to Tyrol. To begin with, he found himself adrift in the Lüsner valley, but from a report of October 10, 1525, by Ludwig of Emershofen, canon (*Kapitelherr*) and parish priest at Klausen, one gathers that Karlstadt arrived there at about that time, against that priest's will but in response to being called by the miners of the Villander ore mines.[61] His stay there was not of long duration, for on obtaining the permission to return to Saxony that he had applied for from the elector of that principality, Karlstadt went back there.

With the increasing pacification of the country after the peasants' rebellion it became less and less frequent for preachers to enter the country from abroad. Restricted as it was to narrow circles, the new teaching lost its foothold in the country and little by little came to have secret adherents only in the larger towns, in smelting works, and individual manor houses. It ceased to appear anywhere in public; quietly and little by little its place was taken by Anabaptism.

2

THE RISE OF ANABAPTISM IN TYROL

THE FIRST DEFINITE information about the existence of Anabaptism in Tyrol comes to us from the "Anabaptist principal" Hans Hut at his interrogation on September 10, 1527, by the examining magistrate Peutinger in Augsburg. Hut confesses to having been baptized on May 20, 1526, by Hans Denck in a little house by the *Kreuztor* in Augsburg. This happened, Hut related, at the advice and encouragement of Caspar Färber, a native of the Inn valley, who had learned the trade of dye-making in Augsburg and had told Hans Hut a lot about Anabaptism and in particular that there were some brothers in the Inn valley, who had let themselves be baptized and were now leading a Christian life. That is how Caspar had prevailed on Denck and also on him (Hut) to undergo baptism.[1]

Among this small group of Anabaptists was also the mining magistrate Pilgram Marpeck, a native of Rattenberg or close by, a capable mechanic[2] employed in the industrial works of the lower Inn valley. "Brought up in popery by God-fearing parents," as Marpeck recounts himself, he became a protagonist of the Wittenberg gospel. "But on discovering that at the places where the word of God was being preached in the Lutheran way a fleshly freedom made itself felt as well, he became a little uncertain and could not find rest among them. He thereupon accepted baptism as a testimony to the obedience of faith, having regard solely for the word and command of God."

It remains uncertain where these Anabaptists—Urbanus Rhegius calls them, surely not in very good taste, *Hundsbader* ("dog bathers")—had come from, whether from the Salzburg region or from southern Germany or, what seems most probable, from Switzerland. In opposition to the orders of the traditional church and thus standing on common ground with the "evangelicals," they fought against the lax morality of the latter and in many points were closer to the traditional church than them. They had the appearance of a truly Christian life, tolerated no vice, took dedicated care of brothers and sisters and had only words of peace and tolerance for their enemies: "Vengeance belongs to the Lord, not to us" was a principle of their church community—to be sure a principle they would later deviate from at times, although even then not entirely through their own guilt.

In 1527, the numbers of these "devout" were greatly increased by newcomers from Switzerland, Bavaria, Salzburg, and Carinthia. Their "teachers and ministers of the word of God" settled on either side of the Brenner Pass, crossed the land in all directions and found entrance in peasants' huts, burghers' houses, and noblemen's mansions. Most likely, also the cowherd Wolfgang from the Sarn valley was just such a missioner of Anabaptism.[3] The miners at Klausen, he declared, had told him not to let himself be turned away from the Gospel but to preach it boldly, and most of them had wanted to accompany him to the interrogation. He also stated that the Gufidaun administrator had sent for him, and that he had preached about four times in houses there. Wherever a congregation desired it, he said, he had preached in the church there. In Bozen, Taufers, and other towns persons of social standing, among them some priests, had approved of his sermons. In March 1527, mention is made of Anabaptists in Rattenberg.[4] In May of the same year the government was informed that Anabaptists were staying at Glurns and Mals and did not hesitate to order Jakob Trapp, the administrator there, to render these people harmless.[5] In an awareness that otherwise, too, "false teachers of that kind are gadding about in the country, engaging in unchristian talk in pubs and at other places and, regardless of the Edict of Worms and of the other imperial injunctions, vociferate against the sacrament of the altar and the other sacraments," on May 31, 1527, a mandate was issued which decreed that such malefactors were to be noted, be they of high or low estate, natives or aliens, secular or clergy. If caught in the act, they were to be arrested and reported to the government.[6]

The most significant persons affected by this mandate were Anton von Wolkenstein and Helena von Freyberg, mistress of the Münichau estate.

Anton von Wolkenstein, whose house is said to have been a place of theological disputation and an "asylum of sectarian spirits" was summoned to Innsbruck to give an account and was only able to obtain his release by pledging June 1527, in front of the governor and the regents, to remain henceforth obediently in unity with the ancient holy Christian church, to let no Lutheran or other sects be preached in his house and to hand all sectarian books over to Georg Basch, the vice president of the province (*Unterlandeshauptmann*) and to the parish priest of Taufers; nor was Anton to order, purchase, or read such writings in future. As regards his further treatment, the decision was left to the archduke to whose grace he was commended.[7]

The government hoped to make an end of Anabaptism for good by the draconian mandate of August 20, 1527, first promulgated in Ofen and made public in Tyrol on November 20.[8] Indeed the mandate did not fully take effect in Lower Austria, and certainly not in Tyrol, where Anabaptism had struck much deeper roots. On October 21, 1527, King Ferdinand writes as follows from Ofen to the regent and councillors in Lower Austria: "We have decided to have issued in our lands 2,000 copies of our Mandate against the Lutheran and other misleading teachings and customs." A total of 1,655 of these mandates were sealed and issued in Vienna, of which 1,200 went to Innsbruck and the remainder to Styria (200), Carinthia (100), Krain (88), Upper Austria (80), and Lower Austria (150).[9] The following day yet another mandate[10] was issued "as a renewed gracious warning" against all Lutheran, Zwinglian and any of the other seductive doctrines of their followers and adherents. In this mandate the king notes: "In spite of all previous mandates we have had sufficient information to the effect that the said mandates are being given little heed and compliance.

Until now the excuse put forward has been that the common man in the street cannot possibly know which doctrines are heretical and which are right, and therefore, it is said, it had not been possible to mete out punishment in accordance with the edicts issued." "In order to henceforth eliminate the reason for such excuses it is commanded that the governing authorities strictly see to it that all subjects and inhabitants of our lands comply with the mandates."[11]

It was only in November 1527, that the Innsbruck government received definite news about Anabaptists (who until then had only too often been confused with the Lutherans). It was informed that in the lower Inn valley, in particular around Calzein and Rothholz, there are some alien persons that "presume to incite our subjects to Anabaptism and other seductive articles." "Because of the strict mandates issued against the Anabaptists, it is commanded that around Gasteiger and Calzein inquiries be made about those Anabaptist persons, their garb, age, etc., to track them diligently, search for them and, if coming upon them to arrest and interrogate them, and to report to the government about their character and intentions."[12] This order was sent to the district sheriff (*Landrichter*) in Rattenberg, to the mining magistrate (*Bergrichter*) at Schwaz and to the sheriffs at Rotenburg and Freundsberg. The archbishop of Salzburg was requested[13] to order the administrator of Kitzbühel, Hans Vinsterwalder, to comply with the written instructions he had received regarding Anabaptists entering the country, "in order that this sect be suppressed, punished, and in due time be eliminated."

The first victim of the measures thus set in motion was the former monk and present Anabaptist Leonhard Schiemer from Vöklabruck, the first Anabaptist bishop in Upper Austria. Already on November 28, the government writes to the district sheriff at Rotenburg: "As you have somebody from Vöklabruck and a ropemaker from Rotenberg (Rattenberg?) in prison there as adherents of the new Anabaptist sect, we recommend that you have both of them interrogated under torture, particularly the one from Vöklabruck, to find out who sent him out, what is their sect and their purpose, also who are their adherents and promoters, and in what way the one from Vöklabruck prevailed on the rope-maker to join the sect; furthermore whether the two local burghers of Rattenberg, who were with them at their arrest, have also accepted their sect."[14]

The same day the Freundsberg sheriff and the mining magistrate of Schwaz are being notified with displeasure that in spite of the issued mandate, Anabaptism has been brought to Schwaz by persons from abroad and has gained ground there and that the orders of the authorities ought to be attended to more diligently than has been the case until now.[15] Similar instructions are sent to Kufstein, Rattenberg, and Kitzbühel.[16] A man the authorities specially had in mind among the Anabaptists at Schwaz was Jörg Vasser, a former monk and presently a *Wasserheber* ("raiser or lifter of water") at the Triefe mine and he is married. He and a goldsmith, who had come to Schwaz shortly before, had managed to escape.

The censured magistrates now developed a feverish activity, and before long the prisons at Freundsberg were too small to lodge all those arrested, so that the dungeons at Schwaz were put at the Freundsberg sheriff's disposal.[17] Among those arrested was the mine foreman Stephan Leder, who was to be kept under surveillance particularly at nighttime to find out if his house was frequented by Anabaptists.[18] At the beginning of November "a true teacher of the Word and of the Gospel of Christ," Hans Schlaffer, was added to those imprisoned.

One of the chief places of refuge for the Anabaptists fleeing the Salzburg area was Kitzbühel. The administrator there promised the Innsbruck authorities that he would "straightaway" comply with their orders.[19] The government was particularly intent on getting hold of a former Kitzbühel cleric who called himself Paul and had gathered a sizable number of Anabaptists around him; he went in and out unhindered at the Münichau mansion, whose owner, Baroness Helena von Freyberg, openly favored the Anabaptists. When his calling drew him forth into the mountains, he would leave behind Hans Roth, a student, who for a time "roamed the mountains," frequented the Münichau mansion, and "afterwards moved to the Reutte, where he preached to the people and baptized several at Münichau."[20]

For her sponsoring of the Anabaptists, Baroness Helena von Freyberg subsequently had to pay with the loss of her freedom and her possessions, whereas most of the other Anabaptists in the Kitzbühel area had to pay for it with their lives. The trial of Leonhard Schiemer began in December 1527. Here only those of his statements will be mentioned that refer to his activity in Tyrol, as contained in his "Confession" of January 14, 1528.[21] He declares that he had moved through Bavaria and had intended to baptize a lot of people at Schwaz; however, he had suspected that brother Reinhardt, whom he had got to know, was going to betray him, for "the monasteries in Lower Austria had tried hard to put him in prison." He felt sorry he had not managed to baptize more people, seeing that he had been arrested the very first night after arriving at Rattenberg.[22] On December 14, 1527, the government addressed unisonal letters to the "two dukes of Bavaria," the cardinal of Salzburg, and the city of Augsburg, as follows: "We are herewith sending your grace a copy of the confession made by Leonhard Schiemer of Vöklabruck, presently imprisoned at Rattenberg, a leading figure in the new sect of Anabaptists. His confession makes plain that some or your princely grace's subjects have embraced Anabaptism through him." Four days later the district sheriff is instructed to "hold off bringing Schiemer to trial" and to keep him guarded in the Rattenberg castle, "as he had been advised by the Lord of Liechtenstein." On December 18, the district sheriff Bartelme Angst is ordered to set a day for the trial of Kaspar Leonhard Schiemer. In a writing of the same date Schiemer is referred to as the "beginner and main originator" of the new doctrine, and the sheriff is commanded to let justice be done in line with the content of the issued mandates, "as a showcase to help ordinary people be on guard in future against such heretical and seductive teachings. On the day to be set two associate judges will be in attendance." "In order to proceed against him more imposingly and valiantly, as an example to others, the district sheriff is to set the trial date soon after Christmas and have twenty assessors in attendance, two from the town and two from the Rattenberg rural district, two each from Innsbruck, Hall, Bozen, Braunegg, Brixen, and the Freundsberg rural district, and one each from the towns of Kufstein and Kitzbühel and from their respective rural districts."[23] A special governmental mandate[24] ordered these judges to be sent without delay.

Meanwhile Anabaptism had raised its head also on the other side of the Brenner Pass. About the middle of December 1527, a message reached Innsbruck to the effect that Anabaptist conventicles had been spotted among the miners and townsfolk of Sterzing. When one of these, a carpenter "from the synagogue of N. Mayerhofer in Lüsen," was arrested in the house of a coppersmith, this was for the government an event of such importance that the chamber procurator Dr. Johann Vintler was immediately dispatched there with a letter of credence in order to "be present at the interrogation under torture scheduled for December 23."[25] In particular, inquiry was to be made, with or without the application of torture, as to who had sent out that Anabaptist, what their sect was like, and what was their intent.

Four other Anabaptists, who also had been part of the "synagogue" in the coppersmith's house and had "brought several to the new sect," had managed to escape in time. A governmental document states "that in spite of the issued mandates the following have all recently been at Sterzing: someone named Mayerhofer, a brother of the Mayerhofer in Gufidaun, with a long, brown beard and wearing a grey coat (*Wappenrock*); a tall, pale fellow wearing a long, black coat with trimming; a short fellow with a small, thin, red beard, and finally someone called B. Messerschmied, who is said to have taken a bad departure from Klausen." "Such ringleaders are to be arrested."[26]

The Innsbruck government sent a letter concerning the activities in Lüsen to the prince bishop of Brixen, and the captain in charge at the Adige river was ordered to be on the lookout in Tramin.[27] Already on December 23, 1527, Bishop Georg of Brixen had on his own initiative issued an order to be on guard for roving agitators, "among whom are also reputed to be some that preach in nooks and corners about the new sect and Anabaptists," and to arrest them without further ado.[28] Mayerhofer, who was being sought at Lüsen, where his father lived, secretly came with his three companions to Klausen, where they held meetings in Ulrich Müller's house and received here several persons into the new sect, as they had also done at Sterzing.[29] They moved on before this became known, and when the episcopal captain Ulrich Wittenbach appeared at Ulrich Müller's house, they could arrest only the master of the house and a woman, the wife of Gilg

Bader. The confession Ulrich Müller rendered at Klausen was sent to the Innsbruck government on December 26, with the question what was to be done with the prisoner and how to go about executing such persons. In the reply from Innsbruck[30] His Princely Grace, the bishop, was directed to keep the prisoners under guard until further notice, and as regards their execution to seek the advice of learned men in the Brixen bishopric. What these would come up with should then be passed on to the government. At the same time the bishop had sent to him all printed mandates concerning the Anabaptists' eradication, with the request to have them promulgated in the Brixen bishopric.[31]

It was from Bavaria that important news about the indigenous Anabaptist movement reached the Innsbruck authorities, mostly from confessions of arrested Anabaptists, and they were pleased to repay the favor by extending a corresponding courtesy. However, the extradition of Schiemer, the former leader of Bavarian Anabaptists, "many of whom he was said to have misled," was refused on the grounds that this "principal" and originator of the sect had also led astray many persons in Tyrol and his case had already been referred to a criminal court.[32]

The court assessors assigned to this trial were each paid two Bernese pounds for the journey there and back, and those attending the court proceedings at Bozen in mid-March 1528, were each assigned half a guilder per day.[33] The mining magistrate in Rattenberg refused to pursue the Anabaptists, declaring this not to be part of his office. The government let him know that "this refusal had been seen as a disgrace by His Majesty and that it had been decided to take serious measures against him," if he were to persist in this attitude.[34]

Schiemer's trial was nearing its end. On January 6, 1528, King Ferdinand confirmed receipt of the prisoner's confession.[35] "Since such rebaptism is bound to lead to nothing but continuous agitation and rebellion on the part of the common people—as becomes evident from the confessions of several persons, who in part also went to death for it—necessity requires that the fire thus kindled be dammed in, before it develops into an uncontrollable conflagration. It is therefore commanded to proceed against Schiemer as a ringleader and principal of the Anabaptists in accordance with the recently issued mandates. In case not enough of the latter have as yet been dispatched (to Upper Austria), a number of reprints should be made and, with seal attached, be publicized and placarded."[36] The district sheriff had let the prisoner have a number of amenities; in particular he was supplied with ink, paper, and writing pens. Schiemer used his leisure time to compose several writings and also found opportunities to send them to his friends. The first of these, "setting forth what God's grace is," was composed on Thursday after *Andreae* (December 4, 1527). It shows us a man who had studied theology and philosophy, who knows his Aristotle and speaks of the *ens cognitum*. "All the world," he says, "and in particular our scribes, bandy and prattle about the little word 'grace,' Scripture makes them aware that there is something called grace, but not having this within them, they are unable to say anything about it. They derive the word 'grace' in the way the universities say, from their Aristotle, from *ens cognitum*,[37] which has its essence only in the intellect or as long as it is talked about. However, once such talking or thinking has ended, their essence, too, has come to an end, and then they call it *entia secunde intentionis*...[38] and say that it cannot be put into German, given that their intellect is so lofty that the German language is not up to it. And if one has a close look afterwards, they are so uppity as if they had ceased to be *realia*, for *res* or *realia* signifies 'something' or 'a thing.' It only lasts while it is thought about, and it finally ends up as nothing. And the people who yap most loudly about this 'not being able' are called masters and doctors."[39] Here some of Schiemer's statements about how the authorities proceeded against his own party might be of greater interest than his further pronouncements about the threefold grace, into which he inserts a very fine elucidation of the Our Father. "People pray to God; 'Hallowed be thy name' and afterwards spit at him below the eyes and into the face and are the first to dishonor his name. They forbid God's own teaching and call it heresy, seductive matter, and rebellious doctrines. That is why the emperor has to let edicts and mandates go forth into all nooks and corners; here the mail carriers go running, and over there the constables; the judge turns up and the administrator; here is an arresting officer[40] and over there a troop of horsemen, and in every house is a traitor. And whoever is not ready to become a traitor himself, at any rate keeps yapping about expelling and killing Christ's brethren. And those not ready to say bad things about them don't have anything good to say either and excuse themselves saying: 'I don't like to do it, but I must not fall into the prince's disgrace'."[41] In a second epistle Schiemer writes: "I would still have a lot to talk about with you, but the day of the Lord has overtaken me. Implore God also for our brother Tischler from the Brirlegg (Brixlegg), who lies in prison at Lofer together with his wife, our sister. You must tell brother N.N. to stop speaking to people about our brothers in such a mocking way as he did at Kufstein. And should Jörg Zaunried come to you and wants to follow me, I would have him get married. I commit my Bärbel to your care, and may she walk honestly and modestly. If the Lord calls me away from this vale of tears, let her remarry if she wants to. What God terms good you must not call evil. Whoever regards the married state as sin is a teacher of the Antichrist." A third epistle "to the church at Rottenburg" contains a fine explanation of the twelve articles of Christian faith, concluding with "a brief foundation for baptism." He writes a "consoling letter to a weak brother" because Paul exhorts us to comfort the despondent.

In his "confession" Schiemer offers to defend his faith against learned doctors. But it did not come to this. After the government had reprimanded the district sheriff at Rattenberg for letting the prisoner have ink, paper, and a pen while in prison, it decreed that on the day of his trial Schiemer was to present to the judges only his confession and recognition, duly confirmed, together with whatever other writings he had composed in prison. The judges were also to read the enclosed royal letter, and should they arrive at a sentence of death, they should have it carried out without delay outside the town. But should they not arrive at a death sentence for him, they were to send him back to prison pending further orders. Those writings of Schiemer's in which Bavarian Anabaptists are mentioned, were to be sent to the dukes of Bavaria.[42]

Concerning the "complex" ground of truth Schiemer had made the following offer: if a learned man were to overcome him with the truth of Holy Scripture and prove his teaching to be false and unjust and not in line with Scripture, they should get the hangman to tear limb after limb off from his body, and, if no limbs were left, to pull out his ribs as well. But if they were to judge him to have been misunderstood and not proven wrong, he would call upon the witnesses hearing his confession, and on all others present to testify to that at the last judgment. "Thereupon the judges condemned him to death by fire; however, the sentence was commuted to execution by the sword (on January 14) and his body was burned to ashes."[43] The district magistrate at Rattenberg, who had sent a report of Schiemer's execution to the government, was ordered to "present himself to the government the following Monday (January 19) to receive the decision concerning the remaining captives. As the Anabaptists' chronicles relate, following Schiemer no less than seventy brothers in the faith testified with their blood to their conviction at that same place.

3

INROADS AND STATE COUNTER-MEASURES

As already noted by Kirchmaier, what makes the year 1528 stand out within Anabaptist history are the numerous mandates issued against them and the fact that many people were being burned or punished otherwise on account of their erroneous belief. To begin with, the trial of Hans Schlaffer was brought to a conclusion. On January 15, the government informed the district magistrate of Freundsberg: "Our opinion is that Hans Schlaffer, a former priest, be put on trial and that twelve observers be convened—two from Hall, two from Brixen, two each from Truer and Braunegg, and the remaining four from your own administrative area." He was to have Schlaffer's confession[1] confirmed and set a date for the trial and was also asked to have the Anabaptists from Schwaz in his prison interrogated. To the question whether the Anabaptists might have plans to stir up a rebellion, Schlaffer was reported to have answered that "in all his days he had never considered stirring up any rebellion or uprising. All the plans he was aware of had been to abstain from evil and from the wicked life of the world. Obedience toward governing authorities was certainly a commandment he had taught. Over against the clerics he represented, 'on the basis of Holy Scripture,' that 'first of all God's word was to be taught to all who are able to hear and understand it and only then to baptize them.'"[2] His confession, too, was passed on to the Bavarian government.

On January 18 [1528], the government ordered the Freundsberg magistrate to set an earlier date for the trial and to schedule it for February 10.[3] He was asked to report secretly what kind of judgment he would expect Hans Schlaffer and Leonhard Frick to receive, whether they would be sentenced to death or in some other way—misgivings to be explained by the judges' reluctance to condemn such people. On the appointed day, sentence was passed on Schlaffer at Schwaz, where he had been taken.[4] His writings mostly contain presentations of his teachings and little about his companions in the faith. In one writing he glories in his friends, mentioning his acquaintance with Jakob Wiedemann, Jakob Kautz, Sigmund Hoffer, and Hans Hut, "now in prison since the birthday of Mary [September 8]." He also says that in Nuremberg he got to know Ludwig Hetzer and Hans Denck, two excellent, earnest men taught by God, and at Regensburg, Oswald Glaidt and Wolfgang Brandhuber, former parish priest in Linz. With all these he had noticed nothing but a fervent zeal for a godly and devout life. No one had directed him to go to Tyrol, he said; he had traveled from Regensburg to Rottenburg with a man called Moser, who takes Meißner china jugs there for enameling. Schlaffer referred to Leonhard Hallenstein in Pritzlegg as his mother's brother, but as Leonhard had been vexed, he (Schlaffer) had moved on to Schwaz. In his testament he accuses himself on account of the sins he committed as a priest: the priest's opulent and idle life, which is like casting straw into the fire while forbidding it to burn. His heart, he said, had been agitated until God opened himself to him and Martin Luther's teaching caused him to read the Bible. An observation in this testament makes it clear that this persecution had lasted from Peter and Paul to Nicolai. Added to the testament are the words: "Thus these two dear brothers, Hans Schlaffer and Leonhard Flückger (sic), were put to death by the sword and gallantly witnessed to faith and sealed it with their blood."[5]

The following trials concerned Hans Schneider and Apollonia Niedermayer at Bozen,[6] the Anabaptist named Kohl in Gargatzon, where Anabaptists had been staying, a goldsmith in Sterzing and a cabinetmaker at Rottenburg. There is a report that more than at other places this sect had taken root among those "connected with the mining industry" at Rattenberg.[7] In Kufstein the "cutler's wife," Jörg Held and his wife are listed as Anabaptists. The captain on the Adige river is notified: "Your letter of February 4, has informed us about the Anabaptist synagogue held on the Rittner Horn by N. Maierhofer; we have also learned that the captain has had Gasser and his gang arrested."[8]

The cardinal of Salzburg is being informed that Anabaptists are retreating from the Salzburg area into the Tyrol.[9] The municipalities of Innsbruck, Hall, Kufstein, Kitzbühel, Rattenberg, Sterzing, Meran, Bozen, Trent, and Glurus as well as all district sheriffs are notified that Anabaptists may be recognized by special distinctive marks on their clothing and by the way they greet each other, and that houses, towns, and market places where Anabaptists reside, are marked by special signs. These are to be carefully noted.[10] Arrest warrants[11] were taken out for leading Anabaptists (*Principaltäufer*) such as Jörg Tauffer or Vasser, and new, sharply-worded mandates were issued against Anabaptists in general. The first of these mandates, dated February 24, 1528, sets down that persons "stained with Anabaptism" may no longer excuse themselves by saying that they had got caught up in the sect before the publication of the mandates in question in Upper and Lower Austria. If such persons want to evade legal punishment, they must before next Palm Sunday present themselves to the authorities, acknowledge and revoke their error and plead for mercy; failing this, they will, if arrested, be prosecuted and punished according to the law. Finally, to stop anybody from still pleading ignorance of the mandates, until Whitsun these are to be read out in church by appointees of the court on every third Sunday and, after that, on every Ember Day.[12]

Palm Sunday came and went, but only a few persons actually denounced themselves. Meanwhile trials of individual Anabaptists were in progress at Meran and Kufstein.[13] Administrator Hans Vinsterwalder reports that a considerable number of Anabaptists have moved into the Ziller valley. There the provost Georg Kentschacher, the Kropfberg administrator, and the Rottenburg magistrate are ordered to take counsel on how to track down such persons. Simultaneously there comes the news that the Swabian League is sending out "400 horses" to deal with, and punish, Anabaptists, and that "on Oculi Sunday this region is to contribute 53 horses on the review ground at Kempten [Third Sunday in Lent]."[14]

On March 5, 1528, the government informs the district sheriff at Schwaz that a printed booklet is on sale there in which "Anabaptism is said to be presented in pictures for those unable to read." Order is given to confiscate the booklet and to track down the sellers.[15] The government also let the mining and district magistrate at Rattenberg know that in spite of all previous endeavors to pursue them some "principal" Anabaptists are still "stalking about" in Rattenberg district and its valleys.[16] Six days later the government sends the king a report about the Anabaptists arrested in Rattenberg (including copies of the sentences passed) and how they have been dealt with until now.[17] At the same time several fugitive Anabaptists were arrested in Kitzbühel.[18] The wife of a fugitive Anabaptist pleads for some of his property to be allocated to the child he left behind.[19]

Because of the numerous inquiries about how to proceed against Anabaptists in certain cases, on April 1, the government issued (while referring to the edict of August 28, 1527) something like an implementation order "as a statute and law of the land." It extends the time accorded for self-denunciation until the Sunday of *Misericordia* (April 26). "Those who avail themselves of this additional time granted, who publicly repudiate their error, take upon themselves the penance imposed by their parish priest, and divulge the identity of their seducers, shall be granted their life and not be subject to a freeman's punishment; they will merely be punished by incarceration for 8-14 days with a reduced provision of food the cost of which they will have to bear." That is also to be the treatment meted out to those presently incarcerated. The punishment for those succumbing to [the Anabaptist] error either before or after *Misericordia* and who after this time period denounce themselves or land in prison, is left to the discretion of the government. Those, on the other hand, who are in prison now or will be in the future and who persist in their error are to be condemned to death by fire; if after sentencing they repent of their sins, their sentence is to be commuted to death by the sword; their property, however, remains forfeited. Those that have seduced and baptized others are to be put to death by fire, whether they recant or not, and their property is forfeited to the government. That is also the treatment meted out to recidivist Anabaptists. The goods of the fugitives are to be seized and confiscated by the princely government's chamber of finances. A special decree is to determine how to proceed with the demolition, burning or barricading of the houses used by Anabaptists for their suppers, gatherings, and preaching.[20] "We therefore command each of you to have this gracious decree of ours read out to the people from the pulpit everywhere in the towns and judicial districts of your administration and to have it publicly displayed afterwards." On April 8, the bishop of Brixen had the very same mandate sent out to all captains, administrators, district magistrates etc.[21] At the end it said: "Pastors should see to it that the people come in for confession and communion at Lent and Easter."

The Anabaptists were now hunted up with renewed zeal. On April 2, the district magistrate of Rattenberg is ordered to track down the priest Virgil Plattner, who "is reputed to be a proper Anabaptist."[22] A warrant of arrest is taken out against Jörg Vasser from Schwaz.[23] On the same day Hans Vinsterwalder is instructed on how to proceed with the prisoners at Kitzbühel. There it prescribes that those released from arrest or set free on bail shall during a whole year carry a burning candle "at procession and Mass" and shall not enter any wine shop and meeting for the duration of one year. For three successive years they are to bear testimony by partaking of the sacrament at Easter. The houses at Oberpannin, Tauer, Sepach, at the Oberlahn and Püchl, at Pfaffenberg and Münichau, where "the sect was having its supper and meeting" shall, if feasible, be burned or torn down to set an example.[24] The Hertenberg sheriff is notified that the Anabaptists are gaining ground in the judicial district of Petersberg.[25]

On April 3, similar directions were dispatched to Hall,[26] on the following day to Stein on the Ritten,[27] and at the same time the district sheriff at Bozen is notified: "The prelates, lords, noblemen, towns and judicial districts of the country along the Adige (Etsch) river, the office of the burggraviate, Vientel on the Eisack (Isarco) river and Vintschgau, who recently gathered at Bozen have requested the

Upper Austrian government in writing that the Anabaptists imprisoned at Bozen, in consideration of their lack of understanding, be given a suitable punishment and be set free with no infringement of their honor. Hence an order is issued to the effect that Anabaptists, if they recant, be treated leniently.[28] On the other hand the prince bishop of Brixen is being given a slight reprimand on the ground that the sentences meted out to the Brixen Anabaptists sounded "too light and sloppy." In future the issued mandates are to be observed.[29] As regards Jörg Vasser, the magistrates at Hertenberg and Petersberg are being informed that he had baptized several at and around Stams (who have meanwhile recanted) and that he, along with his fellows and a woman, has taken to flight and is making his way toward Telfs.[30] A fortnight later a mandate was issued commanding that Anabaptists be neither "sheltered, housed, nor supplied with food or drink."[31] As to the Anabaptist Augustin Wurmb from Brixlegg, who had baptized five persons, the government refused to grant him reprieve; on the contrary, he was to be arrested, his property confiscated and he himself prosecuted as prescribed by the mandates.[32] Jakob Fuchs is told that he has no right to keep the goods of the Anabaptists executed on the Rittner Horn and that he ought to act in accordance with the statutes.[33]

Meanwhile the king managed to coerce from the estates of Moravia gathered at the diet of Znaim their consent to the expulsion of Anabaptists from Moravia. Many brethren who had found there a new abode were now turning their eyes back to their old homeland. When Ferdinand heard about this, he hastened to inform the Innsbruck authorities and to ask them to be on the lookout for returning Anabaptists, a considerable number of whom had already left Moravia.[34] Special attention was to be paid to the following persons: Jörg from Passau, Hans Hut from Bibra, Andre Rieß from Utzing, Michael Milter from Schwabthal, Hans Gruber from Eggenhof, Hans the Swabian, Hans from Langstadt, as well as one called Tauffer or Vasser from Schwaz.[35]

The prohibition of giving shelter to Anabaptists concluded the series of mandates for the year 1528. The government nevertheless had an opportunity to test the correctness of Luther's pronouncement that the sect, instead of diminishing, kept wondrously growing—"growing through the good appearance presented by those alive and the great boldness of those dying by fire and water." In its conversion endeavors the government had to contend with great difficulties, not the least of which was the sluggishness, already referred to more than once, of its own organs and the common people's aversion to the constant shedding of blood. Because of the Gufidaun administrator's nonchalance Anabaptists were able to move about with impunity in his district and hold meetings. The situation in Sterzing was not much different. However, the government remained unrelenting, so there was no lack of Anabaptist trials also during the succeeding months, e.g. of Egidi Marpeck in Rattenberg[36] and of Hans Schwaighofer in Kitzbühel, where, on May 5, as many as 106 persons renounced Anabaptism by oath.[37] Of these, thirty-six relapsed, but thirteen could still be brought to penance.[38] The magistrate at Rattenberg is ordered to have the Anabaptist women at Colsass pilloried and whipped.[39] On June 9, there is a report of Anabaptist propaganda at Vells. There Jörg Zaunried, a *Vorsteher* (overseer) among the Anabaptists, whose name is mentioned in this document for the first time, baptized Michel Kürschner and appointed him, too, as an overseer; and in the middle of August we hear of Kürschner's being active in the Adige (Etsch) area. In Hall, the "*Salzmaier*" Anton Stoß, son of prothonotary Ulrich Stoß, who had immigrated from Saxony, was accused of inclining to the sectarian party.[40] A letter of July 9, 1529, by Pope Clemens VII to the Cardinal and Archbishop of Salzburg[41] expatiates upon the measures taken against the Anabaptists particularly in Lower Austria. On August 19, the government takes note of the report of Mathias Langer in Kitzbühel. Langer relates that on August 10, he had intended to have the execution of Schweighofer and Aschelberger carried out, as commanded, on an open public place.[42] However, a person named Thoman Hermann from Böhmisch Waidhofen had uttered some sharp, wicked words in front of everyone, by which he "would fain have made the prisoners turn around." Hermann was then arrested and his confession made it clear that "he was a true ringleader and Anabaptist and had also baptized many people in this country." Facing the jury on August 28,[43] he was condemned to death by fire and was burned without delay, however, as Langer reports, "the jurors were dismayed and were overheard saying they were not sure if our order and statute for such a case of Anabaptism had in fact been agreed by the estates of the land or not." On September 2, Langer was advised to bring in outside jurors and judges in future cases like this, to make sure that the law was being upheld.

As regards the Kitzbühel judge, who let so many be condemned and executed, the *Geschichtsbücher der Wiedertäufer* relate that he was himself deemed a heretic later on, "and this not on account of his faith but rather so that he, too, might come to shame and disgrace before the world." The clerk of the court, too, was struck by "God's vengeance": "As he was driving round the town in his sleigh in winter, the horse flung him against a street corner so that his skull was shattered. Hence, as brothers Hans Kitzbüheler [Kräl] and Christian Häring came to hear, he did not lay his head down gently."

In October 1528, Anabaptists appear in the judicial district of Carneid.[44] On October 22, the administrator on the Ritten is ordered to search for four Anabaptists listed by name, who are said to be staying with the innkeeper Prior at St. Pilgrim's. In November and December Anabaptists are evident in the judicial districts of Wangen and Vells, then at Grieß and Bozen.[45] Those upon the Ritten were interrogated in December.[46] On December 24, an Anabaptist at Prefels renounces the sect, but there is also recent news about Anabaptists on the Rittner Horn and in the Oetz valley,[47] at Kurtatsch and Michelsberg.[48]

4

NORTH AND SOUTH OF THE BRENNER PASS

AMONG THE MOST active Anabaptists along the Eisack (Isarco) river, on the Ritten, and surroundings was a certain Jörg Zaunring (Zaunried) "from the Inn valley," later Jakob Hutter's companion and keeper of the purse. In the summer of 1528, he baptized many people along the Ritten, at Vils and around Völs. A man named Kirschner, at home known as Klesinger, whom he had baptized, also carried out an apostolic service; he taught in and around Teutsch-Noffen, in the judicial district of Gufidaun, in Kurtatsch and Kaltern, around Leifers and Klausen and was being avidly pursued everywhere. On April 25, 1529, the Kitzbühel sheriff managed to ambush him at a nightly meeting of brethren in Kitzbühel and to arrest him along with seven of his companions.[1] Upon receipt of this information, Mathias Langer was ordered on May 1, 1529, to bring this man to Innsbruck, as he "was an overseer and by his own admission had baptized over one hundred people. There, and not in Kitzbühel, this 'principal overseer' was to be subjected to the law." Taken to Innsbruck by two men driving a one-horse wagon (*zwei Ainspenniger*), he lay there in the *Kräuterturm* prison, refusing all attempts to convert him, and on June 2, he was burned at the stake at the shooting range on the other side of the bridge over the Inn.[2] They were in such a hurry to execute him that the so-called secret articles the court [in Vienna] had sent to the Innsbruck government on June 6, for the purpose of making clear whom they were actually dealing with in the person of Kürschner, could no longer be put to use.[3] The articles had been delivered to the king by a "very trustworthy person of knightly rank."

On the part of the reigning monarch, all necessary steps were taken to stop this sect from spreading. The mandate of February 5, 1529[4] renews the previous decrees and goes on to say that "through sufficient information and daily experience we are made aware that at several places those charged with the administration of justice do so not in accordance with our statutes but according to their own feelings, so that persons, who by rights ought to have paid for their guilt with their life are being let off." Given the fact that several such administrators of justice are disregarding their vows and oaths, with the result "that at present this seductive sect is found more in our county of Tyrol than in any other land, we hereby decree that henceforth all persons, both male and female, who let themselves be re-baptized, be imprisoned and punished by death. If apprehended, then it is in this and no other way that the magistrates and judges in the towns and judicial districts are to pass sentence, and therefore, before sitting down 'to administer justice' they are to swear an oath to God and the Saints, and no one ought to flout this."

We nevertheless hear of numerous trials of Anabaptists also in the following weeks and months. Thus, in February 1529, Wilhelm Stabmüller was tried in Rattenburg;[5] the case against Hans Kofler at the same place was taken up anew;[6] the jurors in Bozen who had acted unruly were reprimanded,[7] and there are complaints about Anabaptists in Klausen and Gufidaun.[8] The government is displeased to hear that the Gufidaun administrator is allowing some Anabaptists to stay in his district and presses for him to be removed.[9] Anabaptists make themselves noticed in the Michelsberg and Sonnenburg districts.[10] From Speier King Ferdinand orders the government to employ fifty soldiers for six weeks or two months and to appoint three inquisitors for the purpose of grappling with the Anabaptist sect in the county of Tyrol.[11] It was a man from Schwaz by the name of Jobst Engest, who made the suggestion to send out a captain with a number of soldiers against the sectarians.[12] On April 1, when it was reported that Anabaptists had shown up in the Ziller valley—actually in Kropfberg—the [Innsbruck] government ordered that "in the districts under suspicion," two soldiers be employed, at the government's expense, for the purpose of "pursuing the ones defiled with Anabaptism."[13]

The most significant Anabaptist centers were Sterzing, Hall, and Kitzbühel. Burghers, peasants, and miners were among the Anabaptists and filled the prisons almost as soon as they were emptied, eager "to pluck the bloody rose for which the faithful heart was longing."

One of the Anabaptists in Sterzing was Ulrich Stadler, whom we shall meet later as a teacher and leader of the brethren in Moravia and Poland. Schweyger's chronicle reports that "in Hall many people, men and women, young and old, have joined the Anabaptist sect. They subsequently renounced this sect due to instruction by Magister Christoff Landtsperger, the then parish priest and preacher." The largest number among those imprisoned in Hall was represented by the Anabaptists whom the Hertenberg magistrate had arrested in a meadow near Mils at the end of August. Among them were two "sisters" celebrated in the chronicles and songs on account of their steadfastness: Annele Maler and Urschl Ochsentreiber, who had been led to Anabaptism by a baker and cloth shearer in Hall.[14] Most of those in prison opted to recant. They then had to make confession, and on a Sunday before the procession or mass had to abjure rebaptism, and on the same and the following two Sundays had to walk "barefoot and bare-headed" in front of the priest in the procession, and remain kneeling before the altar all through Mass. In addition, each had to sign a written renunciation, which went as follows: "I confess that by letting myself be moved to join the seductive sect of Anabaptism I did wrong and from my whole heart I am sorry for it and I hereby publicly renounce and abjure this seductive sect of Anabaptism. I promise and commit myself from now on and for the rest of my life to cleave to the unity of the Christian Church, and I will not let myself be separated from it in any way."[15]

An even greater harvest than in Hall and Sterzing, Anabaptism was reaping in Kitzbühel, where the judicial authority was far away—Kitzbühel was at that time in pledge to the Archbishopric of Salzburg—and the administrators were either not zealous enough or unable to check the movement. More than 200 Anabaptists were rounded up there in 1528.

The order to demolish or burn the houses where Anabaptists had held their meetings aroused the opposition of those whose private rights were infringed upon. That is why mitigating interpretations of the above-mentioned decree were issued: "Item, since Christoph Fuchs, captain in Kufstein, requests instruction, given that he has orders for the houses that sheltered Anabaptists to be burned and that the respective landlords find this difficult, the government hereby directs him as follows: Houses of this kind in towns are *not* to be burned down, but only houses out in the country.[16] Where the house is under a leasehold or rented out, whoever permitted its use for the meeting, is to pay off the rent; however, if the landlord was unaware of it, the house is not to be burned down."[17] Another problem for the government was provision for the numerous underage children left behind by the fugitives. In April 1529, there were between forty and fifty such children without parents in the Kitzbühel judicial district alone: they were put in a house together and a guardian was appointed for them.[18]

One such refugee, who left wife and child, goods and chattels, in order to follow "the trumpet call from Mount Ephraim," was the author of the song "Come ye to me, calls God's own Son"–Jörg Grünwald of Kitzbühel, a "principal overseer" of the Anabaptists.[19] In September 1529, he was staying in Lakstatt in Bavaria (judicial district of Klingen). The captains of Kufstein and Rattenberg and the administrator of Kitzbühel were ordered to be on guard for his return home. He was apprehended the following year in Kufstein and executed there.[20] On December 7, 1529, another twenty Anabaptists were seized. They had been holding their meeting among the bushes on a mountain near Kitzbühel. Among them were nine recidivists who had previously recanted in the Kitzbühel cemetery.[21] Quite a few of them had been baptized by Jakob Partzner, "a former priest, who as an overseer of the sect had fled the county of Tyrol some time ago."

The administrator resident at the Salzburg castle was ordered to watch out for Anabaptists in the Ziller valley, especially around the

Kropfberg. Similar instructions were sent to Rattenberg and Rotenburg with respect to the four main leaders: Hans Streicher, Adam Steiner, Paul Polt and Wolfgang Maier.[22] Among the Anabaptists in Rattenberg, Christian Gschöll was executed in 1529, and his property and that of the other Anabaptists who had fled Rattenberg was confiscated.[23] The care of the thirteen children who had been left behind became the responsibility of the authorities.

The largest number of those brought to the Rattenberg *Malstatt* (place of justice, and execution) derived from the neighboring villages "infected" by Anabaptism: Brixlegg, Ratfeld, Kramsach, Breitenbach, Puch and Imming. The twelve Anabaptists, men and women, who were taken captive on September 20, all came from these villages. Four of the women belonged to respected families. All the efforts of the Barefoot Monk Reinhard, who had been summoned from Schwaz to convert the prisoners, were in vain; so the judge in Rattenberg was ordered to "let justice be done to them."[24] Some of the prisoners eventually recanted; the others were sentenced to death, and the sentence was carried out on December 12.[25] Although both men and women and particularly the recidivist (Nickhinger) were severely tortured, the captain of Rattenberg could get nothing out of them, for they would rather die than become traitors.[26] This "small number" of people handed over to "Meister Hans" (i.e. the executioner) was followed in quick succession by several more, among them the "principal Anabaptists" Polt, Steiner, and Leopold Nicking from Brugg.

In his account, Philip von Liechtenstein informed the authorities that in his opinion there were clandestine Anabaptists also in Schwaz, among them five or six overseers. Mere patrols would be of little avail there; it would be better to hire several trusty persons who would let themselves be baptized and thus could easily find out everything. Such persons might be paid 50-60 gulden on the quiet. Also, he said, there were several churches without a priest, which left people bereft of church services. He concluded by suggesting that the Rattenberg parish, presently served by an incompetent "journeyman priest" (*Gesellpriester*), be staffed properly. Such spies ("moles") as suggested were indeed employed and were promised 40 Rhenish gulden for every overseer apprehended.[27] The archbishop of Salzburg was urged to send a learned and able priest (*Ordinarius*) to Reutte, the main parish that Rattenberg was a part of (until 1786), given that several of the daughter churches had no priest and the king's subjects were left without any religious services. "Your princely highness will be well aware that the new seductive sects can be controlled just as well by good, learned, and capable priests as by stern secular punishments."[28]

To a lesser degree than in the case of Rattenberg, the judicial district of Sonnenberg including the *Pflegschaft* (administered estate) of Wellenburg, was infested with Anabaptists. The Sonnenberg district exercised penal jurisdiction also over the city of Innsbruck. In the late autumn of 1529, bookkeeper Balthasar Vest and his wife were arrested as Anabaptists.[29] Both refused to recant and were executed four days later. Their property, including books and a small house at Tauer were confiscated by the treasury and used to pay the court expenses. The remainder was left not to the relatives, who requested it, but[30] to the Innsbruck burgher Hans Pirger in consideration of the fact that he had formerly let himself be used, for a mediocre remuneration, in Emperor Maximilan's chancery. He had also been employed in that emperor's chapel and while in service had suffered bodily harm by breaking his leg. On November 26 and 27, reprieves were granted to Jörg von Werd, master joiner from Innsbruck, and to Michael Resch, a master cloth-shearer.[31]

Less watchful was the administrator of the judicial district of Petersberg, Ulrich Rungen. In the dark of night, five of the Anabaptists he had apprehended in early July escaped, for which reason he was reprimanded by the government.[32] Anabaptist preachers were turning up at Wenns[33] and around Flauerling[34] but especially in the Oetz valley, in the parish of Sils and at Umhausen. The *Gesellpriester* ("journeyman priest") there was inclined toward the new teaching and was said to have preached in a Zwinglian and Anabaptist sense about the Lord's Supper and the intercession of the saints.[35]

No less intense was the movement on the opposite side of the Brenner Pass. At the end of February Hans Koller, who had been reprieved the year before, was brought in to Sterzing and executed a few weeks later. He was followed on March 29, by the two Steinfelder brothers and young Hofwieser, and on April 6, by Heinrich Goldschmied and Blasy Gengel.[36] On the other hand, Ulrich Stadler was set free from the beadle's house in Sterzing. He denied being part of the Anabaptists. True, he said, he had not received the blessed sacrament for two years, but only because the priest he had been unwilling to confess to twice, had withheld it from him. The government ordered an investigation about this and when this kept dragging on unduly, ordered him released.[37]

As regards the remainder of the Anabaptist movement on the far side of the Brenner Pass, we find Anabaptists mentioned in 1529—to be precise, in January in the judicial district of Michaelsburg and at Taufers; in February at Bozen, Mölten, Sterzing, Sarntheim, and Wangen; in March in the Gufidaun district, then around Michaelsburg, Schöneck, and Sonnenburg; in May in the Puster valley, especially around Metsburg, Bruneck, Toblach, and Michaelsburg; in June near Völs, Bruneck, along the Ritten and Breitenberg mountains, at Brixen, near Bozen, and in the Michaelsburg district; in July at Sterzing, Bozen, Kurtatsch, Brixen, close to the Rittner Horn, and at Peytelstein; in August along the Ritten, at Klausen and Gufficaun; in September at Vill, Neumarkt, Tramin am Moos, near Leyfers, Klausen, and Gufidaun; in October at Gries and Bozen: in November around Neumarkt; in December at Brixen, by the Rittner Horn, at Toblach, and at many places in the Puster valley, in Kaltern, Deutsch-Noffen, and in the Fleimser valley.

In the Michaelsburg diocese the Anabaptist movement became so noticeable already in March (1529) that the government exhorted the lenient district administrator to be more in earnest about it. At the end of April 13, Anabaptists from there were delivered up to the Brixen court[38] and four of them were executed on June 4, among them their overseer Gregor Weber from Pflaurenz, whose name crops up many times in the Puster valley, who was Hutter's most intimate friend and teacher. He ended his life at the stake together with two of his brothers and in the presence of two other brothers and a large crowd of people.[39] His property was confiscated by the government but not without a protest on the part of the episcopate, which as holder of a pledge, raised a claim to the executed man's estate. On June 11,[40] the government informed the bishop of its desire that in future such

Anabaptists be sent back to the Michaelsberg district, which they rightfully belonged to, so as not to infringe upon his imperial majesty's prerogatives as the reigning prince.

On June 9, the number of Anabaptists confined in the Brixen prisons was further increased by a host of such people from Kienz and St. Lorenzen, who also had been apprehended by the Michaelsburg administrator. Most of them were executed. A reprieve was granted to Agnes Hutter from Moos, the sister of Jakob Hutter, who until now had not come to any public notice.[41] Also the former "journeyman priest" Benedict from Bruneck was now handed over to Brixen. While still a priest, he had been inveighing against heretics being put to death: "Getting drowned or burned on account of his faith ought not to disconcert a Christian, for the work of Christ would nevertheless endure forever. Administrators, judges, and magistrates resemble Pilate, who like them had Christ deprived of his office." When summoned to Brixen to give an account because of using such language, he was set free when he promised to better his ways. Before long, though, the Anabaptists' courage, piety, and discipline drove him wholly into their camp.

Just like the Michaelsburg administrator, his colleague in charge at Schöneck set about clearing up his district. A chronicle tells of six persons who "were put on trial at Schöneck," which most likely means that they were apprehended at Schöneck and were put on trial at Brixen. In order to get hold of the persecuted folk in the forests and deserted places where they mostly held their assemblies, many times two or three districts had to summon their combined military might. Even so it was only in very rare cases that they succeeded in removing "the whole nest."

The *Malstatt* (place of judgment, court) at Brixen, too, gave rise to considerable difficulties. The jurors repeatedly expressed an intense aversion to the continuous shedding of blood and would refuse obedience by pretending that they could not burden themselves with the actions of persons who were neither obdurate nor criminal, not to mention that they were sent to Bozen from other judicial districts such as Wangen, Mölten, Sterzing, and Sarntheim and were thus taken out of the competency of their own judges. On February 26, the district magistrate Jakob Kuppfer addressed a complaint to the government with reference to this problem. The reply received went like this: Tell the jurors that the reigning prince does have authority to assign prisoners to any judicial district in his domain, for special reasons.[42]

What still offered maximum quiet and safety to the Anabaptists was the Ritten massif with its deserted areas[43] and scattered hamlets. Here, jointly with those from the Puster valley, they set up a proper community with Jörg Zaunring (Zaunried) as treasurer. There on the Ritten he repeatedly celebrated the Lord's Supper [with the brothers and sisters].[44] Here the administrator Augustin Heyerling raided a meeting and carried off thirteen persons as captives. Among them were Hans Gasser[45] and his wife, who had both been the subject of complaints already in 1528. He was now, being "unwilling to recant and repent, put to death by the sword at Bozen."[46] His wife, as well as several others, was granted a reprieve after hard penitence.

The persecution was carried out all the more vigorously since the government saw the Anabaptists not as just heretics but as rebels and insurgents, whose extermination was regarded as necessary not only to preserve the Christian faith but equally much in order to uphold peace and the order of the state. This is why in the various mandates the viewpoint of the state is definitely not the last one to be given consideration. In the mandate of April 1, 1528, the Anabaptists are presented as a sect that "has led to nothing but a destruction of God's honor, contempt of authorities, disobedience, war, ruin, bloodshed, and sadly, all manner of evil, such that has not been witnessed for more than a hundred years." This ignorance of the real character of Anabaptism, as evidenced by the writings and talks of the court preacher Dr. Johann Fabri and by the actions of the government explains the harshness and cruelty of the measures taken against them. A better understanding of their character and tendencies would doubtless have meant a better lot for the "quiet in the land" (*Stillen im Lande*). Rebellion was far removed from what they were striving for, as was the setting up of a secular government. These people, who were on principle opposed to the "sword" and bloodshed, had nothing at all to do with the Peasants' War, which, by decrying all the discontented as Anabaptists, is so readily placed to their account.[47]

Among all the districts south of the Brenner Pass the Michaelsburg one was the one most heavily afflicted, and it was precisely here that the main Anabaptist leader Jakob Hutter took up his work in Anabaptism's hardest days, undertake an activity that opened up to him all the gates of the separatists, from the outer boundary of German-speaking Tyrol to Kufstein and from the Eisack (Isarco) river to deep in Carinthia.

5
HUTTER AND PERSECUTION IN TYROL, 1529-30

THE ANABAPTIST CHRONICLES USE biblical language when speaking of Jakob Hutter. "Around this time there appeared a man named Jakob." His home was in the small hamlet Moos close to St. Lorenzen, not far from Bruneck in the Puster valley. Following a meagre education at the school in Bruneck he went to Prags to learn the hatter's trade. As a journeyman hatter he then moved about and finally settled at Spittal in Carinthia. It may have been in Klagenfurt that he first became acquainted with the Anabaptist teachings that became so decisive for his later life. He never set foot in either Bavaria or Silesia. In the summer of 1529, when, looking for a place of refuge for his community, he arrived in Moravia, he heard about Gabriel and his Silesian followers.[1] After "accepting the gracious covenant of a good conscience in Christian baptism, with a promise to live in true surrender and walk in God's own way" and "when it was felt that he had abundant gifts from God, he was elected to, and confirmed in, the service of the Gospel"—although it is not certain in what year.[2] In this position he moved about, initially in the Puster valley. One of the first small Anabaptist communities he headed up was the one at Welsperg, which would in turn gather in the house of his relative Balthasar Hutter and in that of the scythe-smith Andre Planer. At the first-named place he baptized ten people in one day. Among the "brothers and sisters" in the upper Puster valley he was known either as Jakob Hutter from Spital (in Carinthia) or as Jakob from Welsperg, among those in the lower Puster valley and along the Eisack as Jakob from Brunecken, "where he had relatives among that sect." He had an undisputed standing among all of them. By May 1529, the government had information about "the synagogue at Welsperg"; hence on May 25, the administrator of Toblach, who was also in charge of Welsperg, was ordered to raid the Anabaptists there, to arrest Balthasar Hutter and Andre Planer and call them to account.

On May 26, administrator Herbst and his men broke into Planer's house just when they were celebrating the Lord's Supper there, and captured fourteen of the brothers and sisters assembled. Some managed to escape, among them Thomas Schilling, already known to us from Kitzbühel and Jakob Hutter. Since Herbst was afraid that the prisoners might be forcibly freed from his castle, they were imprisoned at the Peytelstein fortress and were interrogated there. Their statements were sent to Innsbruck by Herbst. From their evidence it transpired that ten of the captives had been rebaptized[3] and that eight of these were ready to recant if they could be shown to be in error. The evidence given by Balthasar Hutter and Planer made it clear that some had been baptized by the late Gregori Weber and the others had been baptized, housed and accommodated "for money" by Jakob Hutter, he being their overseer. "For money" means that every baptized person had to contribute something to the communal purse. The Lord's Supper, which they refer to as the breaking of bread, was held in the room downstairs. Christian Hutter had been baptized by Jörg Zaunried from Rattenberg in the Inn valley. The government asked Herbst[4] to have the prisoners instructed by two capable priests about the two articles of faith: Holy Communion and baptism, and if the four men and four women were to recant and do penance, to let them go free. But as regards the others, they were to be dealt with in accordance with the princely mandates. On August 21, Christoph Herbst served notice that Baltzer Hutter and his consorts had been interrogated and that Jakob Hutter was a principal overseer (*Prinzipalvorsteher*).[5] Though Jakob Hutter himself had got away, at the beginning of

December 1529, the government succeeded in apprehending, "on account of rebaptism," his sister Agnes Hutter from Moos, in the judicial district of Michelsberg. Some time previously, Agnes had been granted a reprieve, but soon after had fallen back into error. That meant that her fate was sealed, and there was really no need for ordering Christoph Herbst on December 8, to keep instructing[6] her with or without torture, to subject her to criminal justice and let her be dealt with according to the mandates."[7]

The persecution of the "devout in the land" was just about becoming unbearable. The blood of the "martyrs" and burning pyres were in evidence everywhere. The dungeons were brimful of captives, who left behind abandoned and starving children, and no ray of hope for an end to the tribulation within sight anywhere except with God, whom they fervently implored day and night to take them away from this vale of sorrows. That is when the church community remembered that "in the Margraviate of Moravia, in the town of Austerlitz, God had gathered a people in His name to live as one mind, heart and soul, each caring faithfully for the other."[8] "So they were moved to send Jakob Hutter with Simon (Sigmund) Schützinger and some companions to the church at Austerlitz to make inquiries about all that had taken place." And when they came to Austerlitz in the fall of 1529 and talked things over with the elder of the church there, Jakob Wiedemann—"one-eyed Jakob"—and agreed to be of one mind and heart in the fear of God, they unified, on behalf of the church in the county of Tyrol, with the church in Austerlitz.[9] Soon thereafter Hutter returned to his homeland and joyfully told his people about the community of saints he had seen and experienced at Austerlitz; how, in the name of his own people, he had united with those at Austerlitz and how they had taken leave of him and sent him back with peaceful and united hearts. All the devout were full of joy about this. "Thereupon all who had no place or possibility to stay up there in their own county were sent off to the church in Austerlitz by Jakob Hutter and Sigmund Schützinger."[10] Hutter had a minister of the Word, Jörg Zaunried, accompany those who departed, and subsequently sent group after group to Moravia, as well as all their possessions, so as to share everything with the believers there.

In May 1529, Georg Cajacob, i.e. "of the House of Jacob," also called Blaurock ("the one with the blue coat"), the cofounder of Anabaptism in Switzerland, had come to Tyrol in the company of a Tyrolese, Hans Langecker, a weaver from the Ritten area, in order to care for Michael Kirschner's orphaned flock. While Hutter was away in Moravia, George Blaurock sealed his faith with his blood.[11] At every place where he had tarried since arriving in Tyrol—in Glurns and Schlaunders, in Meran and Bozen—he left behind traces of his activity, until he finally came to the desolate tracts around the Ritten massif and to Klausen (Chiusa).[12] The area of his mission extended from there to Neumarkt, his main stations being at Klausen, Gufidaun, Völs, along the Ritten massif and the Breitenberg, at Leifers and in the vicinity of Bozen. With crowds flocking to him the way they did, his activity could not remain secret for long. The government sent to Baron Georg of Firmian as the lien holder (*Pfandinhaber*) of Gufidaun a statement informing him of their displeasure in noticing that the Gufidaun administrator, Hans Preu, failed to observe the princely mandates since he allowed some Anabaptist refugees to stay in his district.[13] Firmian was therefore asked to remove this administrator and appoint a more suitable one. Blaurock was cautious enough to quickly shift his activity to another place. In June we therefore find him in Völs, in Tiers, in the ravines of the Kundersweg, near Leifers and Bozen (Bolzano); in July at Penon, Kurtatsch, Tramin, and Klausen. This is where he reaped the richest harvest and where he also returned from each of his mission journeys. On August 14, Hans Preu was able to inform the government that he had captured "two 'principal' seducers and Anabaptists, Georg [Blaurock] from Chur and Hans Langegger, a weaver from up on the Ritten, and had taken them to the Gufidaun castle to be guarded there," also that he had them interrogated there and was sending their confessions. On August 19, the Innsbruck government replied that they would have expected him to proceed against them as "chief seducers" in accordance with the princely mandates; since this had not been done, he was to ask them who had baptized them, who were their brethren, who they were, and whether they, too, had been baptizing.[14] In order to have this done "in a more stately manner," the administrator in charge of the Ritten area,

Augustin Heyerling, had been asked to be present at the interrogation. The protocol of the statements made by the captives was thereupon sent to Innsbruck,[15] and this resulted in Preu's being ordered to administer justice to the two prisoners, who were holding on to their faith. However, since Preu pointed out that he had no authority to administer justice involving capital punishment, judge Sigmund Hagenauer from Rodeneck was instructed to pass sentence on the two prisoners on the appointed day.[16] They were both condemned to death and "at the Holzschramme not far from Klausen (Chiusa) were burned alive at the stake."[17] This took place on September 6, 1529.[18] With Blaurock's death the Anabaptists lost their "second Paul." To begin with, his church was still held together by brother Benedict,[19] who had already served it during Blaurock's imprisonment by baptizing and preaching at Vill and Tramin.[20] Betrayed by spies and false brothers, a small band of Anabaptists was pounced upon on the Breiten Mountain (*Breitenberg*) above Leifers near Bozen by the district sheriff of Gries-Bozen, and the captives were taken to Bozen. They were unwilling to desist, even though the Barefooted Friars' guardian at Bozen tried hard for more than three weeks to convert them. They were people from the Gamper estate, which also otherwise had been a place for such conventicles. Among them was Simon Kob (Gobl) from the Breiten Mountain with his wife, her sister Margaret and others.[21] Most of them were sentenced and executed at Bozen. At the insistence of the district magistrate, who wanted it to be passed on to Kob's orphaned children, Kob's property was at the king's behest bequeathed to his heirs.[22] In the night of November 16-17 once again, this time at Vill near Neumarkt, four brothers and four sisters of Blaurock's church were captured and taken to Caldirf Castle. At the government's command the Neumarkt magistrate had them instructed by learned priests; and the obdurate ones were handed over to the court of criminal justice, to be presided over by the sheriff of Eppen, Hans Starffen.[23] The trial ended with the condemnation of the accused. In Kareid and Kaltern, too, Anabaptists were being hunted down. In Kaltern, Philip Koffler from Vill, frequently mentioned in Hutter's epistles, fell into the hands of the catch polls. It was in his house in Vill that Benedict had baptized Georg Frick and others. In face of the fate awaiting him, Philip pleaded for mercy. But when he had to speak out the requisite recantation, "he once again fell back." As a result he was placed before the court of criminal justice[24] and was sentenced. The property values he left behind in the judicial districts of Enn, Caldirf, etc. were confiscated by the princely treasury.

The continuous persecution drove the Anabaptists from the northern parts of Tyrol into the bishopric of Trent. On December 19, the Innsbruck government prevailed on the bishop there to take measures against them.[25] Simultaneously the magistrates (sheriffs) and the captain of Fleims, Ulrich of Spaur, were warned against tolerating Anabaptists in any way.[26] In January 1530, it was learned that Anabaptists, who tried to escape into Venetian territory, were being sighted in the Fleims valley and adjoining areas, especially on the high pastures of the St. Pelegrin mountain in the judicial district of Deutsch-Noffen. Attached to this information was the complaint that "some magistrates and administrators, in particular the Neumarkt agent (*Anwalt*), are very slovenly in the way they act and in part adhere to that faith." The agent concerned apologized and let it be known that he had arrested several Anabaptists.[27] The bishop of Trent was strongly urged to "have honest, capable, and learned men in all parishes and pastoral offices."

In order to get hold of refugees also on the other side of the territorial boundary, the (Innsbruck) government asked the king to "make arrangements with those in Venice, lest persons tainted with Anabaptism find refuge in their dominion."[28] If on the one side efforts were made to root out the hated sect, on the other side attempts were made to prevent its departure from the land in order to prevent them infesting the emperor's other patrimonial lands. It was certainly not in the manorial lords' interest to see their villages and farmsteads depopulated. That is why the princely mandates continued to be enforced in all their severity. Nevertheless the sect maintained itself on both sides of the Brenner Pass: on the one side around Schwaz, Rattenberg, Kufstein, Kitzbühel, Steinberg, St. Petersberg, and Ellenbögen; on the other side in the Puster valley, in Enn, Caldirf, Deutsch-Noffen and Gufidaun. At the very beginning of the year 1530, seven Anabaptists were captured in the judicial district of Neumarkt, among them two overseers: Martin Nauk from Deutsch-Noffen and Benedict Gamper from Breitenberg, who were in contact with the brethren in Madrusch and the Fleimser valley.[29]

In the judicial districts of Michelsburg and Sonnenburg jurors were the object of particular disdain, which expressed itself in abusive letters affixed to their doors at night. If there were fewer executions in the course of the year 1530, this was not due to a change in the treatment the Anabaptists received from the government but rather to the fact that the persecuted folk managed to find their way to Moravia, either singly or in groups. Unfortunately we are not adequately informed about the details of this emigration. At any rate, already in 1530, numerous Tyrolese make their appearance in the Anabaptist communities in Moravia. Those who had come from Tyrol would complain about "the teaching being less comforting and edifying than it had been over there in the old county. Many, too, had complaints about church discipline and the rearing of children. Such were the complaints the folk from Tyrol brought to their minister and fellow countryman Zaunring, thus burdening his mind and heart."[30] They remained in unbroken contact with Tyrol, and Hutter, who had by now gone back there, remained their overseer.

Meanwhile the persecution in Tyrol continued its course. In Schwaz, Anna Gasser, sister of Caspar Mayerhofer, was brought in as a recidivist on January 17. Besides her, Hans Glaser from Hall was arrested. As he remained obdurate, he had to suffer the death penalty, as did five Anabaptists who had been arrested on January 27 in Rattenberg.

In Steinach, in addition to somebody called Weber from Pangrazen, the overseers Zaunring, Froner, and Hutter were apt to turn up. Franz of Schneeburg was given the task to put an end to this disorder.[31]

The government was embroiled in a long legal battle with the free imperial city of Augsburg about the extradition of the former Kitzbühel chaplain Jakob Partzner, who the year before had turned Anabaptist and had fled. He stayed in Augsburg with a bookbinder and from there sent two epistles and a song to the brothers and sisters in Kitzbühel. At the government's request Partzner was arrested and interrogated, but his extradition was refused, for which reason the intervention of the imperial government was requested. Partzner was handed over only after King Ferdinand issued the declaration (Revers) of August 17, 1530, to the effect that in its case against Partzner his government desired to "pursue no other course than that of a justified legal case" and that it would practice mutuality in whatever cases might arise. Partzner confessed to having been active as an Anabaptist in Kitzbühel, Rattenberg, and Kufstein and to having misled many persons who then paid for their error with their lives, and declared that from his whole heart he was truly sorry for that. After formally recanting on August 29, he was granted his life.[32]

Partzner's benefactress, Lady Helena von Freyberg, already mentioned more than once as a friend of the Anabaptists fared better. When persecution broke out she moved from her Münichau estate to the lands owned by her husband Onofrius in Bavaria. When she was to be arrested there, the Bavarian government was notified that she had moved to her castle. In reply to an inquiry about this, Duke Wilhelm of Bavaria was told that nothing was known about this nor would she be tolerated. On learning that she was staying at Eppau, the administrator of Altenburg, Carl Fuchs, was given the task of apprehending this person sought "for being a firm adherent of the Anabaptist sect, for harboring Anabaptists and for bearing the main responsibility for the fact that around Kitzbühel so many persons had been baptized and in part sentenced to death." As she could not be found at her house, she was treated as a fugitive from justice and was deprived of her properties. However, friends and relatives of hers saw to it that these were set aside for Helena's sons.[33] She herself was granted a reprieve two years later but was to publicly recant. She was "long enough" in delaying her recantation and in October 1534, obtained permission to be spared a "public" recantation and to have it reduced to one hearing before the regent at Innsbruck. There she declared "in loud, clear words that she renounced her error."

Worse was the fate of young Sigmund von Wolkenstein, when he claimed the same alleviation. He was told that "the case of Lady Freyberg differed from his own in more than one respect": while she had been at liberty, he was in bonds; while she declared unreservedly, decisively, and clearly that she was recanting, he had been found altogether vacillating and doubting in his heart, hence "rightly undeserving of the grace extended to the baroness."

For the purpose of instructing the misled people discovered in and around Kitzbühel in May 1530, the dependable Franciscan brother Tonauer from Schwaz spent four weeks giving missionary sermons. On July 30, were promulgated the norms that were to guide the authorities in their work of uncovering and rooting out Anabaptists. These norms, following up on the mandates of March 2[34] and July 1, 1530,[35] decreed that any foreign, unknown persons and those journeying on unusual paths were to be stopped and questioned[36] regarding their activities and purposes; all houses were to be searched by honest and suitable persons. [Suspect persons] were to have their baptismal and family names taken down and to be questioned "when and where they had gone to confession and received Holy Communion. The father or mother of the house in question was to be asked who had baptized their children and when this had taken place. Whoever refused to cooperate was to be 'seized' and dealt with severely. Enquiries were to be made with the respective priests as to who had come to confession and who had not. This investigation was to be carried out three times a year: at Lent or after Easter, around St. James's day and around Candlemas [February 3]. Foreign persons were to be carefully watched the whole time; they were not to be given shelter, and if it came to light that, 'contrary to the warning, seductive persons had been sheltered,' the houses concerned were to be burned and destroyed, if this could be done without detriment to others. If other people had a share in such houses but were not involved in the error, the houses in question were to be donated to them."

"Likewise, the authorities are to clandestinely promise 20-30 gulden, to be paid by the board of finances, to certain trusted persons, to have them obtain information leading to the arrest of Anabaptists, 'in the hills or houses.'"[37]

"Pregnant Anabaptist women are to be kept in prison, away from their husbands, until delivery; costs to be defrayed from the Anabaptists' property; the confiscated goods to be transmitted to the chamber of finances."

"Judicial proceedings against Anabaptists are not to be public but to be held behind closed doors."

"The Anabaptist mandates are not to be promulgated by the priests from the pulpits but are to be read out by court clerks to His Majesty's subjects on a day when these are called together."[38]

The task of ascertaining, registering, and collecting the goods of Anabaptist fugitives in Kufstein, Rattenberg, and Kitzbühel was entrusted to *Ainspänniger* (i.e. driver of one-horse wagon or cart) Michael Rauch, who was sent out for this purpose in the autumn of 1530.[39]

Meanwhile, at the beginning of the year 1530, Prince Bishop Georg had returned to Brixen. Incensed as he was about the infringements of his administrative rights that had occurred during his absence, on February 1,[40] he sent a note to the provincial government in which he voiced his displeasure about this but also expressed the wish that the sectarians be proceeded against with the same vigor as before, and subsequently the government declared itself ready for this role. In addition, the governors, regents, and administrative chambers were asked, in view of the fact that "the cursed and seductive sect of Anabaptists has not yet been eradicated in our county of Tyrol, in spite of your diligence and manifold punishment," to set up roving bands or detachments that would patrol "mountains and valleys and any suspect places and corners" and in particular would pay visits to isolated and lonely farmsteads, would apprehend any "tainted" persons and incarcerate them. As regards ringleaders and recidivists, these were, "without any further judicial procedures and without mercy," to be brought to justice and dealt with in accordance with the issued mandates. "However, in view of the fact, that both the common people and the other estates form so integral a part of our county of Tyrol and that this way of proceeding might provoke a sense of revulsion, we want to pursue still another course, namely that our government might select, say, two persons of good repute from your midst who would travel through all districts and would communicate in meetings to all assembled subjects that His Majesty will in no way tolerate the sect and is determined to take strong measures against it." "Also, according to confidential information received, some of our officials and magistrates are in fact promoting such new sects; they converse and dispute with them and thus give the common people a bad example, without which they would have remained obedient as their parents had been." Hence this, too, has to be stopped, and it has to be considered how best to eradicate the sect.[41]

Already on February 9, the government served notice that the setting up of a roving patrol would not serve the purpose, nor does the other course suggested strike us as a good one at the present time, for in view of the stand taken by the Swiss Confederation and Grisons (Graubünden) and because of the widespread opinion among the people that the emperor is intending to bring in the Spaniards, generally "considered the worst people in the world" and to first punish his own people on account of faith, it would not be wise to convoke every judicial district and lay this before the subjects while gathered in so large a crowd; "it would be bound to fill them with dismay and horror." Besides, the statement goes on, "a measure of discouragement is to be noticed" because of the fact that after so many serious mandates there has to be recourse to measures that in all probability are bound to prove unsuccessful, being applied to people not afraid of persecution and even of death, who are deaf to any attempts to instruct and convert them and mostly just long to die soon.

The [Innsbruck] government would, however, consider it good for the punishments specified in the former mandates to be meted out in earnest, with no one to be spared. They would know how to take appropriate action against negligent officials; however, in more than one case the incriminating information received had ultimately turned out to be unfounded. So far one had definitely proceeded with sufficient earnestness: "We may loyally and truthfully inform Your Royal Majesty that in these two years there has scarcely ever been a day without Anabaptist matters calling for our attention. More than 700 persons, both male and female, have been executed at several places in this county of Tyrol; others have been expelled and still more have fled abroad, forsaking their property and in part also leaving behind their orphaned children."

What the government proposes and requests His Majesty's agreement to is this: first, that open orders be issued to all captains, administrators, and magistrates in the land commanding that in view of several administrators' lack of application, every magistrate or administrator in the country is to himself go to every parish within his district, ascend the pulpit and have the court clerk read out the mandates issued and exhort the people to beware of the evil Anabaptist sect. Every captured Anabaptist is to be questioned about his co-conspirators and these are to be searched for. Every Anabaptist is to be "dealt with and punished according to the law and as befits his confession." This present article is to be read out in each church along with the mandates. This procedure, the article continues, is in accordance with the customs of the country and will have a deterrent effect on the common people. Secondly, the administrative head of the Adige area is to be specially commanded to properly supervise the administrators and magistrates in his territory.

This memorable document goes on: "If people were not so obdurate, the manifold cruel punishment meted out to old and young, men and women, some of whom not even fully grown up, a punishment people have before their eyes just about every week, by rights ought to so terrorize them that no one would want to join the sect in so irresponsible a way as is quite common."

"We cannot leave Your Royal Majesty in ignorance about the senselessness now commonly met with among these people, which causes them, instead of being terrified by the punishment meted out to others, to rather go to where they themselves might partake of it, or they request to join the imprisoned ones and reveal themselves as their brothers and sisters. And when pursued by the judicial authorities and arrested, they confess to it readily and willingly, with no torture needed, and refuse to listen to any instruction. Only rarely is one of them ready to turn away from their mistaken faith; in most cases all they covet is to die soon." "And when one of them actually recants, he is still not to be greatly trusted, hence neither good instruction nor severe punishment is of any avail with these people. We hope Your Royal Majesty will graciously gather from this truthful presentation of ours that we have not allowed anything to slacken our diligence."[42]

The king agreed to the proposals, and the authorities promulgated them in March 1530. The decree included a reprimand for those authorities who had been acting in a sloppy, negligent, and sluggish way in these matters. A second decree, of the same date and likewise promulgated under the king's name, informs all authorities that the Anabaptists are peculiar in that they do not attend church, do not allow their children to be baptized, do not go to confession nor partake of the sacrament, these being the signs by which they can be recognized. Accordingly, all authorities are "recommended" to have it publicly announced that in accordance with the old-established Christian order everybody is to attend Holy Mass and sermon on Sundays, go to confession at Lent, and have his children baptized, all of which is to be attested by the priest. Whoever fails to do this is to be imprisoned.[43]

The decree of July 1, 1530, served as a bait for informers, several of whom are branded in the chronicles, songs, and epistles of the Anabaptists, e.g. in the well-known song of the schoolmaster Hieronymus Käls (d. 1536 in Vienna): *"Ich reu' und klag den ganzen Tag"* [I feel remorse and complain all day].[44] An award of 30-40 gulden was paid to whomever spied out a brother and caused him to fall into the hands of the authorities.

While the government thus mustered all its powers in order to bring Anabaptism under control, Jakob Hutter would tirelessly and while braving all dangers, move from valley to valley and gladden the believers with "the forbidden word of God." What kept him from being captured was only the loyalty and sacrifices of the "brothers and sisters." Not even severest torture could make them betray the secret of his whereabouts at the time. Shortly before Whitsun 1530, after the execution of brother Grünwald, Hutter sent an epistle to the brethren in Moravia,[45] in which he exhorts them to hold out in the grace received and not to grow weary in the struggle of that perilous time. He sends greetings to his brothers and coworkers Georg Han and Christel (Chr. Alsaider or Chr. Häring) and reports that "once again the godless have savagely torn away from us a devout brother and together with him two other zealous ones." He tells that eight days before Whitsun, on Saturday night (May 28) "we had wanted to come together, but then the noblemen from Enn appeared with a whole crowd of catchpolls and surrounded the houses. However, only two brothers were inside."

While Hutter, summoning all his strength, cared for his church community, in Austerlitz in the winter of 1530, contentions arose that endangered the existence of that community and in the end split it into two hostile camps. What caused it was the discordant understanding of the brethren's statutes on the part of the confirmed ministers of the Word, their clumsiness in deciding difficult cases, opulence in the overseers' household, secrecies in the administration of the property, and the ambition of individuals unready to have their light hidden under a bushel, not to mention various other shortcomings listed, with some exaggeration, in Reublin's letter to Pilgram Marpeck. As he had once, at St. Alban's in Basel done against the Catholic Church, in Austerlitz Reublin now started speaking out against the "annoying abuses of the ministers of the Word." In this endeavor he was assisted by the Tyrolese Zaunring, David from Schweinitz, and others. Reublin was accused of rebelliousness, and without allowing him to give an account, Jakob Widemann, the main minister at Austerlitz, and the elders he had summoned from all the other communities, declared Reublin banned. He and those standing with him were treated as if "disconnected from the church and had to eat separately."[46]

As a result of this action the banned ones and the people holding to them, mostly Tyrolese, Swabians, and Rhinelanders, after first finding accommodation for their sick ones and children with good people in the town, moved from Austerlitz with grieving hearts. Another group who wanted to neither go with them nor remain with those at Austerlitz, trekked back to their old homelands.

Lowly and destitute as they were, Reublin with his people—250 persons—made their way to Auspitz, where the abbess of Maria-Saal in Brünn permitted them to settle and also put the empty parish priest's house at Steurowitz at their disposal.[47] At the same time two messengers were sent to Hutter, who were to inform him and the elders about the split and were to invite them to come down right away in order to investigate what had taken place. Those in Austerlitz did the same. So Hutter and Schützinger came back to Moravia, investigated "where the fault for the dissension might lie and found that those at Austerlitz were in the wrong and the most guilty." However, when Hutter reprimanded them on that account, they "no longer wanted to listen to him." "But he nevertheless showed them their error and how they had gone wrong. In the first place they had acted unjustly by casting out, and separating from, innocent people; second, they had given in to fleshly freedoms and had allowed for private property back; third, they had allowed marriages with unbelievers."

However, Reublin, too, did not enjoy his leadership role for long. Unfamiliar with the "community" he had committed himself to, he had secretly stashed away some money for unforeseen emergencies, was convicted of this and therefore excluded from the community. The direction of the latter was now entrusted to Jörg Zaunring, with the assistance of Burkhard of Ofen, Adam Schlegel, and Bohemian David [Burda von Schweinitz].

Having settled the dissension for which Hutter and Schützinger had been called from Tyrol, they returned to their homeland, where "God had been powerfully at work." Not long after their departure from Austerlitz the new church community was again without a shepherd, for Schlegel and Burkhard were relieved of their service and excluded as "opponents of the truth" and Bohemian David as self-willed and of an unrighteous heart, while Zaunring lost his service because of his laxity. "Without delay the church turned to those in Tyrol both by letter and word of mouth and pleaded for help with the ministry of the Word." Thereupon at about Easter 1531, Hutter and Schützinger set out once more, and now Schützinger was appointed in the place of Zaunring. Negotiations were entered into with Gabriel [Ascherham] and his people in Rossitz and with Philipp [Plener or Blauärmel], who lived in Auspitz, and these led to a unification of the three separate branches—an event greatly celebrated by the *Chronicles*. Hutter's task had been accomplished, and he turned back to the home country he had left behind in distress and turmoil.

6
THE PRINCIPAL MANDATE OF MAY 12, 1532

THE LAND ALONG THE ADIGE AND ISARCO RIVERS AND THE PUSTER VALLEY AS THE ANABAPTISTS' CHIEF CENTERS.

AFTER HUTTER HAD SUCCESSFULLY reestablished unity among the Moravian Anabaptists, as the chronicles report, "the number of people in the church increased daily at all three places. From Silesia they came to Rossitz; from Swabia and the Palatinate they joined Philipp's group, and Jakob Hutter sent many from Tyrol to Schützinger."[1] This was the time when the Tyrolean Anabaptists struggled for their existence. As Kirchmair notes, "in this year in the Empire as well as in the country hereabouts the trouble with the heretics, in particular with the Anabaptists, kept getting worse and worse, and I think that alone here in the county of Tyrol and Görtz a thousand people have been burned, beheaded, and drowned on account of it. For the Anabaptists evinced tremendous stubbornness . . ."[2] True, the Anabaptist chronicles themselves list among that year's victims only Walser Mayer, who jointly with two other ministers of the Word was executed by the sword at Wolfsberg in Carinthia.[3] However, this in no way comprised the total number of victims. The Innsbruck authorities had not forgotten the stern directions received but a few months ago from the highest authority. On May 20, 1530, the country's authorities had been confronted with the following questions:

1. Why have the heretical Lutheran sects been allowed for so long to take root in the country, or where has an overseer or wealthy person or magistrate been punished?
2. Why, in view of the many mandates issued, have the suspected Lutheran preachers been allowed to preach for so long in towns and judicial districts, particularly in Kitzbühel, Rattenberg, Schwaz, Hall, Innsbruck, and Sterzing, without being punished? Why were things not put in order?"
3. Why was the preacher from Stams, who had long since been recognized as "Lutheran," allowed to come to Schwaz? Why was he, as well as a second one in Jenbach (Inpach), shielded and protected, contrary to our issued commands?
4. Why was the barefooted monk brother Reicharten (sic) forbidden in my name to speak out or preach against the above-mentioned Stams preacher?
5. Why were several Lutheran Anabaptists set free, without any corporal punishment, thus disregarding our mandates? Who absolved these persons?[4]

Otherwise, the authorities were everywhere kept busy apprehending fugitive Anabaptists, which at times led to conflicts with the neighboring rulers.[5] At the end of July, Blasius from Crossen on the Oder river, "a true overseer of the sect" was burned alive.[6] The execution costs of eight gulden were borne by the finance board.[7] Ullrich Müllner from Klausen had already in 1528, been accused of having sheltered Anabaptists but found a way of justifying himself; this time, though, he openly confessed to being an Anabaptist and in October 1531, was beheaded at Klausen. Even thirty years later Jörg Kotter of Innsbruck was told by eyewitnesses of Müllner's steadfastness and of how well he "was liked by the people."[8] During July a number of brothers and sisters were executed in Bozen and Kaltern; in the judicial district of Schöneck brother Steinheis was put to death, leaving behind a good farm, which was then confiscated. In Brixen, Mayerhofer from Niedervientl was still awaiting his sentence.

North of the Brenner Pass the Anabaptists found brothers and fellow sufferers in and around Rattenberg,[9] among the miners at Schwaz[10] then at Imst and Petersberg;[11] south of the Brenner Pass in the Adige area, specifically: in the districts of Gufidaun,[12] of Teutsch- and Wälsch-Noffen,[13] in Bozen and Brixen,[14] as well as in the judicial district of Sterzing,[15] in the Sarn and Taufers valley,[16] and similarly in the Hohenberg domain (*Herrschaft*) in the forelands.[17]

In Battenberg they held their meetings in a coal mine, in the Schwaz district in an abandoned adit and afterwards in a house on the Calzein Mountain. In the mines Peter Schilling was their preacher. The mining magistrate in Freundsberg came to have misgivings about how to deal with people condemned to die by the sword. On July 11, he received the following direction: "All rebaptized persons who have not themselves carried out baptisms, who are neither overseers nor recidivists and have been sentenced to die at the stake may be executed by the sword if they so desire. However, when the sentence is carried out you are to let the corpses of those executed in this way be buried like animal corpses, just as has until now been customary in our domains of Rattenberg and Kufstein."[18] There were several Anabaptists at Klausen, among them Hutter's confidant Caspar Schmidt from Bruneck; in the Gufidaun district it was especially people from Teys and Villnöss. In a mountain cave in the latter district Hutter held a gathering, at which 150 persons were present and also partook of the Lord's Supper. Also at Albeins and close by the "smelting hut" (foundry) at Prugg between Brixen and Klausen nightly gatherings of between 50 and 60 Anabaptists were sighted.[19] A government edict of September 29, 1531, voices the expectation that Baron George of Firmian, the wielder of judicial authority, should be able to put an end to this disorder. In the summer of 1531, similar conventicles, numbering 40 to 50 people, made their appearance also in the Branten valley. The thankless task of apprehending the participants fell to Lord Wilhelm of Liechtenstein as pledgeholder of Carneid and feudal lord of Wälsch-Noffen, and to the guardians of Jakob of Niederthor's children as pledge holders of Deutsch-Noffen.

Somewhat less gloomy than in the preceding years was the situation in the Sterzing judicial district, although there was no lack of baptism-minded folk[20] also there. We find them in the Pfitsch valley, in Dulfes and at other places. In the person of Heinrich Kessler they had an overseer here who, supported by a population well-disposed toward the Anabaptists, kept evading the bailiff's meagre surveillance. The baptism-minded folk in Ridau were also part of his fellowship.[21] As stealthily as they came they would also disappear again just as soon as a danger loomed.

The [Innsbruck] government left no measure unused that it deemed suitable for the suppression of the sect. On January 19, it notifies captain Christoph Fuchs and the administrators of Kitzbühel, Rattenberg, Rotenburg, Wilten, Sonnenburg, Axams, Ambras, Hertenberg, Freundsberg, Tauer, and Steinach:[22] "We are hearing that several Anabaptists from this land have been expelled from the land of Moravia and that these now want to come back to this land of Tyrol. It is therefore commanded to forestall this evil and everywhere, on mountains as well as in valleys, to be on the lookout for such Anabaptists, since they are not allowed to enter."

What harmed the Anabaptists more than this ordinance was the decree of July 8, 1531, issued in the name of Ferdinand I, in which the earlier punishments threatening all those giving shelter to Anabaptists are reiterated and persons who denounce to the authorities an Anabaptist overseer are now promised an award of 40 gulden. This was an enticing offer and would fill many a dungeon with both real and alleged Anabaptists,[23] particularly in Klausen, Gufidaun, St. Georgen, and Michaelsburg. On August 18, 1531, this edict was followed by a second one in which all magistrates, sheriffs, and administrators were ordered to proceed with proper strictness, with imprisonment and punishments, against all persons tainted with Anabaptism, to seize as forfeited to the chamber of finance (treasury) the goods and chattels of prisoners or fugitives, to use this property for the upbringing and education of the abandoned children, and to earnestly see to it that all parish priests and preachers read out the issued mandates at least four times a year from the pulpit, so that the people be instructed to be on guard against heretical opinions and sects.[24]

In the Innsbruck government circles, meanwhile the conviction had been gaining ground that not very much was to be achieved with the measures employed so far; that is why in a report of January 12, 1532, the authorities turned to the king with the request that other ways be found. As one such way they recommended a measure that had been decided against in 1529: the setting up of a roving detachment of forty men on foot, headed by a captain, to begin with at least for the judicial district of Sterzing, which was seven miles long but until now had only two policemen. In future, Anabaptist goods were no longer to be given away but were to be sequestered for the chamber of finance.[25] Consent was given for the establishment of such a troop, and on February 6, the mandate stated that "nobody was to house Anabaptists nor grant them any kind of shelter, as these people were doing greater harm than murderers and enemies; so everybody should be ready to subdue and capture them."[26] As this exhortation did not seem of much use, three weeks later a new mandate was issued, in which regret at the fact that in some judicial districts notorious Anabaptists were allowed to roam about unhindered. It was accompanied by a more tempered injunction to be diligent in apprehending those evil and harmful people and to render help and assistance to the authorities in their investigations.

From the confession of the Anabaptist Jakob Gasser, who was laying in prison at Rodenegg and would later be apostate, the police were able to learn that the Anabaptist Jakob Hutter from Welsberg was about to leave the country and move to Moravia, where "an alien faith had sprung up in their church." This, as well as the circumstance that four Anabaptists, equipped with "passports" directing them to Auspitz, had in March been stopped in Sterzing, caused the Innsbruck government to ask the territorial prince to make corresponding provisions. It had also ordered the authorities in Hall, Schwaz, Rattenberg, and Kufstein to watch out for Anabaptists "traveling on boats and intending to leave the country by water."[27] Against Hutter the following arrest warrant was issued:[28] "Jakob Hutter, said to be from Welsberg, a person with a black beard, wearing a military coat (*Wappenrock*) of black frieze, a blue doublet (jerkin), white trousers, a black hat, and bearing a small pickaxe (*hackl*) on his arm." "He is said to be journeying from this country to the county of Moravia and will doubtless, as also happened last year, travel by water down the Inn river toward Austria and from there make his way to Austria [sic—should probably read 'Moravia']." Hence an order is given to be especially on the lookout for Jakob Hutter.

It then became patent from the confession of the Anabaptist Peter Hungerl, who was put to death at Sterzing, that he, jointly with Hutter, as well as the five brothers Grueber, Beck, Schuster, Planer, and Thaler,[29] who were executed together with him, had intended to travel to Hutter's church at Auspitz. The government did not hesitate to ask the reigning prince to "make provision for Hutter, who in this country has brought so many persons into that sect, to possibly be apprehended over there."[30]

The mandate of February 28 was still in everybody's memory when the government, aware of the fact that the Anabaptist sect "was showing no sign of coming to an end, in spite of all the measures taken, and was in fact springing up at several more places," on April 24, asked the reigning prince for yet another mandate against those giving shelter to Anabaptists.[31] It is this action that caused the general mandate of May 12, 1532, to be issued.[32] What comes to expression in it was in agreement with the facts, namely "that, regardless of the mandated fines and punishments, in many places Anabaptist persons are well and adequately provided for. And yet no one within the area of our princely county of Tyrol can truthfully and reasonably claim to have been ignorant of our decrees. Given that this sect is thus enabled to lead a wholly vexatious and profligate life, which we in our principalities and lands are no less than before resolved, with all earnestness and diligence, to put an end to, we hereby command that henceforth all who knowingly shelter and accommodate or in any way assist Anabaptist persons will be immediately arrested and proceeded against with interrogation and torture to ascertain if they, too, are stained by the Anabaptist sect." "And though they may not have accepted rebaptism themselves, because of the shelter they have given they are nevertheless to be punished in body and property, and no one will be spared."

In this year (1532) more than in the traditional Anabaptist area of Rattenberg-Freundsberg[33] it was in the Adige (Etsch) and Isarco (Eisack) region and in the long stretch of the Puster valley that the Anabaptists were finding to be a pitiful dwelling place. For them, the names Gufidaun and Sterzing, Michelsburg and Lüsen, Rodenegg and Peitelstein-Welsperg bring up bitter memories.

At the end of February, forty Anabaptists had gathered for the breaking of bread, when armed catch polls pounced on them and carried seven of them off as prisoners. The others escaped, among them three overseers, one of whom being "a Hutter from Welsperg, who is said to carry a *puchse.*" [a small container] The captives were taken to Brixen and the prince bishop's councillors were asked to have the Michaelsburg administrator hunt for those that got away.[34]

On August 3, the government sent the Welsperg administrator, Christoph Herbst, the following order: "Even though we already earlier earnestly commanded you to keep a sharp lookout for Jakob Hutter from Welsperg, an overseer (*Vorsteher*) in the seductive sect of Anabaptists, to apprehend and submit him to suitable punishment, we nevertheless learn that he recently held a meeting of 80-90 persons in a woods at the bathing pool,[35] that he there propagated that seductive sect and carried out baptisms, with nobody impeding him and handing him over for punishment. We once more urge you earnestly to keep a sharp lookout for the afore-named Hutter and his adherents and do your best to have him apprehended."[36] The reprimand meted out to Christoph Herbst had the effect that only three weeks later he was able to report that he had arrested several Anabaptists in his district and taken them, securely guarded, to Peitelstein castle. Among the prisoners was Friedrich Brandenberg from Cologne, who had accompanied Hutter on his missionary journeys and was later executed.[37] As the authorities reported to Brixen, he stated that Hutter had baptized seven persons at Lüsen and had done the same in the Sarn valley. The Brixen bishop was asked to try and identify the persons baptized.[38] From Brandenberg's confession the authorities also learned[39] that Hutter had misled a great many persons in the country into that error, that "as an important overseer he had been rebaptized himself," that he crisscrossed the country mostly at night and was finding shelter with simple peasant folk and in particular with a peasant called Hansin Schmyren, in the remotest house at Schmyren. Friedrich Franz of Schneeburg is to arrest that peasant and to inquire of him where Hutter might be apprehended. Long before a search had been on for Hutter, Christoph Gschöll, and Hans Tuchmacher (Amon) were also in Gufidaun and Klausen.[40]

On March 22, the Gufidaun administrator was directed as follows: His proposal to stop having the confessions read out in full length and to have capital punishments carried out by the sword at the "Schranne" instead of by burning could not be agreed to. It was the accepted order to have the judgments read out in extract, as was customary. When leading the condemned out it should be seen to it that they do not spread through preaching efforts, and the people were to be kept away by telling them, "Go home, make way; you have no business here": "*ne audiat docentes* [sic: don't listen to teachers]."[41]

It was the magistrate in Sterzing that had the most work to do this year. True, the Anabaptist *Geschichtsbücher* (*Chronicle*) only mentions seven who went into death there for their conviction, namely Lamprecht Grueber and his fellows, then Kunz Füchter, the brethren's treasurer,[42] who "from prison wrote to the church community an epistle, which is still in existence." However, there was a much greater number of victims. Even before the execution of Lamprecht and his fellows four brothers were put to death in Sterzing; several others died with Kunz Füchter, and before the latter also Georg Schröffl from the Michelsberg judicial district. When finally, thanks to the roving patrols, fifteen Anabaptists were captured in November, the parish priest of Hall, Christoph Landsberger, was called to Sterzing to instruct them. Only from a few did he and his assistant Leonhard Menthaler succeed in extracting a recantation, hence on December 15, 1532, the district judge Flamm was ordered to proceed against the obdurate ones as his office required. First, though, he was to try and find out the location of the three leaders: Hutter, Tuchmacher, and Offerus, "given that now in winter they cannot find shelter in woods and forests, and could be apprehended." Flamm was to promise them that, "if they tell the truth, he would recommend them for a reprieve."[43] The result of this and the later interrogation of brother Balthasar Thal was that Jakob Hutter and Hans Tuchmacher had lately found accommodation with Hans Mayer in Antholz, then with Peter Binder in Klausen, and that shortly before Candlemas [February 2] 1533, they had held a meeting in Villnöss in a house called Pitscheid, at which about seventy persons from the Puster valley had been present. This information was immediately passed on to the episcopal officials in Brixen, with the request that appropriate measures be taken with respect to the above-mentioned Anabaptists.[44] Already in January 1533, it had been known in Brixen that Hutter was active on behalf of his sect in and around Klausen. This becomes patent from the reprimand that the episcopal Counsellors meted out to Leonhard of Aischach, subcaptain at Säben, and to the town judge of Klausen, Stephan Rieder, on account of "not watching out for, and apprehending, that Hutter from Welsperg, an overseer in the sect, who is out to mislead the countryside and is so often visible in Klausen." In addition, in April and June 1533, several epistles that Hutter and Hans Amon had dispatched to their fellow members in Moravia, in part simply signed J and H,[45] had fallen into the hands of the authorities. The writers of the epistles were sought in vain. Ludwig Fest from Pinnegg, though, who had aimed to recruit fellow believers in the mines and at other places in Schwaz,[46] was arrested in the Freundsberg area and taken to Schwaz.[47] Being closed to all attempts to convert him, he was beheaded at Schwaz, in accordance with the ordinance of July 3.[48] In Kitzbühel he was followed by Christina Häring, about whom the *Geschichtsbücher* tell as follows: "As she was advanced in pregnancy and in fact close to delivery, they left her at home until the child was born. And though she could easily have escaped ten times and more during those days, she did not do so. So they took her back to the town of Kitzbühel and there executed her by the sword, something they do not usually do with a woman, and afterwards they burned her corpse, as is well known to her brothers Christian and Thomas Häring, who both lived in the church community for a long time."[49]

On Monday, July 14, in Brixen several Anabaptists, men and women, were executed by the sword; they were people from Lorenzen,

Gais, and from Götzenberg, who had fallen into the hands of a roving troop on general patrol.[50] In October 1533, seven Anabaptists were executed in Gufidaun: "They mightily urged the people to repent and wrote several epistles from their prison testifying that no impure, indolent, and slothful heart can hold out when it comes to the test." One of these epistles contains an exhortation for brothers who have children among the "godless" to take them away lest they be corrupted. The other epistle tells that ten are still lying in prison who all want to witness to the Lord with their blood.[51] The same fate awaited some brothers and sisters in Brixen, part of whom Hutter mentions by name in his epistle dated Auspitz, November 21, [1533]:[52] "With a shocked heart and weeping eyes I have read how severely and violently you are being persecuted and that once again several of the dearly beloved brothers and sisters have been captured, such as Valtan (Gsäl),[53] that faithful and beloved brother so very dear to me, and my children all of whom I bore with labor and great anguish through the grace of God: Gretlein, Christina, Ruepel, Stoffel, and also Kontz and still others, who had been imprisoned before and had also given a witness."

At the same time also the dungeons at Sterzing, Schönegg, and Rodenegg were filled. In mid-June 1533, the Anabaptists held a big meeting in the judicial district of Gufidaun in order to consider how their people who "can no longer find shelter and refuge anywhere in the whole country," might be sent off to Moravia.[54] Of the attendees, eighteen were captured; some of them renounced their doctrine, but eleven remained steadfast, and to these, says the report, "we have applied the law as required by the mandate." The *Geschichtsbücher* explain what that means. Nevertheless, as one of the prisoners stated, there were still a "number of brothers and sisters" around Gufidaun. These were the facts that the government communicated to the reigning prince on June 19.[55] It also reports that in the three domains of Rattenberg, Kufstein, and Kitzbühel there was by this time no longer any evidence of persons stained with Anabaptism nor of any signs of its gaining a new foothold. The report states that in Kufstein, the eradication had been carried out so diligently that the overseers and "sectarian" persons are unlikely to look for any further "refuge" there. As regards persons passing through to Moravia, they are, if captured, dealt with according to the mandates.[56] The report further asserts that right up to the present the county government has been proceeding earnestly and diligently to eradicate such sects everywhere in the country. Many such persons, it says, have been apprehended in Sterzing, Rodenegg, and Gufidaun, and the following legal proceedings are now being taken against them: Those who "fall victim to the sect for the first time but recant and are penitent are being reprieved as specified in the mandates. Against those unwilling to renounce we have first applied for several days some bodily discipline by withholding food and lashing them with rods," a punishment that has proved fruitful with some. Those who remain stubborn in their error even after this punishment will be sentenced and executed in accordance with the mandates issued. These are the proceedings we also adhere to with those presently imprisoned. Nor have we omitted to prevail upon the authorities to try and find out how one might apprehend the overseers; we have spared no efforts and expenditure to this end and have also deemed it right to increase the reward (*taya* or *taglia*) offered for their capture from 20-40 gulden to 60-70 or even up to 100 gulden, depending on the importance of the person apprehended.[57] We have ordered the head of the provincial administration (*Landeshauptmann*) and other authorities to recruit various persons that "under the pretence of wanting to join the sect" let themselves be rebaptized in order to thus find out about their assemblies. Appended to his report are the following suggestions: To begin with, the Anabaptists in Moravia should have their existence "cut off."[58] We also think that having capable preachers could greatly benefit the eradication of this sect. However, this is what the government considers the most fruitful procedure: "that the original cause giving rise to this sect be abolished, which, however, is something not to be achieved without a general reformation. That is why Your Royal Majesty's brother, His Imperial Majesty, had good reason to call for a Council to be held." As regards a "substantial counter-action," we would consider it good for Your Royal Majesty to propose at the forthcoming diet that a reward of 50-100 gulden be offered for each Anabaptist captured. The government, the report goes on, "knows of no better or more direct way of apprehending them or chasing them away." However, lest the treasury be unduly burdened, well-to-do Anabaptists were to pay the *"taya,"* whether they recant or not. Should they be unable to pay, the amount was to be taken from the assets of other Anabaptists, regardless of possible protests on the part of pledge holders. Finally, it was suggested that any goods seized be confiscated by the treasury.

Braving all dangers, in July 1533, a small band of Anabaptists from the Gufidaun judicial district, taking twenty-five children with them, set out for Moravia, traveling secretly, mostly at night and along offbeat paths. Even though the Schwaz administrator and the district magistrate of Rattenberg tried to block their way, they succeeded, by traveling in small groups, in arriving safely at the brothers in Auspitz.[59] Only four stragglers fell at the beginning of August into the hands of the authorities.[60] In those same days information was also received that just recently, shortly before August 1, there had been a large gathering in the Hegaw (Hagau) area near Rattenberg and that Hutter had held a second one at the Stamser Joch (Stams Col). By the time the government issued its order to have Hutter and his companions apprehended, he was already beyond the border and on his way to Auspitz.[61] His work was continued on this side of the Brenner Pass by Offerus [Griesinger],[62] on the far side by Hans Amon or Tuchmacher, as he was commonly called.

The strongest church community south of the Brenner Pass was the one by the Götzenberg. That is where on feast days the devout would gather from near and far: from Sterzing and Rodenegg, from the Puster valley and from Taufers. At the same time the Inn valley Anabaptists in Steinach, where Valentin Luckner was their minister, held their meetings near Vomp, Brixlegg, and in the Hegaw.[63] From amidst these brothers and sisters occasionally groups of ten-fifteen persons were sent off to Moravia. Each detachment was told precisely which places and persons they were to seek out. On one of the ten brothers seized at the Götzenberg in September such an itinerary was discovered,[64] which identified the way stations between Wasserburg and Moravia. The councillors in Brixen immediately sent this discovery on to the Innsbruck authorities, and these passed the information on to Duke Wilhelm of Bavaria and to the administrative head (*Landeshauptmann*) of Upper Austria. In Linz they [the travelers] put up with a man named Partener.⁶⁵ The bishop of Brixen was duly thanked for this precious information⁶⁶ and was urged to keep a close eye on Onoferus [Griesinger] and the other Anabaptists in the Puster valley. But by this time Onoferus was already back in the Inn area and celebrated Christmas with the faithful near Hegaw. A troop led by the district magistrate Ernst Brandt, which had been dispatched for the purpose of apprehending the Anabaptists there, arrived too late, as usual. The only person to fall into their hands was an elderly sister, Ursula Holzkirche.

At the end of the year 1533, the clerical and secular authorities were faced with a completely new case.⁶⁷ The bishop of Brixen had informed the [Innsbruck] government that Jörg Scharlinger, the district magistrate at Sillian, had been authorized to set free two youths who had recanted from among the four Anabaptists he had in his prison; however, as regards the two other youths, aged 16-17 years, named Hutter and Schuster, one of whom had fallen prey to the sect for the second time and who were now refusing to be instructed by the priests, justice was to take its course. "However, as Scharlinger informs us, the jurors have grave misgivings about passing judgment on these young people according to the mandates, on account of their unripe age and also of their lack of understanding, for where that is missing, the jurors consider it a grave responsibility to condemn a person to death, especially in matters concerning faith." The government was at a loss how to handle this and on December 3, turned to the reigning prince for a ruling about appropriate punishment for the two youths. To this request was added the observation that until now young maidens had been executed by drowning; other young people had been given a flogging; however, those maidens had been older and had also had a proper understanding. The eventual decision (Prague, December 19, 1533) went as follows: The recidivist was to be judged according to the law; he was to be kept in prison with the other one, both at their own expense or at that of their relatives, and if that proved impractical, supported by common charity, until they reach the age of 18. In the meantime they were, even should they recant and be penitent, to be well instructed by learned persons. They were to be reprieved only if upon reaching the age of 18, they would formally recant and do penance. However, if they remain obdurate even then, they are to be dealt with according to the law.[68] This was also the procedure the Brixen authorities recommended to administrator Ulrich Geltinger, advising him, "you should obtain learned and able secular priests, laymen, and friends of the boy in question to address him with Christian admonition and Holy Scripture and if that should prove fruitless, then have him flogged repeatedly." If that, too, were to prove fruitless, he was to be banished from the bishopric.[69]

The seizure of [Anabaptist] properties involved the treasury in disputes with Tyrolean manorial lords who were holding pledges on those properties and now asserted their claims. The first such case concerned the Höllrigl estate in the judicial district of St. Petersberg and the attempts made by the officials of the Brixen bishopric to claim the properties of executed or fugitive Anabaptists. Without delay the government brought this case to the attention of the ruling prince and let him know that apart from Sir Caspar of Freundsberg and the bishop of Brixen, also the other pledge holders, e.g. the archbishop of Salzburg as owner of Kitzbühel and Count Firmian, asserted similar rights. The archbishop based his claim on a writ of Emperor Maximilian, which had been confirmed by Archduke Ferdinand at Schwaz.[70] King Ferdinand issued a preliminary order enjoining the applicants to refrain from seizing the properties in question until he could work out a settlement with the various pledge holders at the forthcoming diet. It seems that no such settlement was arrived at, for soon afterwards a royal ordinance (renewed in 1536) was issued, specifying that henceforth everything left over of such estates after defrayment of all legal and court expenses was not to be confiscated for His Majesty's benefit but was to be passed on to the children or closest heirs of the Anabaptists in question.[71]

As the Anabaptists experienced it, the tyranny reached its peak in the middle of 1533. The content of the available files gives us no reason to contradict this opinion. The Anabaptist trials mentioned above probably just refer to the severest of the judgments passed on them and by no means exhaust their total number. The files are full of entries that cast a lurid light on the way the Anabaptists were proceeded against. On January 31, the government reproved the prince bishop of Brixen for having reprieved a recidivist and letting him get off with a fine.[72] Before May 24, Hans Gasser from the Rittner Horn was executed in Bozen.[73] On that day his daughter Barbara as well as Margaretha, the daughter of Paul Zimmermann, were being cross-examined. The last-named one was the wife of Caspar Puchl in the Sarn valley; she regards the church as a pile of stones and Mass as an abomination and a stench before God. She says that the priests lie more on the pulpit than tell the truth and that her Anabaptist faith is the true one, that a year ago she had been arrested in Terlan with two others named Leonhard and Agnes from above the Braitenberg, who had both been burned at the stake. She herself had recanted at the time but had since gone back to the Anabaptists. On Palm Sunday she had taken Valten Schneider, presently in prison at Gufidaun, to the hill on the Braitenberg, from where they were chased away, and afterwards into a woods, but had recently been driven out of that, too. About 100 of their people had been together there, she said, Hutter as well as others. She knew that this was the right faith and the way to eternal bliss. They had all wanted to jointly go to Moravia. She said "she was gladly ready to suffer death or torture for the sake of truth—God be praised" and that "she had been baptized by Hans Tuchmacher at Candlemas [February 2, 1532]."[74] Of still greater interest are the confessions of Gertrud Prezin from Sterzing and her daughter Elsbeth, dated June 17, Balthasar Maierhofer from Unterviertel, Apollonia Kniehäusser and Hans Sattler (June 21), Hänsel Gremser (July 1), Vincenz Puchler (July 11), Valten (October 6) and Margaretha Maierhofer (October 10). Lest color and light be spread unevenly, a number of details from these confessions should be mentioned here; at any rate the contents of confessions such as these help to somewhat explain the manner in which clerical and secular authorities proceeded against the Anabaptists. On the other hand it has to be conceded that not all Anabaptists adhered to such extreme doctrines as these. Gertrud Prezin and her daughter confess that they do not believe in the Christian church, it being a heap of stones and a den of murderers, mass and sacraments being an abomination and a stench before God, and infant baptism a dirty bath. They say that they had been baptized a year ago at Falkhanej by Onofrius [Grieseinger], who had proclaimed to them the word of God, and that their faith was the divine truth and a blessed life and that they hold firmly to this. At the present Lent season they have failed to confess to the priest, whom they call a leader of the blind. They refuse to be converted, do not ask for mercy and with God's help would rather die. According to them, the priests do not proclaim the Gospel in church but rather lie; and none but fornicators and scoundrels enter that heap of stones.[75] From this confession, too, we learn that Jakob Hutter is intending to move to Moravia.

Vincenz Puchler avows that the priests' mass means nothing to him, that the Anabaptists want to hold the Lord's Supper in their own way and that they are being taught to regard the images of Christ and the saints as mere idols. He also confesses to having broken a crucifix.

The most detailed confession is that of Luckner; it sheds light on the Anabaptists' life and activities, but it tells less about their doctrines. When Christ the Lord walked on the earth, there was no church apart from Solomon's temple, he declares; the clerics are the first fornicators; not being allowed to marry, they keep whores. The mass, he says, is totally useless and the holy sacrament just flour or bread; it is like the devil's leashes and was invented by the pope, who is a minister of the devil. The clerics' preaching he regards as utterly useless; seeing that they are ordered not to preach the Gospel. Hutter, on the other hand, has been entrusted with this task by the church community, he declares, and God's command is to baptize those that have been instructed in the faith. The priests are false prophets, he says, and the brothers who had been at the Götzenberg have moved on to Moravia; only Hansel Derker and Hansel Maurer might still be in the Puster valley.

Among the proposals that were made for the conversion of the recalcitrant ones is a rather strange one suggested by the government to the Gufidaun administrator on May 31, 1533, namely to pour a bit of holy water into the drink the Anabaptists are given and to cook all their foods with holy salt, to do this for a few days and then see how they respond to that.[76]

On June 4, 1533, Ferdinand sent a missive to the Archbishop of Salzburg "as regards putting down the heresy in the area of Rattenberg, Kufstein, and Kitzbühel."[77] On June 18, he orders the judges at

Sterzing and St. Petersberg, the Gufidaun administrator, and the pledge holders at Ritten, Rodenegg, Lienz, and Kitzbühel to be on guard in forests and valleys and on the high pastures, in accordance with the government's wish that both the heretics and the persons sheltering them be apprehended and that their houses be burned as decreed by the mandates. "Given that there is no better way of eradicating this sect than by imprisoning its overseers, do try to find some reliable and capable man, instruct him to gain the trust of the Anabaptists under the pretence of wanting to join their sect and to let himself be baptized." To end with, a reward (*taja*) in the amount of 60, 70, and up to 100 gulden is agreed to.[78]

The [Innsbruck] government recommends like procedures also to the bishop of Brixen.[79] On June 25, the head of the provincial administration (*Landeshauptmann*) Georg Baron Firmian reports that meanwhile and even before receiving the latest governmental order, he had the mountain crests where Anabaptists frequently meet reconnoitered by shepherds. When these catch wind of something, it is first reported to the local administrators, who will then get moving and occupy the mountain ridges and passes. This would be the quickest way of catching the overseers.

There is an ironic twist to the letter of June 29, that the Brixen bishop sent to the government and which says at the end: "We have no doubts about your having sufficiently experienced by now whatever good the revocation has done among Anabaptist persons and particularly Jakob Hutter and other adherents of that sect."[80] On the following day the government informs the bishop about having received the confessions of the above-named Anabaptists confined at Michelsburg.[81] On July 3, the reigning prince is told about evidence of Anabaptists in the territory of Count Montfort and the abbot of Kempten. His Majesty is asked to call for firm counter-measures to be taken.[82] The government replies to the prince bishop of Brixen that its missive had been misunderstood in Brixen. "All we have in mind is that these persons be dealt with in line with the content of the mandates issued."

On August 5, the government informs the legal staff and councillors of the Brixen prince bishop that a woman called Justina Rumler, surviving daughter of the former Jörg Ruler at Innsbruck and wife of the deceased Gall of Brixen had "disregarding her previously granted reprieve succumbed again to the seductive Anabaptist sect, had left and taken to flight."[83] Four days later, the new district sheriff in Bozen, Ludwig Pock, was invested with the judge's mace. We mention this circumstance because he and Heinrich Peringer, who installed him in his office and in 1535, became sheriff of Bozen and Gries, found themselves in the black books of the clergy on account of having done away with church feast days.[84] On September 9, Wilhelm of Liechtenstein at Carneid is notified from Brixen that once again a great number of Anabaptists is said to be gathered in the Puster valley, that they ought to be kept under surveillance and taken to prison.[85] The Michelsberg administrator is commanded to hold off with the imprisoned Anabaptists. "We are returning to you," it says in the writing, "the little book sent to us; what we want you to do is to find out from Paul Ruemer who wrote that book. In particular, where it says in the last epistle, 'All the brothers greet you—each of them a thousand times,' there is also talk about a window through which a squirrel had got out, and you ask that fellow Ruemer at which place that squirrel got out through the window and what persons were sitting there."[86] They had found a piece of paper on him listing all the "way stations" from Wasserburg right through to Moravia. In the communication of September 15, about this matter to the [Innsbruck] government, which also reports about recent Anabaptist gatherings at the Götzenberg with Hans Tuchmacher present, we read: "According to credible information we have received there are also a good many Anabaptists around Rattenberg, including Jakob Hutter or Onofrius."[87] A few days later the government laments, in a letter to the town of Kitzbühel, the proliferation of the Lutheran sect there and the fact that Paul Kessler, a priest, had been there and had uttered wicked things about the venerable sacrament and about child baptism.[88]

On October 16, Brixen remitted to the district sheriff the testimonies of the Anabaptists captured at the Götzenberg: Ruprecht Hueber, Vincenz Schneiderknecht, and Christian Pediller. Hueber owns up to having once carried children over the Brenner Pass toward Schwaz; at some time in recent years Schneiderknecht had come up from Carinthia with a number of brothers (about 20).[89] From the confessions of the Anabaptists confined in the Michelsburg tower it is to be gathered that also Linhard Schmidt at Müln and his daughter belong to this sect, both of whom ought to be arrested and interrogated.[90] The Neuhaus administrator is reported to be a "shelterer" of Anabaptists; in particular Hans Tuchmacher is said to be a guest of his.[91] The latter had repeatedly also been given shelter at Nieder-Vintl by the Brixen citizen Peter Lanz, who however had been granted a reprieve for it.[92] On November 2, the captain at Puchenstein and the Thurm administrator are being notified that Anabaptists are infiltrating into that area from the Puster valley and they should be apprehended.[93] On December 3, Hans Fuger was sent out to arrest the Neuhaus administrator. It would be best, the government writes to Brixen, to take out that whole [Anabaptist] nest—*Vorsteher*, administrator, brothers and sisters.[94] All necessary measures were taken but did not have the desired success. The administrator Erhard Zimmermann was indeed arrested but was released again on bail, which action earned the displeasure of the government.[95] The latter failed to get hold of either Hutter or Tuchmacher. The former had in the meantime shifted his activities to Moravia.

7
"HUTTERIAN BRETHREN" IN MORAVIA

"On the twelfth day of August anno 1533," the Anabaptist records say, "there came to us, through the providence, grace and mercy of God our heavenly Father, our dear brother and minister of our Lord Jesus Christ, Jakob Hutter. The entire holy church community of God welcomed and received him as though he were the Lord himself." "It gave great joy to all the devout." He, too, expressed his joy by telling Sigmund Schützinger and the elders of the church that "it was not strangers he was coming to but his dear brothers, all of them well-known, and children." They all agreed and asked and exhorted him to faithfully and diligently care for the people, and he pledged to do it. A small "temporal" gift he brought with him was to help pay off the debt to the abbess at Maria-Saal in Brünn and to individual Auspitz burghers, which the brethren had incurred in the period of destitution. A letter Hans Amon had sent in advance to his compatriot and brother Leonhard Schmerbacher[1] was intended to pave the road for Hutter in Auspitz: "I plead with you especially on behalf of our brother Jakob and commend him to your care. I write to you confidentially to faithfully warn you for the sake of the dear brothers and sisters. If brother Jakob came down to you and was made a minister and, as I hope, came to lead God's people, and the dear children of God would trust in him, while on the other hand others were to lose heart and grumble, you must see to it that this does not come to pass and that no root of bitterness [Heb. 12:15] springs up among the servants of God." What Hans Amon had feared eventually came to pass before long and, according to Hutter himself, had already occurred by the time he arrived. On the next Sunday (August 17, 1533) Hutter announced to the people the salutary message from the brothers and sisters who had sent him, and told of the wondrous works God had wrought through him and other saints. Then he mentioned that some had understood his coming to mean[2] that he would move with them to a separate place, but this was not at all the case, he said. He went on to say that now that God had sent him here, he would strive with utmost diligence to make improvements. Several days later he did set about improving some matters but was hindered by Sigmund Schützinger. That is why Jakob turned to Gabriel in Rossitz in order to find out whether or not they wanted to have him as a teacher and minister of the Lord: For him to remain silent and fail to faithfully carry out the task God had entrusted to him was something he could not account for before God. If they had no need of him, he would move on to wherever the Lord would send him. He said he would like to lay this before the people and was ready to do whatever they would decide about him. Gabriel approved of this step.

While Hutter was at Rossitz, Schützinger came to Leonhard Schmerbacher and Wilhelm Grießbacher and told them that he was not ready to give up his service and that he was not going to let Jakob speak a great deal. Both pleaded with him to carry the service jointly with Hutter, but Schützinger was not willing. When Hutter returned from Rossitz and wanted to pass on to the people the greetings Gabriel had asked him to convey, Sigmund snapped at him and wanted to know what he was going to do. In the presence of Caspar from Rossitz, Jakob told Sigmund and the elders what he had on his mind and was requesting, whether he was needed or not. For he did not feel free before God to not use the service he had been given. Sigmund protested that it was to him that God had given the service and that he wanted to continue as the lead. The elders again asked him to give in and carry out the service jointly with Hutter, but Schützinger was not willing. The ministers of the Word were now minded to call the church community together the very next day, but that was hindered by the fact that "many brothers were away working." So they came together the following Sunday (August 24). Schützinger complained that Hutter wanted to push his way in; the latter, however, said all he wanted was to serve the people. That was the purpose for which God had sent him here and that the care of the people was entrusted to him just as much as to Schützinger. At that point brother Philipp jumped up and screamed that if that was what Jakob wanted, he was the worst devil to ever come into the country. Jakob, though, remained firm and asked the opponents how they would like it if, having been away for a time and having entrusted their people to an assistant, on their return they had to play second fiddle to that assistant. The ministers of temporal needs present—Blasius [Kuhn], Philipp [Blauärmel], and Peter [Hutter]—were already in agreement that Jakob and Sigmund should jointly carry out the ministry. Gabriel, however, intervened and blocked an agreement. Hutter requested that the voice of the people be heard, and that was something he could not very well be refused.

On August 31, [1533] Jakob laid forth the reasons for his coming [to Moravia] before his assembled fellowship of believers. Sigmund Schützinger pleaded his election, and Gabriel seconded him and declared that if Sigmund were considered less than Jakob or no more than equal with him in the ministry, he (Gabriel) would be ready to go back the way he had come. In Jerusalem, too, he said, there had been but one shepherd, namely James. If they would now instate Hutter above Schützinger, perhaps because he could talk well, God's punishment would come upon them. Hutter, he said, should not be made into an idol; he appeared to be of a proud and haughty mind and to be less gifted for the pastoral ministry than for that of an apostle. In the end the church community was asked to pass judgment. Peter Hutter got up and said that he could not regard either the one or the other as higher or lower, greater or smaller and that he considered both of them equally valid. Leonhard [Schmerbacher] spoke in the same direction and suggested that for the sake of peace Hutter should let Schützinger have precedence. The people agreed, and one of them said that if Jakob were not here, they would still have all they needed with

Sigmund. Gabriel asked Hutter if he would accept the decision, and Hutter replied he wanted first to consider it before God and take counsel with the elders. Gabriel retorted, "I have nothing more to say to you."

There was great sorrow and anguish of heart among all the brothers and sisters. Jakob, too, was deeply distressed. Several brothers went to comfort him; others thought he was of the mind to lead some of the people away to another place. On Tuesday September 2, the people were again called together, and now Hutter announced that he wanted to accept the decision for the sake of love, peace, and unity but not for the sake of justice. He apologized and said the brothers had not understood him rightly. Thereupon Gabriel said, "We can all understand German. There was no need for you to give this answer."

A fortnight later Schützinger fell sick, so Jakob proclaimed the Lord's word, and the elders asked him to preach his next sermon about community; this he did on the following Sunday (September 28) and spoke in the power of God about God's true community. But this caused some to again mutter against him and to harden their stand against him.

The following day Jörg Vasser wanted to turn his temporal goods over to God's church and brought his beds, chests, etc., to the communal storeroom. When the ministers went through these things, it turned out that his wife had kept back her own money and some of her children's money, and because of that she was sternly admonished and disciplined by the ministers, by her husband, by Sigmund, and the whole church community. Then it occurred to Hutter that Schützinger's wife might likewise be such a Sapphira, and he told the elders that if they would support him in the strength of God, he would take up the matter and go into it. They agreed and asked him to begin in his own room and after that to examine the chests and beds of all the elders. So they also came to Sigmund's room and there found an excessive supply of bedlinen, shirts, and other things, and along with them four pounds of Bernese currency. When asked by Hutter if Sigmund had known about this money, he said yes and still pulled out about 40 gulden from under the roof, which greatly shocked Jakob and the elders as something not to be expected from Schützinger as a teacher of the community. Jakob confronted him with his dishonesty, and the following morning (October 3) he was placed before the church community to be judged. It came as a great shock to all God's children, and brothers and sisters began to weep aloud. In accordance with the word of God, Schützinger, as is just and right, was excluded and given over to the devil. He himself admitted that he deserved this and asked for grace and mercy. On the same day Vasser's wife, too, (who by God's grace was later readmitted) was separated from the church.

Hutter now impressed upon the church community how unjust the decision was, which they had arrived at against him. They had declared him unfit for the ministry. He exhorted them to call on God to raise up for them a devout shepherd and minister. "So we then began to pray for eight days and nights and also sent two men to Rossitz to let Gabriel [Ascherham] know of their need. He, too," suggested Hutter. "And as we had persevered in praying to God, He sent Jakob to us and joined him to us in great love, for him to be our bishop and shepherd." This took place on October 12. However, as Braitmichel relates, "when love and godliness, as well as true light and discernment was increasing among us and the holy church community was living in peace, the devil could not rest but strove to find causes to destroy the love among us. . . We had gathered on Sunday, October 26, in order to hear the word of God, when who would come sneaking in wearing sheep's clothing, all dressed up and hypocritical, but Philipp [Blauärmel], Blasius [Kuhn], Gabriel [Ascherham] and Peter Hutter."

In his "Epistle from Moravia to the holy church of God in the Puster valley, the Adige country, and the Inn valley"[3] Jakob Hutter himself wrote as follows about this meeting: "We called the church community together two hours before daybreak, and I wanted to consider the Lord's word with them in view of the great need that was there, and still is. I was deeply concerned, though, as I sensed and perceived what was to be seen and heard in the church. In view of the many unmarried brothers and sisters among us I had intended to speak about marriage, so that each of them might all the better find the right attitude. And since I was meant to speak the truth, I was also quite worried lest I might talk too much for some people's liking. In particular I felt afraid of Philipp and Gabriel; however, I felt even greater fear before God; so I determined to speak with true circumspection and modesty. Now when I had called the people to prayer and we were all about to come on our knees, there came to us without our knowledge or consent Philipp and Gabriel and Blasy [Kuhn] and Peter Hutter from Rossitz, and we welcomed them as brothers. I asked them to speak out what they had on their minds. So they started and testified that they had come for the sake of peace and unity and in their words presented themselves as angels of God and lambs, but inwardly they truly were ravenous wolves and subsequently were found to be liars, slanderers, blasphemers, false shepherds and prophets by the whole church of God, for which reason they were in God's strength, spirit, and truth excluded from the church and given over to the devil. "As regards the how and why," Hutter says, "the messengers will tell you; at any rate, we have not dealt with them lightly and hastily but have examined everything carefully and well in God's true, holy light, spending about five days on this business with great pain and a lot of trembling before God."

Braitmichel tells us what it was all about. Hutter asked [the intruders] what they had on their minds. Philipp then began:

1. Why had we separated from David from Schweinitz and had not reaccepted him?

2. Why had we excluded Bernhard Glasser?

3. Why do we say that Sigmund's election was not from God?

This led to heated arguments and counter-arguments so that "the church community could not find a firm grounding. People would call each other liars until Gabriel and Philipp finally came right out with the evil, which always tries to remain hidden. For Jakob challenged them in the strength of God: "You have accused the church, and if your accusations were true, we would be the worst of scoundrels." Philipp denied it and called Jakob a liar. Jakob replied, "The lie will remain on your head!" Philipp went on, "What I did say is that you are an idol and that the people worship you, and that is really true!" This caused a great uproar among the brothers and sisters who shouted at him as with one voice, "You lie!" Thereupon Philipp began to tone down what he had said. Finally they stood up and said, "dear church members, we have nothing against you but only against your minister. Now this is why we suggest: Choose several men from among you who are to judge in this matter." As nobody replied to this, they left.

The following Monday the community chose eight men, divided in two groups of four, who were to give an account to the two other communities. Philipp received these delegates with words of abuse, telling them it was on account of money that Jakob had been made an idol, and that Schützinger had been excluded out of envy and hatred. The following day a message came from Rossitz to the effect that Philipp's and Gabriel's communities would alone judge the matter and that it was to them that Hutter's people would have to give an account. Now while the latter were considering this message in a large evening gathering, scouts sent by the two opposing camps came creeping in to listen to the discussion. When Jakob became aware of them, he had them stand forth and made known to them what the community had decided. One of them wanted to know whether we had excluded Gabriel, and Jakob replied, "We no longer regard him as a brother nor as a minister." Now the wolf could no longer hide in sheep's clothing. One of them, Hans from Strasbourg, sprang up and called Jakob a liar and false prophet. Then Jakob Hutter asked the brotherhood to judge whether these men had come to seek peace, and a brother began to speak and said that since these men had come to us under the pretext of peace but in reality they came to slander and revile the church community, so they ought to be regarded just like Gabriel and Philipp." Further negotiations between the hostile camps led to no avail. Philipp and Gabriel with their adherents were excluded from "the church of God." The latter found it good to set down in writing the reasons for doing this,[4] and for the same reason Hutter was being defended in a separate apology.[5]

As the *Geschichtsbücher* relate, brother Jakob Hutter, by the help and grace of God, then brought true community into a proper order, "for which reason we are called Hutterites even today."

From their former fellow brethren the Hutterites were now meeting with bitter hatred. As the *Geschichtsbücher* tell, "In this year of 1534, Jakob Hutter and his church community suffered much tribulation from the renegades—a great deal of calumny and slander, in particular also from Philipp and his people. For whenever a lord, burgher, or farmer engaged brothers or sisters from both communities to work for him as his needs required, the Philippites would neither work, sit, eat or drink together with the Hutterites, even when jointly provided with food by their employers. Even though the Hutterites would much rather have worked quietly by themselves, they still accepted work, as well as any food and drink they were given with great thankfulness as from God, and the number of believers increased day by day."

The letter [of November 1533] in which Hutter informed his friends and companions in Tyrol about the recent events in Auspitz had been delivered by Peter Voyt. In the week before the feast day of Simon and Jude (October 28) the latter brother led to Auspitz a group[6] that brothers Hans [Amon] and Offerus [Griesinger] had sent from Tyrol. Right afterwards several brothers and sisters with some children from the Adige and Puster valleys reached the church community. Next arrived brother Klaus from Carinthia with seven brothers, who then came to faith in Auspitz; then came brother [Ulrich] Stadler with his children. Peter Hutter came with twenty-four persons, and eighteen arrived from Hesse, so that the Lord, as Hutter writes, in the short time of 3-4 weeks added more than 130 souls to the church community, who were baptized and received into membership there. True, those who had come from Hesse did not cause Hutter much joy. As the *Geschichtsbücher* explains, "there was at that time a minister of the Word, who had brought with him a group from Hesse—Hans Both."[7] He was minded to snatch some of the faithful out of the Lord's hands, but he did not succeed, for the church looked to the Lord and not to him or any other human being. Because he held the false opinion that there were no such things as angels or devils and refused to be corrected, he and all his adherents were excluded from the church of God. And though Hans Both had previously declared many times that he was well aware that Philipp and Gabriel were in the wrong and therefore could not be his brothers, he nevertheless, after receiving his judgment, went to Philipp and became a dear brother to him. "This is what most plainly revealed his deceitful heart. If he could have split the community it would have delighted him greatly."[8] In

1534, a new trek of baptism-minded folk, led by brother Bastl Glasser, set out from the "upper country" (*Oberland,* i.e. Tyrol). However, it was not without hindrance that they reached the goal of their migration—the holy community of the church. At Hohenwarth in Austria (between Krems and Meissau) they were arrested and taken to Eggenburg, from where they were only set free after enduring much torture. Hutter addressed to them a comforting epistle,[9] already full of dark forebodings. For it seemed that not only in Tyrol but also in Moravia their last hour was at hand.

8

THE TRIAL OF THE WOLKENSTEIN FAMILY, 1534

THE CASE against Helena von Freyburg was not yet concluded, and the one against Erhard Zimmermann, the administrator of Neuhaus an der Ache was in full swing, when the government received news that also the family of Lord Anton von Wolkenstein adhered to the Anabaptist teachings. Erhard Zimmermann's case presented no problems. This administrator, it seems, had become familiar with the teachings of the Anabaptists through Hans Amon the 'cloth-weaver' and treated the adherents with moderation and forbearance; indeed, he had even granted shelter to individual members. But since he answered the questions to their satisfaction put before him by the commission of inquiry concerning infant baptism, the sacrament of the altar, the intercession of the saints, etc., on February 15, Lord Friedrich Füeger was commissioned to set the prisoner free on bail and on condition of paying for the costs accrued and of providing a security of two hundred gulden. This money would be forfeited if he did not appear when called before the court.[1] The Innsbruck government informs the captain and the secular authorities in Brixen[2] that from the confessions of the administrator of the Neuhaus castle and of the Wolkensteins' cook, it is to be gathered that these two regard also some persons in the [Brixen] bishopric as Anabaptists, in particular Michael von Teutenhofen, who, when informed by Zimmermann that a number of Anabaptists were staying near Neuhaus in Pfaffenbach, had told the administrator to keep it quiet.[3]

Anabaptist tenets had taken deeper root in the house of Anton von Wolkenstein, who at that time resided in the parish of Taufers and Bruneck. Already in 1527, Anton had had to promise the Innsbruck governor (or regent) to keep away from the Lutherans and other sects and to remain faithful to the old-established Christian doctrines. However, he did become an adherent of the new teaching, and the members of his household were convinced Anabaptists. An anonymous informer accused also him and his wife of being Anabaptists, and added that they had not been to confession nor partaken of Holy Communion for several years.[4] Thereupon, [Sir Friedrich] Füeger was ordered, on January 10, "to make discrete and well-founded inquiries with the incumbent parish priest" to find out the truth of the matter. The Taufers magistrate, Hans Egel, reported on January 20, 1534, "that he had learned from the priest in Taufers and his assistant priest, that Lord Wolkenstein had for a long time neither been to confession nor received the sacrament, and that the same applies to his wife and cook. All three are regarded as having adhered to the Anabaptist sect for quite some time."

The captain and authorities in Brixen even reported that it could be assumed that the "cloth weaver's" [i.e. Hans Tuchmacher or Amon] wife was being accommodated in Anton von Wolkenstein's house. The cook was said to have indicated that the "cloth-weaver's" wife "was in childbed." "Since we knew that the aforementioned Anabaptist leader's wife had recently been with child, we wanted to have you informed about this."[5] Thereupon, the Deputy Marshal in Innsbruck, Erasmus Offenhauser, was ordered to proceed straightaway to the Puster valley with two *Ainspännigen* (i.e. two drivers of one-horse wagons), to arrest Anton von Wolkenstein, his wife and cook, to take the two women to the Taufers Castle, and Lord Wolkenstein to Innsbruck.[6] In Taufers, Erasmus was to question them in the presence of Füeger, lord of the castle there: for the lady, sternly, but without torture, but for the cook, if unwilling to confess, with torture. Their statements and confessions were to be written down and brought to

Innsbruck. In order to avoid public notice, orders had been given "for the above-mentioned one-horse drivers to transport those Wolkenstein persons as quietly and unobtrusively as possible all along their route, as the drivers know very well how to do." The lady of the house and the cook were to be questioned as to why they had not gone to confession nor received the sacrament; whether, where, and by whom they had been re-baptized, whether Anton von Wolkenstein, too, was an Anabaptist, etc. Sir Friedrich Füeger was instructed to assist and support the deputy marshal. On February 3, the latter was ordered "to also arrest Anton von Wolkenstein's son, 'Paulsen' (actually: Sigismund), since he too, was said to be tainted by Anabaptism."[7] Ten days later, the government informed Friedrich Füeger that they had incarcerated Anton von Wolkenstein, his wife and their son Paulsen on account of errors in Christian faith, and had handed their real estate over to the second son to administer.[8]

Among those who came under investigation in connection with the proceedings against the Wolkensteins were also two police agents who had been spying on the Anabaptists. As Brixen informed the Innsbruck Regents' office, of the four persons who had been denounced, "two turned out to be secretly recruited spies and investigators of ours, who, with our knowledge and consent had joined up with the Anabaptists, had themselves rebaptized and might occasionally also have sheltered and accommodated some of them—all for the purpose of thus bringing the 'cloth-maker' and other fugitives behind bars."[9] On February 15, 1534, Friedrich Füeger is instructed to free Lady Wolkenstein's cook, since she is not an Anabaptist, but concerning the lady, "as she had been rebaptized and confesses to being an adherent of that sect, she is to be visited by persons well versed in Holy Scripture in order to turn her away from the Anabaptist error."[10] On the same day the government lets the Brixen authorities[11] know its reasons for imprisoning Anton von Wolkenstein and his wife. Both spouses, it says, had been found in gross error in their beliefs. "Since it is *ex officio* the ecclesiastical authority's task to bring them away from that error, we are passing this task on to you as the competent authority and request that you ask one or two persons well versed in Holy Scripture to bring themselves here to Innsbruck and to Taufers. The exhortatory talks are to take place in the presence of a secular person, a task for which we regard Ulrich Geltinger as suitable."

Anton von Wolkenstein was incarcerated in the *Kräuterturm* in Innsbruck. The episcopal authorities gave the parish priest of Brixen and the St. Lorenzen priest, as well as Ulrich Geltinger, the task of dissuading Lady Wolkenstein from her erroneous belief. They were to arrive [at Taufers] on the morning of Wednesday, January 25, 1534.[12]

The same day Paul von Wolkenstein was being interrogated. As regards the third question, he replied, "I have not let myself be baptized nor have I thought about it or intended to accept another baptism."[13] He maintained he did not know when the Anabaptists had come [to the Wolkenstein house], for this, like many other things, had been kept concealed from him; besides, he had mostly not been at home. When the Anabaptists did come, they had stayed in the lady's apartment. He told of having once been present at a meeting in Auspitz (Moravia)—"out of curiosity." But it had so "pleased" him that he departed and did not get himself entangled with the Anabaptist sect. The ones that had induced him [to contact the Anabaptists] had been Thomas Liendl and Schlesinger. It was indeed in company with them that he had departed, but he had not got involved with them. As regards baptism, he wanted to leave it the way God had ordered it, he said.

Three days later Michael von Teutenhofen, brother-in-law [should be: son-in-law] of the accused [Lord Wolkenstein], addressed a petition to the government to the effect that since official duties had caused the priest of Hall, who was supposed to go together with him and the deputy marshal to see Anton von Wolkenstein and the latter's son, to return home again: he (Michael) was to be permitted, in particular because of having on behalf of his brother-in-law stood out against His Royal Majesty's will to visit his brother-in-law even in the absence of that priest in order to help him, being an old man, "pass the time a little."[14]

To begin with, the talks with Lady Wolkenstein that took place in Taufers on February 27 and 28, yielded no result. According to the report, "no effort had been spared to dissuade her from the error, but in the end she remained stuck on the two articles of the sacrament of the altar and of baptism. Her position and belief does not differ from that of her overseers and the other brethren, nor does she want to recant; she does, however, request to be freed from prison and to be granted a year's time for reflection at home."[15]

Anton von Wolkenstein, too, proved at first inaccessible to any conversion attempts, hence the Innsbruck government reported this to the ruling prince with the request for a decision with respect to the two prisoners.[16] On March 22, the government informs Friedrich Füeger that Hans von Wolkenstein and Michael von Teutenhofen had begged leave to confer with their mother and mother-in-law, respectively. Seeing that they were cherishing the hope of a conversion, the government thought these two could be granted such a permission; however, the parish priest of Taufers ought to be present at the discussion. On March 26, King Ferdinand wrote to the [Innsbruck] government: "If the accused refuse to recant in spite of all exhortations, it is our opinion that they should then be dealt with in line with the contents of the promulgated mandates. For we are in no way inclined to exercise any measure of clemency or mitigation in the punishment meted out to such persons but want them to be treated just like the common people." In the end the designated suffragan bishop of Brixen, Licentiate Albrecht Kraus, had been brought in to assist with Anton Wolkenstein's interrogation. Councillor Dr. Johann Winkler also took part in it. The reports about the interrogation are dated March 26, and April 17 and 21.[17] As regards rebaptism, Anton stated already at the first interrogation that he had been baptized as a child and did not find in the Gospel any reason for still needing another baptism. He said he had not aided and abetted the Anabaptists. Three years ago he had talked with them and they with him on whether he might be persuaded to join their sect. His wife, he said, had had a lot of contact with them and had been rebaptized, but against or without his will. He had kept to his own apartment and had not busied himself a great deal with his wife's affairs, but had in his own rooms read, prayed, and done whatever God and his conscience had exhorted him to do. As regards Holy Communion, he said he wanted to partake of it in both kinds, but if not allowed to do that, he would humbly ask His Majesty to agree to a temporary suspension regarding these matters and not to compel him to partake of it in just one kind.

The second conversation focused mainly on Holy Communion under two kinds, whereupon Wolkenstein asked for time until April 21. Albrecht Kraus asked Teutenhofen to point him to Eck's *Enchiridion* to which he replied by requesting that he be spared that kind of thing. In the third talk, too, the question of Holy Communion was dealt with. In the end Wolkenstein declared himself ready to partake within a quarter of a year of communion under two kinds: if the priest were to deny him this, he would be willing to take it in one kind, publicly, so as to satisfy His Royal Majesty. In the end he had a number of articles placed before him, several of which "he wanted to express himself with neither yes nor no."[18]

In the meantime, Hans von Wolkenstein, Michael von Teutenhofen, and Wolfgang Wiser, preacher at the cathedral chapter (*Domstift*) in Brixen, had in the presence of administrator Egel, carried on discussions with Lady Wolkenstein. At His Majesty's command Erasmus Offenhauser was sent to Taufers as well, "in order to gather more needful information about the Anabaptists."[19] Already on May 9, the designated persons were in a position to send in Lady Wolkenstein's recantation.[20] Thereupon Füeger was on May 12, directed to pardon her in His Majesty's name, provided she remained firmly determined to renounce Anabaptism; however, she would have to swear to keep the peace, and to publicly and in the prescribed manner renounce her error from the pulpit, to take on penitence from her priest, and to promise never more to adhere to the sect in question. Should she not keep to that, she would have to atone for it with life and limb, as someone reneging on the oath to keep the peace. She would also have to pay for the accrued costs of feeding her in the Taufers prison. Teutenhofen's influence on the change in Lady Wolkenstein's position is not to be doubted. It is also evidenced by his being a cosignatory to her promise to keep the peace. She applied for leniency as regards the public recantation but was quickly told that she could in no way be spared this. Hence in June 1534, she entered the pulpit of the Taufers church and followed the priest in speaking out the recantation as formulated by the government:

"I, Elspet, wife of Anton von Wolkenstein, confess to letting myself be induced to join the seductive Anabaptist sect and what it entails; for this I am sorry with all my heart and I acted wrongly by doing it. Now I recant and I publicly swear, promise, and pledge henceforth and my whole life long to cling to the unity of the Christian church and in no way henceforth to sever myself from it."

The repeated talks that Anton von Wolkenstein had with his spiritual advisers and probably even more the influence of his friends and relatives caused also him to convert. In Teutenhofen's petition in favor of his father-in-law it says that the prisoner has made concessions as regards all the articles in which he had erred against the usage and tradition of the Christian church, that he abstains from his intent to partake of Holy Communion under both kinds and agrees to henceforth take it in one kind in accordance with the order of the church. After obtaining these concessions, Michael von Teutenhofen requested the prisoner's release since the latter felt it particularly difficult to recant in public and due to the leniency of such a public recantation, which Lord Wolkenstein regarded as downright shameful. Since Teutenhofen gave an assurance in the prisoner's name that the latter, "as soon as he regained his freedom, would within one month partake of communion according to the order of the Catholic Church and that he would let himself be guided by her in everything," on June 28, 1534, King Ferdinand decided to "let the prisoner be released after paying for the food received." However, before his release he was to be instructed at Innsbruck that should he fail to live up to the assurance given by his son-in-law, he could expect no grace to be shown. "The county of Tyrol and all our other patrimonial dominions would then be denied and forbidden to him."[21]

On July 17, 1534, Anton von Wolkenstein was standing in the large council chamber of the Regents' office and listened to his release being read out. These are the words he was asked to repeat as his vow: "You are to pledge on your nobleman's word of honor that you will never in a wrong, unlawful way exact retribution or take revenge for your imprisonment and all that pertains to it; and on the praiseworthy government of His Royal Majesty; and on the common land of the princely county of Tyrol, or on any of those responsible for your imprisonment; also that you will pay for court expenses and for the food received. You are not to depart from here until such payment has been made, and you must comply with, and carry out, everything your son-in-law Michael Teutenhofen has promised His Royal Majesty on your behalf."[22]

After giving his pledge, Anton left Innsbruck and went to join his wife in Brixen, where she lived under the supervision of her son-in-law, who was providing surety for her. Now it was the turn of young Wolkenstein. He had been arrested in May 1534, and was imprisoned in the Michaelsburg fortress. His confession was sent to Brixen. This was greatly resented by the Innsbruck government[23] as this would take him out of the area of the judge who had jurisdiction over the case.[24] The situation was worsened by the fact that the prisoner escaped from his Brixen confinement and was only rearrested several months later in the Salern judicial district. After four months' imprisonment the episcopal councillors notified Innsbruck[25] that Sigismund von Wolkenstein was requesting to have his case dealt with and was ready to convert if spared a formal recantation. The councillors received the following reply, "We want you to know that, just as it was with his mother and Lady Freyberg, it is only by recantation that he can regain freedom." This still failed to intimidate Sigismund, and he presented his request, which had the support of the episcopal office in Brixen, to the king.[26] He pleaded the favor granted to Lady Freyberg but was given the negative reply already referred to above.[27] A recantation was obligatory. The following year (1535) young Wolkenstein repeated his request but did not obtain a better reply. Now he declared himself ready to recant. With that in view, the Brixen authorities let him prematurely go free and for that reason were reprimanded by the reigning prince. It was to be feared that he might once again take to flight without having recanted; besides, the common people in Tyrol might easily get the bad impression that people were not all being treated the same way.

So Sigismund von Wolkenstein was rearrested and was set free only in June 1536. Making use of his intention to join in the war with a troop of horsemen, his relatives made another attempt to exact a recantation and to have him granted full freedom. This time King Ferdinand was more inclined to grant this, especially since Sigmund's cousin, Wilhelm von Wolkenstein, declared himself ready to provide surety for him.

Through a number of reports the government learned that the Anabaptist movement in Tyrol had still not subsided. At the beginning of February [1534] four Anabaptists were imprisoned in the tower at Michelsberg.[28] Three weeks later a report said that Nicolaus Trotter at St. Jürgen was tainted with Anabaptism.[29] At the same time news came in about Anabaptists in Sterzing.[30] On February 26, Brixen notifies the Innsbruck government, "We have been informed that in the coming spring, as soon as the waterways become navigable, Hans Tuchmacher is planning to send to Moravia" all the common folk they have brought into the sect in the Puster valley and at other places. As we hear, though, Tuchmacher and the treasurer are to remain here in the country.[31] Most likely from February of that year we have a decree of the ruling prince to the effect that in future whatever is left of Anabaptist estates, after the costs of their trial and execution have been paid, is no longer forfeited, and sequestered on behalf of, His Majesty but is to go to the children or nearest heirs. However, no fugitive Anabaptists are to benefit from this.[32] On March 1, the bishop of Brixen, at the request of Abbess Clara at Sonnenburg, grants the fugitive Anabaptist Michael Waldner at Elm safe conduct for one month in order to settle his negotiations.[33] Brixen supports the request made by the guardian of the children of Ulrich Müller (executed 1531 in Klausen) for restitution of the latter's confiscated property.[34] On March 3, 1534, the Innsbruck government informs Christoph of Liechtenstein and Christoph Fuchs that the Anabaptists are preparing for departure to Moravia in the coming spring and that their treasurer has already made inquiries about obtaining ship transport,[35] for which reason all riverboats are to be watched closely. But only six days later we learn that nearly all the valleys around Sterzing are full of Anabaptists, that three overseers have arrived from Moravia and are staying in that area and around Schwaz[36] and that they intend to move into the Etsch (Adige) area.

The outbreak in Münster is probably the saddest chapter in the history of the Anabaptist movement, and the actions of those monstrous enthusiasts had horrible consequences. It provided all the powers hostile to the Anabaptists with the very sharpest weapon. Everywhere it was being stated: that we can now clearly see the pious, holy bearing of the Anabaptists is nothing but hypocrisy and their abhorrence of the sword is a mere pretence.

When perusing the files and edicts issued against the Anabaptists in Tyrol, one almost thinks one is reading the writings of the Swiss [Protestant theologian, Heinrich] Bullinger. Also those territories and governments that until then had been less rigorously opposed to Anabaptism turned away with disgust from the picture presented by the heavenly kingdom in Münster. Before long the Anabaptists had to discover that even the last place of refuge that until then had offered them hospitality was now closed to them—the margraviate of Moravia.

The missive that the reigning prince sent to the [Innsbruck] government on March 26 says: "The enclosed articles will let you recognize what is the ground and foundation on which the overseers and ringleaders of this damnable false and seductive sect are standing, namely that it directly aims at the destruction and annihilation of any authority and integrity, also that they renew themselves and increase from day to day, and that if they now manage to gather in great numbers they will surely make bold to go on from mere intent to an active suppression of all authority and decency or at any rate to arouse rebellion and insurrection among the common people."

The letter points out that many persons, deceived by the sectaries' pious appearance, have joined the sect unaware of the ringleaders' true basis. "We have truthful and certain information that in the bishopric and town of Münster this sect has become so rampant that numbers of Anabaptists have taken violent action against those holding on to the established faith in Christ. For that reason the adjacent electors and other princes who, though also adhering to the new Anabaptist sect, in fact dislike it as much as everybody else does, have taken to arms with their people and are setting out to suppress the whole thing." "Unless we bravely and earnestly set about uprooting this sect, it will lead to irretrievable apostasy, perversion, and loss of our realms and lands. It is already evident that the Anabaptists are being expelled out of the Empire to the ends, and they are moving in droves to our territories of Lower Austria, everywhere seducing and poisoning the people." Order is therefore given for all the previously issued mandates and edicts to be strictly upheld. "You should also," the authorities are told, "under our title and authority reissue those mandates in all the areas under your administration, have them posted and read out from the pulpit by priests and preachers, so that the common people are made aware of what those false teachings are aimed at. "Whoever, disregarding this, our paternal warning, still holds to this sect, will be proceeded against most sternly and with no further chance of reprieve." The same applies to all who shelter and accommodate the sect's overseers and members. In the towns, too, burgomasters and councilmen are to see to it, on pain of losing the freedoms granted, that no foreign person is given shelter and accommodation, unless they have previously convinced themselves that the person in question is not tainted with that sect. At the end King Ferdinand expresses the hope that he will now succeed in eradicating the sect. "Nor do we want to withhold from you our gracious exhortation that all of us be diligent in soon doing away with so seductive a sect, and we cherish the hope of achieving the same goal with the counsel and assistance of our Bohemian crown. That will in no small way lead to a better and more effective uprooting of this sect in our other patrimonial dominions."[37] In a postscript we read: "We are also of the opinion that within the princely county of Tyrol in all the towns and judicial districts where there are operators of barges on the Danube waterway, you shall order these not to accept Anabaptist persons as passengers and before taking on anybody to first inquire of him whether he be tainted with Anabaptism." Care was also to be taken that no false and seductive books be offered for sale; they should be neither bought nor sold. In accordance with the prince's command the [Innsbruck] government issued a stern mandate on May 9, [1534][38] and this was followed by a similar one in Brixen on May 26. The government of the upper Austrian lands had pointed out to the Brixen prince bishop's captain and councillors that it was now all the more necessary to watch out for insurrectionist persons like the Anabaptists, since the present distress and dearth, as well as the warfare now going on in Swabia, could be expected to render the common people everywhere more difficult and rebellious.[39]

As part of the effort to prevent any concourse of the dreaded

Anabaptists, on May 21, [1534], the administrator of Steinach was ordered to have his sheriff, attended by several armed men, "in moonlit nights, when the Anabaptists are most wont to move about, lie in ambush on the most suitable mountain passes. Within his district through which they would have to pass, he was to do everything possible to subdue these insurrectionist sectarians."[40] The costs incurred by such measures would be refunded by the treasury.

One can imagine the elation in Brixen when it was learned that Jakob Hutter had been apprehended in Linz. The happy news was straightway (May 25) relayed to Innsbruck.[41] An immediate inquiry made from there in Linz[42] brought to light that it was just an empty rumor.

Earlier on this might well have been the fate of brother Offerus [Griesinger], who in those very days reached Auspitz with a band he had led away from the Inn valley. "Brother Onoferus," Hutter writes to those imprisoned at Eggenburg, "has arrived with many other brothers and sisters. The Lord has in a wonderful way shown them a way through. We have heartily rejoiced about their arrival and have praised God for it. There are now not many brothers and sisters still left in the upper country."[43] And also these few, mostly residing in the Adige (Etsch) area, were getting ready for departure to Moravia, under the leadership of the indefatigable Hans Tuchmacher. In the meantime, in Moravia there was an eminent change taking place, which Hutter had already hinted at in the above-mentioned letter: "We are the whole time reckoning with still greater tribulation and persecution than we are suffering at present. May God be with us!"

9

PERSECUTION IN MORAVIA

THE ATTACK AGAINST THE ANABAPTISTS, prepared for quite some time and repeatedly foretold by Hutter, was delayed until the early spring of 1535. In the week of the first Sunday in Lent a regional diet was convened in Znaim, at which King Ferdinand was personally present. This assembly deliberated on refusers (*Absager*), on weights and measures, Jews and taxes, and finally also on Anabaptists. With respect to the latter, King Ferdinand had the Lord Steward inform the Moravian estates of the well-known fact that the Anabaptists in the Netherlands, after initially conducting themselves modestly and submissively, had subsequently proceeded to turn everything upside down. Seeing that neither the Lutherans nor the Zwinglians nor any other sects were willing to tolerate these deviates among them, His Majesty desired and requested that they no longer be tolerated in Moravia either.

What Ferdinand I had so long been striving for he achieved at this diet. Greatly pleased, he informed the Upper Austrian government from Vienna that at the recent [Znaim] diet the honorable estates of Moravia had promised him they would no longer tolerate the Anabaptists but would have them expelled.[1]

By St. George's Day [April 23] they were to quit their settlements and "eat their bread somewhere else." The abbess of the King's Cloister at Brünn was the first landowner to have the Anabaptists vacate her lands—at Auspitz and Steurowitz. In the same way the lord marshal Johann of Lipa, manorial lord of Kromau and Göding, in obedience to a repeated command, called on his Anabaptist people to give way and move off with all they had. Johann of Lipa, a man with a sensitive heart, asked the brothers to voluntarily vacate Schackwitz and his lands and to spare him having to use compulsion. The Anabaptists countered this demand with a written complaint which they handed to this powerful landowner, whose heart was touched by the fate of those good people. In an earnest and dignified way they pleaded their inability to so speedily leave their settlements without exposing their acquired properties, settlements and lands, not to mention the sick among them, to an uncertain fate. It was also, they declared, hard and totally unjust to drive somebody away from his property by force and without adequate reason. The prince and the lord marshal were to consider fully what they were doing; they were being reminded that above them, too, there ruled a higher power to which they were accountable. To the best of the Anabaptists' knowledge, up to that time nobody had had any reason to complain to the authorities about them. If the lord marshal or the reigning prince were to ask them for tribute or taxes, they were ready to pay these as they were able, if only they were allowed to go on with their work and their religion.

This remonstrance was submitted to the authorities; however, as the cardinal of Trent's letter of May 25, 1525, to Innsbruck, to which the complaint was attached, makes evident, was given no consideration whatsoever. Further orders from Vienna were demanding that the expulsion be carried out in dead earnest.

An eye witness—the already mentioned Caspar Braitmichel, who would pass away as a minister of the Gospel at Austerlitz in 1573, tells about it as follows:[2]

"When expelled from Auspitz in 1535, the church community had to depart from their house there; they moved to the land of the lord marshal, manorial lord of Moravian Kromau, at Schäckowitz, built a shelter and dwelling and lived there for a number of weeks. However, the Moravian estates were given a strict royal command to the effect that no brother was to be tolerated any longer. In particular the lord marshal had been sternly commanded to immediately expel the brethren from his grounds if he wanted to avoid royal displeasure and punishment. As much as he disliked it, it had to be done. So he sent out his stewards, and they summoned the neighbors in the villages round about, who came with weapons in hand, drums beating and flags flying to the brethren's house in Schäckowitz, to carry out their lord's command. So finally when it could not be otherwise and no further delay was to be obtained, the devout had to go forth into misery." "Jakob Hutter, as their minister of the Word, took his bundle on his back. His assistants did the same, and all brothers and sisters with their children walked off in pairs, following Jakob, their shepherd." "Thus they were driven out into the open field like a flock of sheep. They were not allowed to camp anywhere, until they finally arrived on the Lord of Liechtentein's land near Tracht. There they camped on the broad heath under the open sky, with many poor widows and orphans, sick people and young children."[3]

So as to improve the fate of his people, Jakob Hutter, "for himself and on behalf of all the brethren driven out onto the open heath for the sake of God and of the witness of Christ," wrote to the governor Lord Kuna of Kunstadt Lukow the well-known epistle,[4] which gives a moving picture of the sufferings of those poor persecuted folk: "Now we are out on the open heath, harming no one. We do not want to hurt or wrong anyone, not even our worst enemy. Our conduct and way of life, our words and deeds are there for all to see. Rather than knowingly wrong a man to the value of a penny, we would let ourselves be robbed of a hundred gulden. Rather than strike our worst enemy with our hand—to say nothing of spears and halberds—we would let our own lives be taken. Our words and deeds consist in living peacefully and unitedly in God's truth and justice as true followers of Christ. We are not ashamed of giving an account of our way of life to anyone. But whoever says we had moved onto the heath with many thousands as if we wanted to go to war and things like that—whoever talks like that is a liar and scoundrel. If all the world lived like us, all warfare and injustice would have an end." "There is no place we can move to. May God in heaven show us where to go. We cannot let the earth be denied to us, for the earth is the heavenly Father's. May He do with us according to His will."

The appeal to the Moravian lords, which concludes the epistle, had no success whatsoever. Because of the intemperate expressions against the ruling prince occurring in it the petition was regarded as Lèse-majesté and only resulted in a worsening of Hutter's situation. He was searched for in the camp on the heath, among the bushes along the Thaya river, in the surrounding villages, on the Maidenberg and in the household at Schäckowitz, where the sick had been left behind, but everywhere to no avail. Being unable to find him, they got hold of Wilhelm Griessbacher from Kitzbühel, a minister of temporal needs, and took him to Brünn, where he was eventually burned at the stake. But for the church community's timely insistence that he take a distance, that would also have been Hutter's fate. Asked to go to Tyrol and there "to gather for eternal life those whom the true arch-Shepherd Jesus Christ calls his own," he entrusted his office in Moravia to Hans Amon (Tuchmacher) and took leave from the brothers and sisters, who let him depart with sorrow and sadness.

The *Geschichtsbücher* reports (p. 118): "As those left behind were unwilling to part from one another without good reason, they moved from place to place, not knowing where to go. Finally, when they were refused all provisions and even water, it could not be helped: they had to separate into groups of eight or ten, each committed to one brother's care. So they moved—some here and some there, not knowing where they might be able to rest their heads in peace." From these days derives the song:

> Vagrant Thy wretched folk now stray,
> who from their homes were chased away.
> There's no one to defend them,
> comes no one to befriend them;
> no, to their death they'd send them.

One group was fortunate enough to find accommodation at Steinabrunn in Lower Austria and was joined by further groups; others were received on the manor farms of landowners who did not feel bound by the decision of the Znaim diet. Even Johann of Lipa did not hesitate to let the brethren use the Schäckowitz house for their sick, aged, or incapacitated members, and together with other nobles of like mind. He would speak up for the Anabaptists in government circles. Thus, though the "community," Hutter's ideal, had been broken up, the brotherhood remained intact and was kept going in numerous small groups, who, led by communal shepherds, lived scattered throughout the country. Some, who could not bear the need and misery the community had been plunged into or could find no shelter of any kind in Moravia, turned back toward their old homelands. An attempt to obtain Duke Ulrich's of Württemberg consent for settlement in his country remained unsuccessful, even though the Anabaptists offered and pledged to be subject and supportive to him with body and property.[5]

10

PERSECUTION IN AUSTRIA AND BEYOND IN 1535

It was around St James' Day [July 25] that Hutter, acceding to his community's urging, departed from Moravia, not without promising to let them hear from him before long. "I have gone from you in accordance with your will and demand, your advice and decision." "You are well aware of the reason for it." He continues, "I also know that you have been greatly longing for a message from me, and it has been delayed long enough. Yes, I know well that I promised you that I would hurry as much as possible to let you have a message; it did not slip my mind for even one hour. However, brother Jeronyme is not acquainted with all the paths here, and for a long time we could not get in touch with brother Kränzler, as he has been lying ill at Sterzing; besides, he, too, does not know his way about in the Puster valley. We have made haste to visit each other so as to let you have news soon. . . The Lord has blessed our journey and has let us find our way right here into the Puster valley and the Adige area (*Etschland*); we have arrived at our brothers and sisters, who have greeted us with peace and godly love and have related to us how things are everywhere. And now we have diligently gone back and forth, up hill and down dale and have visited those hungering and thirsting for the truth. . . Several have accepted the truth and submitted to God. . . Already the almighty God and Father has once again established a church community here, and the Lord daily increases His people. And day and night we have a great deal of work to do in the Lord, and there is need for more of us ministers here and for suitable brothers.... The decision compelling me to move up here is not a vain one; it did not come from the flesh either but from God.[1]... That more of us from down there should be up here is not something I have said or written in the sense that everyone should come running along according to his own will. If anybody were to come along like that, we would not receive him."

"As far as we know, the godless tyrants and enemies of the truth, who have power to kill, do not yet know that we are here. May God grant from heaven that they be blinded and remain unaware of it for a long time."

How could this wish of Hutter's have possibly been fulfilled? Since the beginning of April [1535] missive after missive had gone out to the country's authorities, pointing out more and more urgently the perils of having the land flooded by these Moravian brothers. Even before the days when Hutter journeyed to the "upper country" (*Oberland*), the cry had gone out from there: Anabaptists from Moravia are roaming the country![2]

Worried that the expellees from Moravia might gain "through-passage and shelter" in some others of his patrimonial dominions, already at the beginning of April King Ferdinand ordered the Innsbruck government to carefully watch out for any Anabaptists coming in or passing through, to apply the legal punishments to captured overseers and ringleaders but to deport those entangled with this sect through simple-heartedness.[3] In line with these directions, on May 2, Adam of Holenegkh, regional administrator at Steier, issued from Graz the order "to be on guard in all towns and markets, in the Vorau quarter, in the Mürz and Enns valleys, in the Austrian area above and below the Enns river that extends toward Moravia." Wherever Anabaptists are encountered, they are to be arrested right away and this to be immediately reported to the provincial administrator.[4]

In the same sense, and in response to King Ferdinand's demand, the administrator of the bishopric of Passau issued on April 22, a prohibition against giving shelter and accommodation, either openly or secretly, to any of the Anabaptist persons departing from Moravia, against conveying them on water or dry land and engaging in trade or fellowship with them. With the bishop of Breslau and the princes of Silesia, too, the pressure exerted from Vienna (June 6, 1535) to deny entry to the Anabaptists leaving Moravia (as a result of the decision of the Znaim diet) and not to tolerate them at all had its effect, for they offered to diligently see to these deviants getting driven out of Silesia, in particular out of the territories of Glogau, Schweidnitz, and Jauer, and to root them out if they failed to comply with the deportation orders.[5]

When groups of Anabaptists, who could find no place in Moravia, turned north, they found the boundary closed. Passau and Bavaria also carefully guarded their border marches. On August 14, dukes Wilhelm and Ludwig of Bavaria issued an order to "be on guard against Anabaptist persons who after staying for a time in Moravia had now been expelled from there, to arrest them and deal with them in accordance with the laws." The Passau administrator was told that he was meant to deal with such Anabaptists in the same way he was doing with his own prisoners.[6]

In spite of all these measures many of the brothers deriving from southern Germany and Tyrol did manage to find their way to their old homelands. On June 19 [1535], King Ferdinand informs the Innsbruck government that the Anabaptists moving out of Moravia are said to "be intending to fan out and seek shelter all over our patrimonial lands."[7] Nine days later the Innsbruck government informs Cardinal Bernhard of Trent that in line with the issued orders they have immediately sent out corresponding directives to all authorities in the land.[8] On July 21, a certain Anabaptist returning from Moravia is reported to be repentant and to be pleading for mercy.[9] Hutter's presence in the land had not yet become known. At the end of July he surfaces in the Schöneck judicial district. He gathered his church community at the Götzenberg, then in a cellar in Hirschwang. On August 24, a large meeting was held in the woods above Erenburg, at which occasion nineteen persons were baptized. It was at the beginning of October and from Brixen that the government obtained the first news of Hutter's presence. On October 10, the regents and episcopal Counsellors there served notice that "Jakob Hutter and other five or six Anabaptist overseers had returned from Moravia to this land—to the Puster valley and then to Sterzing and Bozen, had already held two assemblies and persuaded several persons to join their heretical sect; that they intended to hold another church meeting on All Saints' Day [November 1], in the judicial district of Taufers or at Götzenberg, further that they were holing up at St. Lienhart or St. Andreasberg, as well as at Lüsen, Rodenegg, Taufers, in the Räsen district, on the Götzenberg and at Herschwang; also that Hutter's wife is at the last stage of pregnancy and close to delivery and that she is set to lie in childbed here in the judicial district of Schöneck."[10]

The government immediately issued orders to the administrators in and around Bozen, Sterzing, Rodenegg, and Taufers: "As it is to be expected that Hutter and his companions are wont to keep close to the boundaries and, if pursued, will escape into the adjoining judicial district, their pursuit is now to be allowed also on foreign lands and enabled mutually."[11] On October 26, the Brixen authorities inform the government in Innsbruck that all captains, administrators, and magistrates have been instructed "how and in what way they are to further proceed with regard to Anabaptist overseers. We have also alerted the Gufidaun administrator to the presence of Anabaptists in his district at and around Gufidaun and asked him to join the others in having his men on high alert."[12]

On November 5, the Innsbruck government instructed the Gufidaun administrator to be especially on the lookout for the overseers and Jakob Hutter, who, "now expelled from Moravia, have returned to this land—to the Puster valley and other places and are said to have found refuge, shelter, and support in the area of Gufidaun."[13]

The prevailing mood is faithfully pictured in the three last epistles Hutter wrote to the "elect church community" in Moravia, in which he exhorts them to loyally persevere right to the end like those who had just recently held out faithfully and had bravely testified to the truth— probably a reference to Wilhelm Griesbacher, executed in Brünn. Here, Hutter goes on, we, too, have experienced sadness and pain, for great injustice and unrighteousness is becoming rampant. Nevertheless the Lord's children are verdant and growing in divine righteousness and truth, like a lovely garden after a rain in May.

This letter, however, already starkly confronts us with the whole seriousness of the situation in which Hutter found himself with his companions: "I am further letting you know that we are no longer here in secrecy and concealment, for the godless men are aware of us and are most hostile, and there is a great hue and cry about us, for the godless, thieving parsons, the guardians and messengers of the devil, those cruel hell hounds clamor about us from the pulpits, warning the people and letting them know that we are here in the land and up on the mountains, and they command people to attend their accursed services, idols and sacraments. They are threatening with beadle and hangman, and the godless sodomitic sea is roaring and raging. I fear it will not rest until devout Jonah is cast into it and swallowed up by the cruel whale."

As already seen in his earlier letter [to the chief administrator of Moravia], here Hutter also inveighs intemperately against the ruling prince and the pope: "This whale is the cruel tyrant and enemy of the truth, Ferdinand with all his attendants and the accursed pope with his cursed hell hounds. But God is going to command the sea, and his own will be rescued from the godless men's power."

"Dearly beloved brothers and sisters, we are now daily, hourly and momentarily expecting the magistrate's beadles and the executioner's catchpolls and all manner of tribulation. We have inwardly prepared for this and do not expect anything else. May the Lord give us strength and power to hold out in his truth."

In the end Hutter warns the church community to be on guard against traitors. "Two of these," he says, "have gone down to Sterzing; in Innsbruck they have betrayed to the government everything they know.[14] Before long the traitors intend to come to Moravia; the godless men here want to send them to you. Therefore do not trust them and be on your guard." Without doubt these "traitors" are to be understood as the "agents provocateurs" frequently appearing in the files of the last two yeas.

Hutter's third letter from the Adige country and the Puster valley, taken to Moravia, by brother Christl Schmidt,[15] is equally full of laments about the prevailing distress. "There is great deprivation and persecution also here and a terrible clamor about us, but God has still helped us through every single day. At many places we are daily and hourly expecting constables and magistrates, by day and by night. They are threatening us and are well aware of who are our brothers and sisters at a number of places. The godless magistrate Peter Maier at Vientl has arrested his own daughter and son-in-law and their servant girl—three dear "siblings." But the servant girl has escaped from Schöneck castle "with her soul untainted." The son-in-law is still imprisoned at Schöneck. As for the daughter, the rogue Paul, her brother in the flesh, has taken her to Greifenburg in Carinthia, where the devil has made him administrator." Hutter concludes by pleading, "Don't let yourselves be misled or frightened away from God's truth."

Hutter's third letter from those days—the last one he sent to Moravia in November 1535, through brother Jeronyme [Käls] shortly before his arrest,[16] already shows us the grave danger Hutter was in.[17]

So many were the snares set for him that he could not avoid them in the end. When, compassed about by beadles, he and his pregnant wife spent the night of St Andrew's Day at Klausen in the house of the former sexton Hans Steiner on the far side of the bridge over the Eisack river, he was surreptitiously pounced upon in the dead of night by the prince bishop's administrator at Seben and the town magistrate Sieber and their armed men, was cast down and arrested together with his wife, an "outside girl," Anna Steiner from St. Georgen, and the old sexton's wife, and was taken to the episcopal fortress Brandzoll near Klausen. The capture was the result of a prearranged "plot" between the government and the episcopal officers to the effect that "during the night of St. Andrew's Day [Nov. 30] raids were to be carried out in several villages and judicial districts in the Puster valley, around Bozen, Sterzing and Klausen, where the Anabaptists are said to find accommodation and shelter." According to the *Geschichtsbücher* it was through fraud and treachery that brother Jakob Hutter was captured.[18] The fact was immediately relayed to Brixen and from there by couriers to Innsbruck, where the news of the capture of that "principal overseer" was received with gratitude and great pleasure. The order was given that in view of Hutter's not being an ordinary prisoner but an overseer of great importance, from whom a great deal might be found out, seeing that for several years he had caused a lot of havoc in this land, he was to be taken from Brandzoll to Innsbruck. For this purpose the deputy marshal Offenhauser with a one-horse waggoner was dispatched to Brandzoll to take him over from the administrator. The latter, as well as the district magistrate of Sterzing had secretly been ordered for the sake of greater security to "on the quiet provide Offenhauser with several trusty, well armed, and reliable persons, as many as he might ask for, to help him convey the prisoner safely to Innsbruck."[19] The interrogation of Hutter's wife was to be carried out in Klausen by the town judge.

In view of Hutter's importance the regional government agreed with the episcopal interference with another authority's jurisdiction.[20] They considered the assessment of the Gufidaun prisons being inadequately guarded as sufficient reason for taking the prisoners to Brandzoll instead of Gufidaun. Less happy about the procedure were the judicial lords and pledge holders of Gufidaun: Georg Baron Firmian and his relatives; however, on December 7, the government assuaged them by explaining that a few days ago the authorities had agreed with the bishop that "in a certain night all regional and episcopal administrators in the Puster valley and at other places were to raid the houses under suspicion and do their utmost to capture the said Hutter, because of reliable information of his sojourning at the places in question."[21] Besides, there had been an advance agreement that the fact of one judicial district encroaching on another district's territory should not be seen as an infringement of that other district's jurisdiction. True, it had also been agreed that prisoners were to be handed over to the legal authorities of the district they were arrested in. However, seeing that Hutter was not a common prisoner but an overseer who had misled many persons and brought them to torture and death, and in view of the bad state of the Gufidaun prisons he had been taken to Brandzoll simply for the sake of greater security. This incident was not to be prejudicial to the rights and privileges of the Gufidaun domain, and it was the government's hope that the baron would see the matter no differently from His Grace, the ruling prince.

In Hutter's traveling bag were found letters that Hans Amon

(Tuchmacher) had written from Moravia. Together with the confessions of the arrested women and a report of the Michelsberg administrator about Anabaptists gathering in the woods of Onach and Herschwang, the Brixen bishop forwarded these letters to the Innsbruck authority[22] and these arranged[23] for the Gufidaun administrator to take over from Brandzoll the custody of Hutter's wife and to keep her under guard at Gufidaun until further notice.[24] As the old sexton's wife is not tainted with Anabaptism, she is to be released in return for paying the costs and promising to keep the peace. As regards the Anabaptist gatherings noted by the Michelsburg administrator and Caspar Künigl from Ernburg, a raid is to be delayed until at least an initial interrogation of Jakob Hutter, who had his hideaway here. Old Fischer in Prags, with whom Hutter some years previously, before he got into the sect, had trained as a hatmaker and was said to have left behind an ill repute, is to be questioned about this. With these provisions Hutter's affair entered its final phase.

11

HUTTER'S TRIAL AND EXECUTION

ALREADY ON THE fourth day after her capture Hutter's wife was being interrogated at Klausen by the town judge, Lienhard Mair from Creuz. The government had conveyed to him the fifteen questions at issue. Katharina Hutter was the legitimate daughter of Lorenz Purst. In 1532, she had been a servant to Paul Gall in Trens and was led here to the sect by Gall and Paul Ruemer and others, some of whom she states were already tried and executed while others had fled to Moravia. In Trens she was baptized by Jakob Hutter, she says. Then she had gone with him to Moravia, where at Whitsun 1535, Hans Tuchmacher had married her and Hutter.

Around St. James's Day [July 25], she and Hutter, accompanied by schoolmaster Jeronyme [Käls] (also baptized by Hutter), had left Moravia and over the Tauern Pass had made their way back up here. They had gone to Taufers and for a time remained in the woods. From there they had gone to Waldner at Ellen, who, however, had turned away from the truth and had gone back to being attached to outward things (*Zeichenmensch*). Then they had gone to Ober at Herschwang, who had welcomed them like a dear brother. His wife, too, as well as two male servants by the name of Marton and Wolf Junghans, had been baptized by Hutter. From Herschwang they had gone on toward Lüsen, to Prader, who, however, was not an Anabaptist himself, as were his wife and son. Here they and Jeronyme would often find shelter and accommodation. The above-named persons had been baptized by Hutter in the woods at Lüsen. About a fortnight ago (hence at about November 19), Hutter had at Trens baptized seven or eight persons said to have been miners, and this took place in a cellar in the house of a wagon-maker, called *"zum Schaffer,"* who, however, was no Anabaptist himself. From there, according to Katharina, they had, together with Steiner's daughter Anna, gone again to Ober, but upon learning that "they were being searched for everywhere," they had set out afresh and gone into the woods and had at night walked along the road to Klausen. At midnight they had arrived at the sexton's house there, intending to leave again in an hour or so but not knowing where to go. Hutter had said to them that he wanted to go to the Nielauer at Villnöss or to Jörg Müllner "or wherever God might protect them," as the Nielauer woman was their dear sister and Jörg Müllner with his wife had been baptized the previous fall. Also Niclas Niederhofer in the Schöneck district and a young servant girl at Kienz had become Anabaptists, and the former [i.e. Niclas] had repeatedly given them shelter.

As to Jakob Hutter's property, "he had been giving his money out to poor widows and orphans or to other poor brothers and sisters in need of it," his wife testified. "As far as she knew, none of the brethren's overseers were in the country here at the moment—all were in Moravia."[1] The statements of the other prisoners interrogated on December 3, contain nothing worth noting.

On December 9, in the severe cold of winter Hutter was conveyed to Innsbruck. The Anabaptist Jörg Rock (Mayer), who was beheaded at the shooting range in Innsbruck in 1561, the place of execution also of Hutter, related (and this statement is also found in the Anabaptist *Geschichtsbücher*:[2] how he "had heard that when they took Hutter to Innsbruck, they put a gag in his mouth to keep him from testifying to the truth."[3] In the report the [Innsbruck] government submitted to the king on December 13,[4] it states: To begin with, we questioned him without torture and three times in succession had him instructed about his erring ways by the preacher Dr. Gall, but as he totally rejected that instruction and would not accept it and did nothing but scold and curse, we had him questioned concerning several points at issue, and we shall remit to Your Majesty his statements and confession. Since the bishop (of Brixen) has forwarded to us the enclosed letters that Hans Tuchmacher and others have sent to the aforementioned Jakob Hutter from Moravia, we have found out by examining and questioning Hutter both amicably and under torture that he negates and rejects the whole Christian order of the churches—confession, the holy sacrament, and others, and furthermore, it is not found subsequently that he and others leaders be of the mind and opinion, namely that he and other overseers intend to use force to push through their plan to propagate Anabaptism wherever they might find success. Before proceeding further with him, seeing that he is a bishop and overseer, who has moved hither and thither in Moravia, is well-known and has preached there, we now wish to await Your Majesty's decision as to whether Your Majesty would also have him questioned regarding some details of what he has been doing in Moravia and whatever else Your Majesty might be pleased to have done with him.

Moreover, since the other overseers are said to be still in Moravia, such as Tuchmacher, Onoffrus, Zaunried, and still others who are familiar with the highways and byways are here in our land, it is to be expected that upon learning of the said Hutter's capture some of them might secretly return to this land and here continue to propagate their sect among the common people. Hence Your Majesty might graciously consider having it strictly ordered and commanded in Moravia that the aforesaid overseers and Anabaptists be pursued lest they again return to this land and go on scattering evil seeds here.

The prince bishop of Brixen hastened to convey to the government the testimony of old Fischer in Prags, which did not incriminate Hutter, as well as some items, about which Hutter was also to be interrogated.[5] One of these questions asked, "whether he had not in the past year come to Braunegg riding a horse and dressed like a merchant, had attended the sermon of Steffan, the former assistant priest there, and after listening to it had returned to the inn and there commented that the priest knew the truth quite well but had his mouth stopped up and was not allowed to speak the truth." "It is also well known that the common people in this country have showered and supplied him [Hutter] with large treasure in the way of coinage, silverware, and jewels, and it is to be assumed that he has not shared all of that among his brothers or sisters."

Given that Tuchmacher had written from Moravia asking him to greet the brothers and sisters along the Adige river and in the Puster valley, Hutter was to be asked who these were. Finally he was to be asked how many persons he had baptized altogether. On December 24, the [Innsbruck] government let the bishop[6] know in reply that the last twelve days the accused had not been further interrogated nor dealt with otherwise and that only preacher Dr. Gall Müller had access to him to see whether he might not on Scriptural grounds be turned away from his Anabaptist error; however, once the holy Christmas feast days had passed, they would have him further proceeded against, and whatever he would testify and confess would be passed on to Brixen.

Shortly after Christmas [1535] the royal resolution (Vienna, December 24) arrived, which effectively sealed Hutter's fate.[7] It states: "We are especially pleased by your letter and feel confident that Hutter's capture will greatly contribute to the eradication of the Anabaptist sect. That is why we have in the end decided to in no way pardon the aforementioned Hutter, even if he should turn away from his error, recant and do penance, but rather to proceed against him as one who in our principalities and lands and at other places has misled many persons, causing them to fall away from our true holy Christian faith, forsaking their eternal blessedness, as well as getting them to lose their honor, body, and goods. He should be subjected to the punishment he has deserved in such rich and manifold measure." The resolution goes on: "Seeing that Hutter has for a long time—for eight or nine years—moved hither and thither and has everywhere implanted his seductive sect not only in our margraviate of Moravia but also in our other Lower Austrian lands—in the mountains of Styria and Carinthia and in Austria both above and below the Enns river, you will no doubt have attended to questioning Hutter how he came into this sect, in what principalities and lands he had been gadding about month after month, what persons of noble birth he had baptized, and with whom he had found shelter and accommodation. He also is to be questioned under torture as to the meaning of the numbers in one of the letters to him from the church in Moravia."

In the margraviate of Moravia, says the prince's letter, orders have already been given to search for the overseers "lest the evil be carried by them to Tyrol or other areas. It would be the government's task to apprehend those persons mentioned in the letters and to send "in the way most appropriate," Dr. Gall to the Adige area, the Puster valley, to Bozen and generally to wherever needed, so that the common people be warned.

An ultimate conversion of Hutter seems to have been expected; for we have before us a list of "questions put to the Anabaptist overseer *N*" from the year 1536, to which an "Anabaptist recantation" is appended.[8] That end was not achieved with Hutter. He was incarcerated for weeks in the *Kräuterturm* and was here visited by the town priest of Hall and other theologians, as well as by erudite laymen who tried their best to obtain confessions from him, but it was all in vain. So the government took recourse to harsher measures. On New Year's Day 1536, the captain of Kufstein, Christoph Fuchs, was ordered: "Since until now we have not managed to make Jakob Hutter, overseer of the Anabaptist sect, desist from his errors by means of good Christian teaching," Fuchs was to immediately dispatch to Innsbruck the two beadles "who had beaten his imprisoned Anabaptists with rods" and if possible was to come himself in order to be present at the chastisement.[9] But Hutter was determined to neither give in on matters of faith nor to betray his companions. By decree of January 26 [1536] the sheriff (district magistrate) of Sonnenburg was ordered to take over the prisoner and let justice proceed with him, but to first question him again under torture about the articles in question. This directive was to take place at seven o'clock in the morning on the day to be set by the sheriff, and the secretary of the district court and the other persons required were to be present.[10] This was the introduction to an orderly conclusion of the trial. So the story that turns up more than once in Anabaptist writings and so also in the *Geschichtsbücher*[11] to the effect that Hutter was placed in freezing cold water and after that taken to a hot room and there beaten with rods, that brandy was poured into his wounds and there set afire, also what has been told about other kinds of "buffoonery and tomfoolery" practiced on him may be exaggerated. What is certain is that he endured all degrees of legal torture and remained constant to the very end.

His sentence subjected him to the heightened penalty of being burned alive. Before putting him to death, though, the executives raised misgivings whether it was advisable to carry out the sentence in public and thought it more expedient to put him to death by the sword in the early morning, before daybreak and with no large crowds present. The decision obtained from highest quarters was to the effect that "His Majesty would in no way allow Hutter to be put to death on the quiet, before daybreak and with the sword; he was to be executed publicly and by fire in accordance with the sentence pronounced and the content of the issued mandates," and that is what actually took place.[12] In a letter (Mödling, June 1, 1536) the Anabaptist Jörg Vasser tells that a trades woman had come to see him and had told him of "brother Jakob's uprightness and of the exceedingly great crowds of people that had been present."[13] After guiding the church community for three years, "he died on Friday before the first week in Lent[14] [sic] in 1536, and gave a great demonstration through his death, for God was with him" (Hans Amon). A trusted brother carried the news of Hutter's death to the brethren in Moravia.

On the day after his death the government instructed the prince's treasury: "Given that on November 29 of the past year the Anabaptist Jakob Hutter was brought to His Imperial and Royal Majesty's prison in the *Kräuterturm* here and has now on February 25, been taken out of there again and executed in accordance with the law, the said Hutter has thus lain in the prison here for a time of 87 days. During this time our council servant Martin Hayler has provided him with food and drink and is now demanding 12 kreuzer for each day. Please see to it that the said Martin Hayler is paid the sum of 17 gulden and 24 kreutzer."[15] As late as April 29, the treasury is still complaining about the heavy costs occasioned by the "late Hutter's" trial.

In reply to repeated complaints by Baron Firmian and administrator Adam Prew, Hutter's wife was finally transferred to Gufidaun. There she was to be provided with a learned, sensible, and devout man for the purpose of dissuading her from her "erring ways." However, before such a man arrived she, assisted by her friends and the negligence of the warden, managed to escape from the tower of the castle. On May 15, Hans Amon informs Jörg Vasser in a letter that "our Jakob's Traindl has got away and so has the sister from Michelsberg, and they have both remained devout." The government on its part was highly displeased with such negligence and reserved the right to proceed with suitable punishment against the guilty ones.[16] In a letter of February 5 [1536], the government had asked the Gufidaun administrator to find out just how it stood with the recantation Hutter's wife had submitted at Rodeneck, the result of which she had been pardoned. It is not possible to say with certainty whether this statement is correct. Two years later Hutter's wife fell once again into the authorities' hands and was executed at Schöneck.

For the Anabaptist Jakob Hutter, who attained such prominence among his companions in the faith,[17] is credited with the great merit of reestablishing the order and discipline that had become lax among the Moravian Anabaptists, of having established, over against multiple special interests that had been gaining ground, a community life that had in many ways become breached, of having cleansed the church community of impure elements, and of having brought under control the abuses that elsewhere caused communities to break up. True, in the eyes of his bitter adversary Gabriel Ascherham,[18] Hutter was merely an inflated, ambitious person, who "got the better of Sigmund [Schützinger] and was unable to hide his ambition. The allegedly so rich fruit of his time in office and his establishment of community in fact consisted in the destruction of the love and oneness among the previously united groups of people. Let others say whatever they want about Hutter," he, Gabriel, would assert this Hutter to have been "an evil man" and "though he might have allowed himself to be boiled and fried, all that he (Gabriel) could say about him was that he failed to prove those qualities in Moravia but rather exacted revenge against all who spoke up for Sigmund. He had burst in on the church community with his poltergeist. That was not the spirit of St. Paul of which boasted, but the spirit of the devil, as he had once been told by a woman. Other people had had to pay for his roistering. Hutter (Gabriel maintained) had perished under the guise that it was for the sake of the Gospel, which, however, was not the reason: it was because of his chastisement."

A fairer judgment is derived from Philipp [Blauärmel], who, though also belonging to an opposing party, is much more cultured [than Gabriel]. He averred publicly that during the time he had himself been active in Moravia no one had cared as faithfully for the people in both spiritual and temporal matters as Jakob had done, that he had never been found unfaithful and had always served the Lord loyally and with success. It was through Jakob, Philipp maintained, that God had gathered and sustained his people.

Even worse than with Gabriel, Hutter comes off with his compatriot Christoph Erhard, the Salzburg councilor and theologian, born in Hall.[19] Erhard is followed by Curaeus, Meschevius, Fischer, and others. It is left to our days to provide a picture of Hutter's work more in keeping with the truth.[20]

In answer to the question what exactly had Hutter been teaching, reference might here be made to the Schlatten Articles,[21] which the moderate Anabaptists of southern Germany and Austria held in common. Jeronyme Käls "Confession and Account regarding various Articles of the Christian Faith,"[22] which he and his fellow prisoners tendered to the judge and the authorities in Vienna in 1536, can be regarded as reflecting Hutter's own words. Hutter's spirit also comes to expression in the "Account and Testimony" of the brothers who were carried off from Steinabrunn and were destined for the galleys in 1540.[23] The doctrinal structure finds its completion in the "Account of our Religion, Doctrine, and Faith" put together by Peter Riedemann in 1543 (printed 1565).[24]

True, the hope expressed by Ferdinand I in the above-mentioned letter [of March 30, 1535], to the effect that Anabaptism could now be completely suppressed and rooted out in Tyrol failed to be fulfilled. In the very same years we are still finding traces of Anabaptist activity in Weißbach, Lüsen, Herschwang, and at other places, though there is evidently a momentary slackening in active propaganda. Perhaps because this was to be observed, did the government once again obstruct the suggested setting up of a "roving band," while on the other hand Jeronyme Käls lamented the shortage of ministers of the Word in the church community.

FROM HUTTER'S DEATH TO EXTINCTION, 1536-1626

1

POST-HUTTER: OFFRUS GRIESINGER, 1536-1538

Jakob Hutter's death was no doubt the hardest blow that fell upon the baptism-minded folk in the area of the Austrian lands. After Hutter's death there could be no doubt that Moravia — and not Tyrol — would have to be the center of the entire Anabaptist movement. Moravia was now the "chosen" land from where year after year numerous apostles were sent out: to Poland and Hungary, to the different regions of Germany, and not least to Tyrol itself, in order to rally the old adherents and gain new ones. There was still a favorable soil here for the activity of the separatists; for yet another whole generation they remained intent on winning the broad masses of the people for their cause in order to then refashion the church life in their native country as they felt it should be. It is only from the inception of the so-called "golden age of the church community in Moravia" that they are no longer concerned with establishing formal Anabaptist communities in the "upper country" (*Oberland*) but rather to "catch" as many people as possible and convey them "down" to Moravia. That is why in the last decades of the sixteenth century such emigration became more and more extensive. To Moravia went the stream of those elements who were unhappy with the situation in their own country, Moravia being a land where not only divergent confessions were able to live unhampered side by side, but where the industrious Tyrolese found foodstuffs so low-priced as to be renowned in all neighboring countries. They also found sufficient scope for their industrial activity and skills, with no need to starve to death as was the case in the "upper country"—a complaint one comes across in numerous confessions. The migration to Moravia only came to a halt when the Anabaptists were expelled also from there and that unique refuge became forever closed to them.

Hans Amon, the "clothweaver," had taken over from Jakob Hutter the guidance of the church community in Moravia. Hieronymus (Jeronime) Käls, a "most excellent, learned schoolmaster" was to take over the leadership in the "upper country" (*Oberland*). It was he, together with two companions, Michel Seifensieder from Wallern in Bohemia, and Hans Oberecker from Affers, who was sent there by Hans Amon. However, on the way there all three of them were captured on January 8, 1536, in the "horrible sodomitic city of Vienna" and were also tried and executed there. Käls' task now fell to Leonhard Seiler, who was likewise caught by beadles and taken to Mödling, where he was imprisoned for nearly a year.[1]

While in fetters Käls still managed to write to Amon[2] that the church community in the "upper country" had but very few ministers of the Word, and counselled him to be well aware of this situation. He stated that he "presently knew of no single minister already confirmed by the laying on of hands." The church was given such a minister in the person of Offrus (Onophrius) Griesinger, who from now on until his death stands in the center of the Tyrolese Anabaptist movement. He hailed from Frassdorf in Bavaria and before joining the Anabaptists (in 1532) had been a mining clerk in the Salzburg area. Soon after being chosen a minister he was captured but managed to escape and began to be active in the Sarn, Puster, and Inn valleys. The authorities took out a warrant against him describing the "aforementioned Onoffrus Giesstätter (that's how he is often referred to in the court files) as "a man of medium height, beardless, wearing a loden (i.e. coarse woolen cloth) coat, two pants and over them two stockings of brown cloth; he has baptized quite a number of persons in this land of Tyrol."[3] A second arrest warrant notes that "he is reported to gad about in the Brixlegg." A *taja*[4] (reward) of 60-70 gulden, eventually even 100 gulden, was offered for his capture, and the judicial authorities in Sterzing, Gufidaun, Rodeneck, Kitzbühel, St. Petersberg, along the Ritten and at Lienz were asked to recruit spies in order to catch him. However, in spite of the authorities' ardent zeal they failed to get hold of Griesinger. Around Christmas 1533, he could even dare to "convene a large fellowship" in the Hagau near Rattenberg.[5]

The sheriffs or district magistrates Ernst Prandl at Rattenberg, S. Capeller at Frundsberg, as well as the Rothholz magistrate set out on a joint operation against him, but Griesinger got away by escaping to Moravia. In 1534, he led a group he had gathered around Rattenberg down to Moravia and united with Hutter and his brethren at Auspitz. As Hutter wrote to the prisoners at Hohenwarth, "brother Offrus has arrived with many other brothers and sisters. God be praised! The Lord has led them down here in a most wonderful way. . . There are now no longer many brothers and sisters left in the region."[6]

After Hutter's death all the baptism-minded folk in Tyrol looked to Griesinger in Moravia for leadership, and he did not hesitate to follow their call and to continue the work of Hutter. Before long Amon was able to pass on joyful news from the Adige (Etsch) country to the prisoners in Mödling:[7] "Offerus has arrived there, and many up there are turning to Christ." In the Lenten Week of 1536, at a joint patrol "through the woods" undertaken by Christoph Ochs, the Michelsburg sheriff, and Ulrich Gerlinder, the Schöneck administrator, Griesinger together with a number of fellow believers was discovered and surrounded. However, because of the patrol's insufficient numerical strength, he could not be taken to prison. This, though, was his fate right afterwards. For on April 23, 1536, the Innsbruck government informed the Brixen authorities that "Onoffrus, formerly of Bozen, had been captured but had got away again." The Brixen councillors are therefore commanded to look around for suitable and trustworthy persons for the purpose of tracking down Offerus, he being a great instigator and promoter of Anabaptism. If captured, the successful reconnoiters were to be paid, as a special bonus, a reward of 80 gulden if bringing him in alive, and 40 gulden if dead.[8]

The news of Griesinger's escape caused great joy in the church community in Moravia. "As regards Offrus," Amon writes to the prisoners in Mödling, "this is what happened: They had captured him, as well as his Aendl [i.e. his wife Anna Langer from Pinswang] and also Hänsl F. They took a true, courageous stand but escaped—honestly and uprightly, we hope. Offrus escaped through a hole previously made by a thief. The tyranny up there [i.e. in Tyrol] is tremendous, but there are many zealous people."[9]

What made the authorities feel all the more scared by these happenings was the fact that a report—albeit a false one—was spreading to the effect that the "clothweaver," too, was once again in the land and was said to have found clandestine accommodation in the Brixen area. At Lüsen sixteen Anabaptists were captured who had been set free earlier on as they had admitted being in error and had recanted. They had now succumbed to the sect for a second time and had attended its gatherings here and there in mountains and valleys.[10] Nevertheless, they envisaged setting up a roving patrol was now postponed until later.[11]

One Anabaptist the authorities had already been searching for since the beginning of 1534[12] was Caspar Kränzler. As a result of the constant patrols he was now taken prisoner. On May 15, 1536, the Innsbruck government notifies the Sterzing district magistrate (sheriff) as follows: "Since you have informed us of having captured an Anabaptist named Kränzler together with five other persons and also have remitted to us a letter written by the Anabaptists in Moravia to the brethren of their sect in the Adige (Etsch) region, we order you to question— under torture and in the presence of the jurors—the above-mentioned Anabaptists and in particular Kränzler, as to when and how they came back into this country, where they have been dwelling and what the Anabaptists in Moravia are planning to do." In a letter to the district magistrate Josef Grebner in Sterzing the government expresses the hope that some of those prisoners may still be "converted." For the district magistrate had served notice that "the actions of the preacher who had instructed them about the error of their beliefs had not yet proved effective among them."[13] A sensible and learned cleric was to be sent from Brixen to

Sterzing for the purpose of undertaking the work of reform. The repentant ones might then be set free but would have to pay for their feeding expenses and swear to keep the peace. The obdurate ones were to be dealt with according to the law, and "in the meantime the prisoners were to be put on a reduced ration of food and drink."

For the purpose of converting these Anabaptists a barefooted friar from the St. Clara Monastery in Brixen was sent to Sterzing.[14] However, his attempts to convert the prisoners did not achieve a perfect result. As Hans Amon let the prisoners in Mödling know, Kränzler and a woman Anabaptist from the Jaufen valley were put to death.[15]

As regards Griesinger's activity during the succeeding time, it became noticeable mainly in the Lüsen area. Around Easter time [1536] two Anabaptists who had recanted once before, Braun and Tonig, attempted to convert a number of people. On St. Margaret's Day [June 10] Griesinger turned up in Valmereis, accompanied by eight other Anabaptists, and succeeded in baptizing five persons.[16] On August 4, a gathering was held at "Weißenbach above the Passeyer," and eleven days later 100 baptism-minded persons came together there, fifteen of whom received baptism. A few days later (August 17) eleven persons were captured and taken to Brixen.[17] The town-and-district sheriff (magistrate) Grebner was ordered to arrange for a day and place for the prisoners to be handed over to him. These were to be interrogated about Griesinger's whereabouts in particular.

A few days prior Gilg Schneider from Lüsen had been arrested in Innsbruck. He confessed to having been baptized by Hans Tuchmacher (Amon) in Passeyer and to having intended to set out with three companions on the following Sunday from there to Moravia.[18]

It appears that Deputy Marshal Erasmus Offenhauser was gaining considerable merit by capturing Anabaptists, for on August 26, the [Innsbruck] government ordered him to be granted a garment of honor in recognition of all the trouble he had gone to with the Anabaptists.[19]

On October 23, [1536] Christoph Ochs, district magistrate (sheriff) and administrator of St. Michelsburg, sent to Prince Bishop Georg in

Brixen a detailed report about breaking up an Anabaptist conventicle on the Götzenberg. He writes:

> On several days of the past week I went out with the court clerk, court messengers, and some beadles to search the mountains near Lüsen. At Götzenberg above Ehrenberg we came upon Anabaptist premises with fires either extinguished or still burning with secretive markings as well as a dwelling place.[20] I suspected I might find here the treasurer—Hansl Mayr from Schöneck[21]—but instead of him I found Anna, daughter of Peter Troier, the Schöneck magistrate, and wife of Niederhofer in Terenten. At first she did not want to reveal her identity. Until further notice I am keeping her under guard in my house.

Given that this person is a woman and not particularly rational (sensible) and has merely been led astray by her husband and the [sect's] overseers, that the aforesaid Troier has served the bishopric for a long time and is still serving it, and lastly to avoid turning him into an enemy of mine, it is my obedient request that Your Princely Grace not take any rash action against this person, for just keeping her locked up for a while will surely make her turn away from this sort of thing.

The following night I once more went into the house with the court clerk and messengers, and if I had only come half an hour earlier, I would have bumped into two total knaves who had wanted to take a child away from the house; however, the other devout folk who also were in the house had prevented them and gave us a good report. These two fellows are definitely still abroad in the mountains here, but I am unable to find the place.[22]

Sheriff Ochs was given the reply that in order to avoid rumors spreading among the populace, he was to have the Niederhofer woman taken to the castle and to have her interrogated there, both with and without torture. Her interrogation took place on November 2, [1536]. She confessed to having been baptized by Jakob Hutter in her home on St. Bartholomew's Day (August 24) of the past year [1535]. The heavenly Father had sent his people to her, she said, and they had taken her away; she would not say who they were. She had stayed in the woods, and the brothers had brought her food and drink, but she did not know who were. Her overseer had come from Moravia, she said, but she had not asked who he was or where he was from. Nor was she willing to say anything about his personal appearance; the one thing she could say was that it was not the clothweaver. Nor was she willing to say who had taken her to that house at Erspan on the Götzenberg, where she had been arrested. She had also been with the fellowship above the Peisser [sic—Passeyer].

The jurymen decided that this "confession" was to be sent to the gracious lord (bishop) in Brixen, but that at the same time it should be pointed out that this Anna had a feeble mind and a weak body and should therefore be spared questioning under torture. The jurors were of the opinion that if imprisoned for a while, she would abstain from her erroneous belief.[23]

Two days later her father petitioned for his daughter to be set free and reprieved.[24] On November 15, she herself submitted a request for reprieve. Seeing that it was her feminine weakness that had made her join the Anabaptists and that her father was willing to provide surety for her, her request received the support of the Brixen authorities, who did not always prove so lenient. On October 21, they reprimanded the district magistrate (sheriff) in Sterzing for having released an arrested Anabaptist, after the latter had recanted merely before him as judge, but not in public. The magistrate's defense was deemed a poor one in spite of his pleading that the suffragan bishop of Brixen had given him leave to proceed like that.[25]

In order to apprehend the remaining Anabaptists in the Lüsen area, it was decided on November 14, to take them by surprise just as had previously been done with Jakob Hutter.[26] The advice of the Innsbruck government was to be obtained regarding how to carry out the raid.

Most likely the husband of the apprehended peasant woman, Niclas Niederhofer, had already been arrested jointly with his wife. At Schöneck, where he lay imprisoned, he too submitted a plea for reprieve.[27]

Just as in the Lüsen area, also in the Puster valley and in the Michelsburg judicial district baptism-minded persons kept cropping up time and again.[28] As regards the Anabaptists in the Brixen bishopric, on December 20 [1536], Prince Bishop Georg issued a mandate with a renewed stern command to desist from sheltering Anabaptists and to rather report them immediately to the authorities.[29]

Various friends of the Anabaptists who had accompanied these to Moravia, were not greatly pleased with the way of life there and hence returned to their native country. Thus on Monday before Ascension Day (May 22, 1536) Cristel Kuedegen stood before the administrator of Rainegg, Hans of Serntheim, and asked for leave to again settle down in his district.[30] The protocol drawn up about this matter states: "Christel Kuedegen, having spent some time with the Anabaptists in Moravia and having made his living there, but without letting himself be rebaptized or taking a liking to their way of life, has appealed to His Majesty for pardon and has obtained it. Hence, on condition that he affirms by oath that he did not join the sect nor let himself be rebaptized, he may have leave to be received back into the municipality he had been part of." He was dealt with accordingly. He had to promise, though, to henceforth not let himself be drawn into such a seductive sect; if he failed to hold to this, he would be prosecuted as somebody who had dishonored his oath and promise.[31]

That this was not a rare case is made evident by the petition that the widow of the deceased Georg Ebner submitted to the [Innsbruck] government in 1535. "In the past year," she writes, "my deceased husband and householder, Jörg Ebner, unfortunately succumbed to the seductive sect of the Anabaptists. He repented for this and, throwing himself at His Majesty's mercy, presented himself at the Michelsburg Castle. After recanting and paying the required penalty and costs he was set free." She claims, though, that, "as the property he shared with me was insufficient to cover the costs," she had helped him out with a portion of her own property to pay a surety—in the amount of 100 gulden—against his ever again succumbing to that sect. However, pity to say, her husband had once more been drawn into that sect, had been arrested and condemned and put to death in Brixen.[32] Now, however, the Brixen authorities were demanding the surety, 50 gulden of which she had already paid, and the secretary of the regents' office had informed her that her request for remission of the remainder of the surety could not be granted and that it would have to be collected in the most appropriate way. The widow now turned for help to the government of upper Austria, which authority sent to the councillors of the Brixen regents' office an order to the effect that as Georg Ebner had suffered the supreme penalty and paid with his life, they should not press the case against his widow and henceforth leave her in peace.[33]

On the basis of earlier mandates the goods of executed or fugitive Anabaptists were confiscated. Thus on May 23, 1536, the Lüsen magistrate (judge), Hans Sergandt, was ordered by the Brixen Prince Bishop Georg to confiscate the goods left behind by the Anabaptists Braun and Tonig.[34] Since such cases occurred quite frequently, this, as expressly mentioned in an edict of the reigning prince, gave rise to a popular opinion "as though we had punished the Anabaptists more on account of the goods and chattels they left behind than for other reasons." In order to counter this erroneous opinion, on November 18, 1536, Ferdinand I directed the Innsbruck authorities to henceforth hand over such goods to the children or nearest heirs of executed or fugitive Anabaptists.[35] However, "no emigrant or fugitive Anabaptists were to derive any use or maintenance from such assets."[36] On December 2, 1536, the Upper Austrian government informed the Prince Bishop's councillors in Brixen about this, telling them that, given that His Princely Grace had a claim of lien on the principalities of Heunfels, Schöneck, Michelsburg, and Uttenheim, he should have His Royal Majesty's command be proclaimed also in these domains. In the absence of Prince Bishop Georg, who was spending some time at the court of Queen Maria in Brussels, the councillors at the regents' office in Brixen turned to Cardinal Bernhard, bishop of Trent, for his opinion "whether he would hand over the Anabaptists' assets to their children or nearest heirs." On December 15, the Cardinal replied,[37] "that until now—God be praised—there had been no Anabaptist case in his bishopric; should such a case occur, though, he would not digress from His Royal Majesty's decision."

Up to that point the government had used the sequestered Anabaptist assets to first of all cover the costs of the numerous Anabaptist trials, and these financial burdens were to rest on those confiscated properties also in the future. On December 9, 1536, Ferdinand I issued a decree specifying that the costs of dealing with the Anabaptists, either by putting them on trial or in whatever other way were to be defrayed from their assets.[38] On December 23, this order was communicated to those holding liens on any of the reigning prince's lands.[39]

However, we do find cases where the government showed scant regard for the principle that the Anabaptists' assets were to go to their nearest relatives; e.g. on February 4, 1537, the Kufstein Councillor and Captain, Christoph Fuchs of Fuchsberg and Jauffenberg, was ordered by Innsbruck to "confiscate the goods and chattels of Thomas Pauhofer's sister, said to be tainted with Anabaptism, and to use them for putting up a barn at our Kufstein castle." Thomas Pauhofer protested against this sequestration and maintained that his sister wasn't an Anabaptist at all. He asked the authorities to examine the matter more closely and to desist from making use of his sister's property.[40]

Meanwhile the persecution of the Anabaptists continued. Anabaptists were being noticed in Gufidaun, Rodeneck, and Terlan. Four persons were arrested in Bozen, among them Anna, daughter of Langer from Pinswang, presently the wife of Onofferus Griesinger. The others were Lorenz Kofler, a stonemason from Sterzing, Anna, daughter of Hans Steiner from St. Jörgen near Bruneck, and Brigitta, wife of Hans Gruber from Asling. On January 8, 1537, the Innsbruck government directs the district magistrate (sheriff) at Gries and Bozen, Ludwig Pock, to first "interrogate these Anabaptists, to then have them instructed by discerning persons and, if they will not recant, to deal with them in accordance with to the law."

The women imprisoned in Bozen on account of Anabaptism all managed to escape from there. On April 2, 1537, the Innsbruck government sent to Georg, Baron von Firmian, the chief administrator of the Adige area, an order "to secretly search for the six Anabaptist women that at nighttime got away from the Bozen sheriff and to also investigate the cause of their escape."[41]

A considerable number of baptism-minded folk were still lingering in the Sterzing judicial district. At any rate this is indicated by a governmental directive of February 17, 1537, ordering that for a quarter or even half a year, one or two suitable spies ("moles") be employed for each section of the district, for the purpose of tracking down Anabaptists. But only quiet and discreet persons were to be engaged for this.[42] In the ruling prince's opinion the Sterzing magistrate (judge) proceeded in a much too dilatory fashion against the Anabaptists. That is why on March 3, the prince sent a reprimand from Prague to the vice regent and councillors in Innsbruck to the effect that "at many places the authorities had dealt in a downright negligent way with Anabaptist persons, from whom, being the ringleaders of their sect, a good deal could have been found out. "In particular we have been informed about the great dilatoriness of the Sterzing magistrate, which lets one suspect him of having an understanding with the Anabaptists or of being an adherent."[43]

Four days later the Adige region's chief administrator Georg of Firmian informs the Innsbruck government that the Anabaptists "are again becoming active and are propagandizing." The reply stated that "for the purpose of punishing, uprooting, and annihilating them in this country we have acted with greater valor and zeal than has been shown anywhere else. On their account we have repeatedly and again just recently, issued mandates and orders to be on the lookout for Anabaptists not only in the judicial districts but also on the waters of the Inn river, so as to have them arrested and punished. We have also come to a consent with the Duke of Bavaria as regards their suppression and to an agreement with the councillors in Brixen as regards the strictness to be used for their eradication in the Brixen bishopric and in the Puster valley. Through God's grace things down here in the Inn valley are very quiet at the moment, as regards the Anabaptists. Without doubt you as the chief administrator in your area will do no less than we are doing to eradicate them also there."

The Anabaptists were especially numerous in the Bozen area. Here between Christmas 1536, and April 10, 1537, brother Kunz, who had come up from Moravia together with the shoemaker Caspar Huber (he was also sentenced and put to death in 1537), was executed.[44] In quick succession several Anabaptist meetings took place here. In the last week in March, shortly before the arrest of

Huber, such a fellowship gathering was held at Lüsen and a second one a few days later in the area above Bozen, at which the peasants succeeded in arresting Griesinger but failed to keep him prisoner. As regards these events, the secular councillors in Brixen sent a report to the Innsbruck authorities on April 4. In a written reply (April 9, 1537) the latter voice the expectation that the Brixen authorities might nevertheless manage to eradicate the "evil, accursed sect" and in the name of His Royal Majesty urged them to continue their endeavors. The letter also points out that at his recent patrol the administrator only had sixteen attendants with him and that this is insufficient and the reason that Onofrius, of much greater consequence than the others, was able to escape. "And you (i.e. the Brixen authorities) should know how to deal with the parishioners of St. Lorenzen, who have not come to confession nor have partaken of the Holy Sacrament at this present Easter time. Should anyone of them prove to be tainted with the poisonous Anabaptist sect, you would know how to proceed against them. We enclose for you a copy of a letter from the chief administrator, from which you will learn that the magistrate at Greiffenstein arrested nineteen Anabaptists and imprisoned fourteen of them. It seems to us good for these to be proceeded against with corporal and lethal punishment in line with the imperial and royal mandates and in no case to be [merely] punished by an imposed fine."[45]

Only five days later the Upper Austrian government addressed to Brixen a renewed challenge to be unsparing in both diligence and expense in the eradication of the Anabaptist sect." Moreover, Gilg Schneider, who had deceitfully stated that he had been unable to receive the Holy Sacrament and who is now again imprisoned, ought to be questioned as to where it might be possible to get hold of Onofrius.[46]

When he had last been arrested, in his possession was found a "list or register of all subjects that had aided and abetted Anabaptism." The Innsbruck authorities who naturally had a great interest in gaining access to that list, ordered the Brixen councillors to pass it on to them and to prosecute the persons named there in line with the ruling prince's mandates.[47] However, they should "refrain from tearing down and burning their houses." A copy of the list was to be forwarded to Innsbruck.

The regional government was discontented with the district sheriff at Bozen, Ludwig Bock, and therefore suggested to the ruling prince that the Ritten administrator, Augustin Heyerling, being not only capable but also familiar with the Italian language, be nominated for that post. In their opinion, at such times he should be able to reconnoiter the Anabaptists and deal with them appropriately.[48]

Afraid that a great number of Anabaptists might try to flee to Moravia, the government issued a command to inspect the ships and arrest any Anabaptists encountered.[49] There are records of individual cases of Anabaptists being pursued who were "journeying by water." On April 25, 1537, Erasmus Offenhauser is paid one gulden for his efforts in this matter.[50] Once again the question of setting up a "roving troop" in the territories of the Prince Bishop of Brixen and the Cardinal of Trent was brought up. On May 2, the chief administrator Georg von Firmian is notified that at the advice of the Cardinal of Trent and with his knowledge it had been decided to set up for one or two months a roving troop or band of thirty armed men to root out the Anabaptists.[51] The cardinal was informed that his proposal had been accepted and that Augustin Heyerling had been nominated captain with a salary of 30 gulden. Each of the troopers was to be paid 4 gulden a month.[52] As regards the costs, the princely chamber of finances was to contribute one third, and both Trent and Brixen the remaining thirds. The suggestion of having Augustin Heyerling take the place of the present sheriff of Gries-Bozen was also given repeated consideration; the authorities "were taking great exception to Ludwig Bock's lack of diligence and were highly displeased with him."[53]

Of great interest is the testimony the imprisoned Anabaptist Jakob Moser from the Flaas judicial district gave on the *Erichtag* after Ascension Day (May 15), before Bartel Haller, the Neuhaus judge, to the effect that eight days before Candlemas Day (February 2), he had been baptized in his house by Onofrius. The Sacrament of the Altar, he said, was purely from the devil, and so are infant baptism and confession. The imperial and royal majesty and other authorities are nothing but godless men, for they protect not the devout but only the godless. On the previous Whitsun Day (May 10), he had left their church meeting with Aschberger, which had taken place in the woods above the Raumwald. Present at this meeting, he testified, had been the overseer Onoferus, Hans Rainer and Balthasar, his own (Moser's) brothers in the flesh, both of them purchasing provisions on behalf of the church community, and the six women, who had got away at Bozen, including the wife of Onoferus, who also had escaped there, as well as somebody called Hans Alpaganer, and some devout men and women whom he did not know. Onoferus, he said, had sent down to Moravia his [Moser's or Onoferus's] manservant Peter Urban Tagwerker, Hans, the son of the Terlan sexton, Matthäus Schefter, and Margret, Niclas Holzmain's sister, as well as others he did not know. Those still remaining in the Puster valley also intended to move to Moravia. He and Rainer, Moser stated, had used a *Drembl* to break the iron grating of the Bozen prison; and that is how the six women had got out. The latter, he said, had made their way via Senesigen (Jenosien) and through the Sarn valley to the Puster valley.[54] Mention is also made of a church meeting that took place in Jakobswald near Flaas.

For the *Exaudi* Sunday (May 13), Cardinal and Archbishop Matthäus of Salzburg had scheduled a provincial synod at Salzblurg. Ferdinand I sent to this synod his own preacher Doctor Gallus Müller and the Councillors Sigismund von Thun and Reinprecht von Paiersperg on May 9, providing them with detailed instructions about "what they were to represent and carry out on his behalf." They were to point out that His Majesty regarded the sacred councils and synods as the most suitable means for eradicating the error of heresy. The synod was to come up with salutary decisions to remedy the abuses that had crept into the church, preventing a further falling away from the Christian faith, while still giving apostates a chance to convert. "Seeing that the present schisms, errors, and heresies have their origin mainly in the abuses that have crept into the church and that the Regensburg Reformation has in part already made provision for their redress, we have nevertheless come to see it as additionally necessary for some articles to be brought forward at this synod, in order that more effective action may then be taken at a later general council. To begin with, considering that since the Regensburg Reformation no such councils have taken place, the provincial and episcopal synods are to take place and to be held much more strictly."

Ferdinand's instruction goes on, "in particular among the Franciscans, there arose a terrible abuse that no daughter is being accepted in the monasteries without a considerable financial contribution, and this has to be stopped so that the laity, be they rich or poor, are all the more motivated to bring up their children to be fit for monastic life." For the same reason monastics were not to receive inheritance to the disadvantage of the secular members of their family but should rather renounce their rights in favor of others, given that the clerical institutions ("divine houses") are quite adequately funded. Any useless luxury in these houses is to be avoided. Clerics are to be strictly enjoined to attend to their priestly office and to divine service in the church with greater devotion and discipline than before. During such service they are not to sing overly fast but in a slow, understandable and devout way so as to be understood. They are to be with heart and soul in their divine service and not just with their mouth, and to be decorous in their walk and attire. No preacher is to be admitted without first having his suitability tested as regards ability, experience, and respectability. In all cathedral churches, in the churches in cities and larger market towns from which preachers are to be appointed, alongside the parish priests, the common people are apt to receive not only the word of God but also consolation, advice, and help in whatever they face in life. Not only on feast days but also on free evenings they are to proclaim both the gospel and the epistle of that day.

"The common people are to have the ceremonies and usages of the church and their significance explained to them, and in connection with every article of the synodal resolutions the canonical punishments which derelict clerics will receive are to be read out, so that in future no one will be able to excuse himself by pleading ignorance. Every priest is to be enjoined to be in possession of a Bible of his own and to read it diligently after attending to his usual duties in the church."

Clerics are to be strictly forbidden to indulge in excessive eating and drinking. Excommunications are to be pronounced for valid reasons only. Parsonages and other clerical benefices are no longer to be assigned by way of protection and to persons unfit for the post in question. In future, benefices are no longer to be restricted to only some of the parsonages; "rather the church's income is to be used solely for the benefit of those who merit them." "Particularly in our Lower Austrian lands many parsonages are totally barren and unkept – mostly because the tithes which are due to the parsonage are being sequestered by both laymen and clerics for their own use and the common people are therefore left wholly unprovided for, also as regards the sacraments. In view of that situation, our councillors are to insist at the synod that the incumbents of all parsonages are adequately provided for and are in a position to support themselves honorably. And the learned and skilled clergymen suited for pastoral care and preaching ought to be given an opportunity for successful activity at parsonages presently left vacant."[55]

These articles demonstrate that the ruling prince was earnestly concerned to do away with the very real wrongs and evils within the church, which were being lamented in the various regions and population sectors. The numerous confessions in the government's hands contained many a valid complaint which could not be denied. And it was not the worst elements among the people that crowded around the "enthusiastic" prophets. By setting out to meet the justified complaints about the distressed situation in the church, by caring for the instruction of the people and for the raising of the moral standard among the clergy and by urging the latter to attend more earnestly to its duties, the government did more for the uprooting of the separatists than even the most bloodthirsty decrees could achieve. Of course, there was no lack of these either. The ensuing government orders were still concerned with the setting up of a "roving troop,"[56] but Heyerling refused to lead it. In a letter (of May 26) to the Cardinal of Trent the government now suggested the judge (magistrate) of Völs, Caspar Wolf Dietrich, as the suitable man for the job.[57]

From the confession of the Anabaptist Jakob Moser the authorities had gathered that a church gathering had only recently been held in the Puster valley. Hence on May 23[58] the government ordered this confession to be sent to the administrator and magistrat of Michelsburg, asking him to "try and get on the track of the Anabaptists there." Through excessive zeal some persons were apprehended who most likely had nothing to do with the Anabaptisits. Thus on July 4 [1537] the Villanders magistrate informed the episcopal captain at Brixen that Balthasar Unterrainer, imprisoned in Gufidaun, had been interrogated but without discovering in him anything Anabaptist.[59] The government found out, however, that he had taken victuals to the Anabaptists.[60]

It remains unclear if Cyprian Rindler, who in August of that year [1537] was in prison in Brixen because of engaging in improper discourse and disputing, belonged to the Anabaptists. On August 18, Ferdinand ordered[61] the Brixen councillors to deal with Rindler as they saw fit.

In the Oetz valley toward the end of November or beginning of December 1537, Sebastian Huebmaier (alias Glaser) and Hans Grünfelder from Lüsen were arrested and taken to Imst. Grünfelder had been a minister of temporal needs and later minister of the Word among the Anabaptists in Lüsen and in the environs of Michelsburg and Schöneck.[62] In an attempt to convert them, Dr. Gall was sent to Imst. His endeavors, however, proved in vain; "it's been fruitless," he wrote on April 4, 1538.[63] In his confession Huebmaier testified that it was only around Michaelmas [Sept. 29] that he had arrived in this country, "in which he had not been previously." He said that he had mostly stayed in the woods, that he had preached and proclaimed his teaching to a number of brothers of his sect but had not baptized anybody. Grünfelder had been baptized by Griesinger two years ago and had likewise remained mostly in the Puster valley.[64] Yet a third Anabaptist, called the old Oswald, was imprisoned at Imst. About their death Griesinger reported as follows to the church community in Moravia. "In heartfelt love we (Griesinger and Lochmaier) have to let you know about our brothers Bastel Glaser, Grünfelder and old Oswald from the Oetz valley. With great joy they have testified to the Lord's holy word and to the truth, as you have already known though not in detail. I am unable to fully describe their joy to you. Up to a thousand people were present at Bastl and Hänsl's execution. Hänsl shouted with a loud voice, exhorting and warning the people, and so did Bastl—right up to their death, and jointly with old Oswald. The people were deeply shaken by it. It's true for the wise man to declare that there will be no reprieve for the old and grey-haired ones [Ecclesiasticus 16:8]. It's reported that, being unable to fully burn their bones, they cast them into the water. We trust that this witness has not been in vain."[65] Bastl Glaser is the author of two songs: "Lord God in highest throne" and "O Lord, do end my suff'rings."[66]

According to the *Geschichtsbücher der Wiedertäufer* a fourth Anabaptist was put to death in the year 1537: Jakob Zängerle, but there are no extant files about him.

An exceptional case is represented by a disputation, arranged by four parish priests from the lower Engadine valley, to which the priests and parishes of the Upper Engadine "adhering to the old Christian faith" were invited. The knight Jakob Khuen at Nanders, "who has the four parsons very much on his heart," asks the government to present the parsons at Nanders and St. Niclas, who are both "faithful adherents of the old faith" and whom he is afraid he might lose, seeing that they long to get away from their impoverished parishes, with a coat each. The government forbade its subjects to attend the disputation; anybody turning up in spite of this order was to be arrested.[67]

Toward the end of the year 1537, two Anabaptists—Oswald Hellrigl, formerly a Lutheran, and Christian Thaler, both from Telfe, were arrested in St. Petersberg. Hellrigl, who, like his companion was being instructed by Dr. Gall, recanted only a few days later.[68]

The merits that Gall (Dr. Gallus Müller) acquired especially through the conversion of Anabaptists were fully recognized by the reigning prince. On March 5, 1538, the Tyrolean chancellor Beatus Widman addressed from Znaim to Cardinal Bernhard of Trent a letter, in which he urgently appealed to him to let Müller have a better post. Widman speaks of having brought the skill of Dr. Gallus, former parish priest in Tübingen, to His Majesty's attention and of having requested to keep him in Tyrol, seeing that "there is a severe shortage here of erudite and eloquent theologians, indeed there is probably no one in the country apart from Dr. Eck." The cardinal is requested to come to an agreement with the Innsbruck government as to how best to accommodate such a man. "He would do a lot of good at Schwaz, would be a necessity at Hall (with no need to tell why); and it would be honorable and most useful to have him at Innsbruck because of His

Royal Majesty's children and the government.[69] His majesty, the letter goes on, had considered "letting him have the preaching post in Hall"[70] which is said to yield about 200 gulden, and it would be possible to still add something from other churches or clergymen, in order to hoist the sum up to 400 gulden. I have advised His Majesty to rather have a regent's position less for the sake of keeping in Innsbruck *talis medicus anime et defensor religionis* [such is a doctor of the soul and defender of religion]."

Already in the next weeks Dr. Gallus was to test his skill on one of the "Anabaptists' chief overseers," Leonhard Lochmaier.[71] In the last days of April 1538, the latter had fallen into the hands of Eitelhans Grieninger, the administrator of St. Petersberg. On Mai 9, the government wrote to Grieninger as follows: "We have received your letter of May 1, concerning the arrested Anabaptist persons, by name: Leonhard Lochmaier from Freysingen, who had been a priest but is now an Anabaptist overseer; Georg Uhl, ore miner from Lenpach near Brixen; Hans Näss from Tyrol; Ruepp Haas, Cyprian, and Veit Kuhn "zu der Hueh," all three from the Oetz valley; also Veronika Clasen, Ursula Hellriglin, Anna, daughter of Jos Mark, and Margareth, daughter of Joachim Kofner. Our command to you is to guard Lochmaier well, to send him to the clerical court in Brixen together with his companions, and to instruct the escort to keep careful watch on him lest he get away."

Veit Kuhn right away declared himself ready to recant and was granted a reprieve under the usual forms. As to the remaining eight, Dr. Gall was to try and turn them away from their faith. "Against those that do not recant," the instruction goes on, "you are to proceed according to the content of our mandates and the criminal laws."

On May 15, 1538, the Innsbruck government informed the clerical councillors in Brixen, "We want to let you know that Lienhard Lochmaier, the Anabaptist overseer and preacher, has recently been arrested, together with someone else, in the judicial district of Petersberg and has submitted a confession[72]—see the enclosed writing. After yesterday bringing the said Lochmaier here to Innsbruck, we have come to the conclusion that, since he is a priest and was apprehended in the Brixen bishopric and it is therefore incumbent upon your clerical jurisdiction to bring him to trial, it would be best to have the said Lochmaier conveyed to you in Brixen, on condition that you proceed against him with serious punishment, seeing that he is an overseer, has caused a lot of evil through his preaching and has misled many people."[73]

Lochmaier had been a Catholic priest for eight years, until in 1526, won over to Anabaptism by Jörg Krautschlögl, who in the following year was burned at the stake together with his wife. In 1528, Lochmaier joined the church community in Moravia and preached there as well as in Upper Austria below the Enns river and in the Slovakian parts of Hungary. After Hutter's death he was active together with Griesinger in the upper Inn valley and the Pitz valley, until falling into the hands of the authorities. He was now taken to Brixen as a captive by "chamber messenger" Mannshalter with his one-horse wagon (*Ainspanige und Kammerbote*) and by Georg Prenz.[74]

The capture of Lochmaier encouraged the authorities to carry out more general and comprehensive patrols in order to apprehend also Griesinger. On May 20, the district magistrates (sheriffs) of Rattenberg, Schwaz and Sonnenburg, the magistrate of Rottenburg and the legal counsel at Thauer were ordered to provide fifteen able-bodied and armed persons for patrolling the mountains.[75]

Brixen, too, used all means available in order to finally bring Anabaptism in the bishopric under control. On June 27, the clerical councillors in Brixen inform the Innsbruck government:[76] "Seeing that the Anabaptists, led by overseer Onopherus, are once again turning up in our bishopric, especially in the Puster valley and on the Götzenberg, and are by no means idle with their damnable sect but rather keep escorting a number of His Majesty's subjects with wives and children out of the judicial districts of Michelsburg and Schöneck, one ought to have them pursued by trustworthy persons over mountains and through valleys and root them out. With respect to this pursuit," the councillors complain, "His Majesty's subjects are not to be trusted, for the Schöneck administrator declares pointblank that he does not have one single man to be trusted in his district, and the Michelsburg sheriff spoke in a similar vein when this matter was talked about, both of them being present at the discussion because of their expert knowledge." In order to proceed more effectively against the Anabaptists, the Brixen councillors request: Firstly, that stern mandates be issued in His Majesty's name and all subjects be commanded to refrain from sheltering and accommodating Anabaptists and from aiding and abetting them in any way, failing which they would have three squads of lansquenets billeted on them; secondly, that bridges everywhere be guarded so as to apprehend any Anabaptists that might want to return. In the third place, the Brixen councillors voiced and conveyed to the Innsbruck government, a "counsel" of their own, saying:[77] "On the basis of the information that has come to hand about the Anabaptists, we have got in touch with administrators and magistrates and taken counsel with them about how this sect might be eradicated and done with, and we have come up with the above-mentioned ways and means, for unless we are determined to take stern and courageous action against it, one has to be afraid of this cursed sect taking widespread root and becoming totally rampant. Hence we herewith bring this to Your Grace's attention and request to hear your assessment and advice with regard to it. In the meantime we have enlisted lansquenets and ordered them to diligently reconnoiter and be on the lookout for Anabaptist persons so as to apprehend as many of them as possible. The enlisted lansquenets have been ordered to occupy mountain passes and bridges wherever necessary—to be specific: the Rundler Bridge, Mühlbacher Klause, the bridges at Ober- and Nieder-Vintl, at Phunders and Pfitsch, at St. Sigmund and Kaltenhaus."

"In addition, Christoph Ochs, sheriff and bailiff at Michelsberg along with three or four good lansquenets, has been ordered to survey the mountains for Anabaptists, and while this is in progress, the bridges and passes are to be guarded also at nighttime, so that Anabaptists intending to move to other places may be apprehended. The lansquenets employed for this purpose are to be paid generously."

"In the same way the magistrate at Rodeneck, assisted by the administrator there, will be diligently on guard, particularly on the occasion of the Corpus Christi procession" (June 20).

"There is to be patrolling and reconnoitering every night until next Wednesday (June 19). In addition, Ochs and Paul Troyer with five lansquenets have been ordered to occupy bridges and passes at night and to lay snares into the middle of them."

"Similar measures are to be taken at the Rundler Bridge, at the gate of the Mühlbach bridge, the Nieder-Vintl bridge and at the other afore-mentioned places."

"The government is to be reminded to make similar arrangements at Sterzing, the Brenner Pass, and at other places such as Gufidaun etc."

On June 26, 1538, the Innsbruck authorities replied to the above "counsel" that they had been pleased to take note of the arrangements made. "If notified in time, we, too, would have been inclined on Corpus Christi Day to undertake patrols at Sterzing and the other places you list. As things are, this is now being missed. If you intended to carry out similar measures in the future, it would be appropriate to let us know about them in good time. But we nevertheless want to be on our guard at all bridges and mountain passes. For the purpose of apprehending the overseer Onofrius, a few days ago we carried out in the lower Inn valley a nocturnal raid on a meeting of the church community, but to no avail. Even though we have already repeatedly issued mandates against the Anabaptists, we nevertheless want to re-issue them; we are afraid, though, that it will be fruitless. However, seeing that it is mostly because of a lack of understanding, a lack of able preachers, and at times also because of the unpriestly living style of some clerics, that the common people have been enticed into that seductive sect, it seems good to us to make necessary changes. Accordingly we want to bring Dr. Gall Müller into the Puster valley and have him preach there for about three weeks. As regards the priests, you ought to see to it that they give a good example to the subjects and present God's word to them in a fitting manner, so that the people have no grounds to cling so obstinately to these evil sects among them. We are also informed that you confiscate the goods of the Anabaptists. However, you will doubtless remember that His Royal Majesty had resolved to no longer usurp the Anabaptists' goods and chattels but rather to hand them over to their children and nearest heirs, deducting only the expenses incurred."[78]

Under the same date Dr. Gall was commissioned to go for three weeks into the Puster valley and first of all to Sterzing for the purpose of working there against the Anabaptist cause.[79] He had 26 gulden assigned to him for food expenses and also had the "one-horse carter or carrier" (*Ainspanniger*) Wucherer placed at his disposal.[80] The administrators at Michelsburg and Schöneck and the burgomaster and council at Bruneck were ordered to see to it that "he be met with all due discipline and respect for his activity so that he might proclaim the word of God all the more impressively." Similar directives were sent to the parish priest of St. Lorenzen.[81]

At the same time the burgomaster and council at Hall, the sheriff at Rattenberg and the captain at Kufstein were notified that there were again Anabaptists in their areas and particularly that the overseer Onoferus was moving about freely in the mountains there. They were ordered to search for him.[82]

On July 3, the town and country magistrate in Rattenberg was ordered to "deal with the arrested Anabaptist Lamprecht according to the law."[83] The following day a report was received that in the Oetz valley, in the Petersberg judicial district, a committee had formed for the eradication of the Anabaptists, with the aim of shutting down the houses in which Anabaptist meetings had been held, and this was agreed to.[84]

Meanwhile the suffragan bishop Albrecht of Brixen and Dr. Gallus Müller had persistently tried to convert Lienhart Lochmaier. Already on July 13, the Brixen councillors were able to pass on joyful news to the Innsbruck government: "We had the suffragan bishop and others examine and address the prisoner, and especially now that Dr. Gall has arrived here (in connection with other matters), we have so worked on him that he has softened and agreed to recant and to publicly confess his error."[85] At that same time the recantation formula was being put together.[86] The government replied that the Brixen councillors were to hold off in their actions, for Dr. Gall wanted to write a copy of the revocation himself and submit it. On July 18, 1538, suffragan bishop Albrecht and Dr. Gall submitted to the Innsbruck government a plea for Lochmaier's reprieve. On July 24, the government replied: "Although it is not for us to grant clemency to Anabaptist overseers even if these recant, we have nonetheless, because of your intercession and since you think that a reprieve would accomplish much good, forwarded your letter to His Royal Majesty and have asked His Majesty to graciously let us know his decision."[87] In their letter to Ferdinand I the government requests that Lochmaier, if he recants, "be granted his life," since "this would do a lot of good among simple folk, as well as among rebaptized persons who have not yet been revealed." On August 8, 1538, the government additionally informs the king that the vice regent and chancellor in Brixen had related in writing how Leonhard Lochmaier had in the parish church and in their presence spoken out his public revocation in a very heartfelt and devout manner and had shown indubitable signs "of doing it wholeheartedly and that, if granted a reprieve, this would be very good and useful for doing away with that sect." In conclusion the government requests that for a time Lochmaier be still given instruction by Dr. Gall and that he then be again "permitted to carry out priestly functions."[88]

On August 15, 1538, Ferdinand I responded to the government's request, writing, "Even though the general laws and our promulgated mandates would give us ample justification for denying a reprieve to the said Lochmaier, as an [Anabaptist] overseer, we nevertheless, seeing that he has voluntarily confessed and has spoken out his recantation with devotion and from his heart, want to graciously exempt him from punishment. However, he is to be adequately tested and enjoined to remain in Brixen for a whole year after his release, so that in the meantime the constancy of his walk and conduct be made manifest."[89]

On August 21, 1538, this information is passed on to the regent's office and the councillors in Brixen. "However," the royal letter goes on, "seeing that in the Petersberg district the said Lochmaier has brought into the sect several persons, who are still mired in it in spite of all the efforts of Dr. Gall, it would be good to send Lochmaier down to them to get them to break with it."[90]

In the meantime the hunt for Offrus Griesinger had been going on unceasingly. On August 26, the Schöneck administrator and the Michelsburg sheriff made all arrangements for a renewed painstaking patrol.[91] On that day Christoph Ochs informed the Brixen councillors that a scout (spy) of his had told him that the overseer Onoffrus with his wife and about thirty brothers were together at a certain place." On August 29, Brixen reported having received news that in the past night "the overseer Onopherus had been apprehended and arrested in a mountain hut."[92] The Schöneck administrator was to be ordered to immediately have this overseer sent here to Brixen under heavy guard. Likewise, His Royal Majesty, the government of Upper Austria, the cardinal of Trent, as well as "my gracious lord in the Netherlands" (where bishop Georg was sojourning at the time) were to be notified. Together with Griesinger a man named Schneider had been arrested. In Griesinger's satchel various writings, scribbled slips of paper, and the "New Testament book" were found. A copy was made of the various writings and paper slips and, together with the report about Griesinger's capture, was forwarded to the Innsbruck authorities.

On August 30, the clerical and secular councillors in Brixen ask chamber procurator Ulrich Schmotzer[93] to seek out Cardinal Brundusianus, legate of His Papal Holiness, if he is still in Innsbruck, and "on our behalf apprise him of the arrest of that overseer, who had been pursued for so long." All this shows the great importance the ecclesiastical and temporal authorities attached to Griesinger's arrest. As he had several times already escaped from prison, the Innsbruck authorities alerted the Brixen councillors to this fact. He was to be guarded most carefully and diligently, regardless of expenses;[94] he was not to be trusted. Meanwhile Christoph Ochs and Paul Troyer were asked to "put together the articles, on the basis of which Onopherus was to be examined."[95]

While the country's authorities voiced loudly their elation about the capture of the most dangerous one among the Anabaptist apostles, a change had occurred in Lienhard Lochmaier. When the suffragan bishop and vicar-general Dr. Jörg Stammler came to see him, informed him of his reprieve and read out to him the government's letter, he replied that he had not asked Dr. Gall to intervene on his behalf with His Royal Majesty and that he felt unable to thank him for doing that. When reminded of his revocation, he said he had done it crazed by fear and terror and did not know how he could have done it and that he "had repented of it twice as much as he had hairs on his head."

When reminded that he was meant to go out and convert the imprisoned Anabaptists, he replied that he would in no way turn them away from their rightful faith and would hold on to it himself.

At the same time Lochmaier tried to get into contact with imprisoned Griesinger.[96] There is reason to suspect that it was the news of that overseer's capture that so powerfully shook up Lochmaier's heart. On September 6, 1538, the Innsbruck government was informed of what had happened.[97] In addition to the above facts we learn from that report that Lochmaier had attempted to gain his freedom by filing through the chain that fettered him. A report about Lochmaier penned by Dr. Gallus Müller had also been sent to King Ferdinand. By return of post—Linz, September 8—Ferdinand ordered the Innsbruck government to hold off with respect to Lochmaier's reprieve.[98] On September 10, the government of Upper Austria writes, "We are horrified to learn that Lienhard Lochmaier has apostatized and fallen away. Seeing that now nothing but troubles are to be expected from him, from Onofferus, Schneider, and the other arrested Anabaptists, the councillors should without delay proceed against them with punishment.[99] In this sense the government also reported to the king: the two overseers ought not to be "sustained" for a long time, but should have their due punishment meted out to them. "There is nothing else we could suggest to Your Royal Majesty than to have both of them burned at the stake." A similar message was sent (September 13) to the Brixen councillors.[100]

Lochmaier's change of heart served to also speed up the case of Griesinger. On September 4, the Brixen councillors had been asked to question Griesinger about "who else in this country is part of this sect, what their names are and in what district they live, whether the sect's outward appearance is hiding various clandestine practices, or perhaps they are not scheming to start a *Bundschuh*[101] or new insurrection." As the scrap of paper found on Onofferus was so unclear that it was impossible to know whether the persons there listed were tainted with Anabaptism, he was to be questioned about it both under torture and without.[102] At the same time trials were in progress against the arrested Anabaptist woman Christina Grienbacher from Khiens[103] and against Leonhard and Veronica Gartner. At the royal court the capture of Griesinger caused immense satisfaction, as may be gathered from Ferdinand I's letter of September 6, to the episcopal councillors in Brixen. "The fullest possible information is to be obtained about this overseer's doctrine, sojournings, and conspiracy to have Griesinger closely questioned about "what had fundamentally been his and his confederates' mind and intention, as regards stirring up a rebellion and the like, also who had aided and abetted him in his escapes." "And since we learn from the writings enclosed with this that many persons under our authority as well as others have links with this sect, we want to make an exact excerpt from these data and command in all our lands that the persons involved be apprehended, incarcerated and punished in accordance with the mandates issued. In particular see to it that the arrested Onofrius is well and closely guarded in his prison, and see to it that whatever he confesses is reported to us."[104] Griesinger's interrogation was attended by chamber procurator Dr. Ulrich Schmotzer, who himself put the questions to the prisoner.[105] Already on September 7, Griesinger's testimony ("confession") was sent to Innsbruck;[106] on September 16, it was also forwarded to King Ferdinand.[107] On the same day the Brixen councillors deliberated on how to go about the execution of Lochmaier and Griesinger. They asked Innsbruck for advice on whether these were to be put to death in public or secretly. The latter way, they suggested, was preferable for it had to be feared that "Onophrius with his quiet and gentle way of speaking might move a lot of people, and for that reason we are inclined to let justice take its course with them secretly in the early morning hours."[108]

Doctor Gallus Müller gave Lochmaier his warmest attention right to the last minute. As may be gathered from a letter of prebendary and chancellor Han, Gallus Müller did his best to bring Lochmaier to a renewed revocation. As Han puts it, "the good Doctor Gall is taken in by Lochmaier's dissembling and forbearance—a quality not usually found among Anabaptists. In reality he is a crafty teacher who for nearly ten years has plunged many devout people into misfortune. If he were to get out again, he would be even worse than Hutter, who caused such a lot of harm. If he is set free again, all one can expect is that he will once again join the Anabaptists, among whom he has his pregnant wife. And if he then kindles another fire, Doctor Gall is going to say he wouldn't have believed it."[109] To his wife Bärbl, Lochmaier sent a letter written by Griesinger's hand, in which he thanks her for her love and sends greetings to Hans Amon and Ulrich Stadler. In remembrance of his revocation he writes, "God has helped me up again. I know I have grieved you deeply; forgive and pardon me!"[110] Of Griesinger's five extant letters three were written in prison. In the first one he writes: "It is probably through weakness that Leonard has fallen; but—God be praised—he once again professes the Lord." In the second letter he tells: "We should have been executed earlier, but something has suddenly stopped it—we don't know what." In the third letter he relates that they had wanted to force him to divulge the names of the persons who were driven out and especially of those who had given them shelter. They also wanted to know how numerous the Anabaptists were and whether they were going to take revenge. He had replied that "if we did we would not be Christians but merely fake ones like you." "I was ill for eight days from the torture. At the moment we are still lying here and are waiting for the Lord."[111]

On September 18, 1538, Ferdinand I lets the Innsbruck government know that in his opinion, too, there should be no further delay in letting the law take its course.[112] But it still remained to be decided whether the execution was to be a ceremonial or a secret one. On September 21, the Innsbruck government tells Brixen: "When in 1536, Hutter was to be executed and the same question came up, His Majesty was unwilling to let him be put to death on the quiet and with the sword."[113] The two prisoners were left in uncertainty for four more weeks. On October 24, the Innsbruck government writes to the captain and the councillors in Brixen: "Since as yet no action has been taken against the two overseers, we have, lest His Majesty be taken aback or displeased, sent to you Dr. Schmotzer to talk the matter over with you." In the end Griesinger's execution was carried out between 10 and 11 o'clock in the morning on October 31.[114] As Lochmaier wrote to the church community in Moravia, "they took him like a sheep to the slaughter. He spoke to the people—very gently and lovingly, and urged them to repent. Some among the people "acknowledged Onophrius to be a devout man."[115] He is also known as an author of spiritual songs.[116]

The sentence on Lochmaier was carried out later. In his last letter to the church community in Moravia he writes, "How things are with me, and why I should be imprisoned so long, God alone knows. I had comforted myself with the thought I might bear witness jointly with devout Offrus. But God the Lord denied it to me. I am waiting day by day like a wretched sheep. The priests still have to wreak their devilment on me and take away my ordination; only then are they allowed to hand me over to the hangman."

This divestiture of the priestly ordination, which only a bishop is entitled to carry out, was delayed for a time, because on October 3, 1538, the suffragan bishop had died and the prince bishop himself was outside the country. Only after his degradation was Lochmaier executed, by the sword and "several days after Offrus," as the Anabaptists' *Geschichtsbücher* relate.[117] Like his companion in suffering Lochmaier, too, was the author of spiritual songs, two of which are still extant.

In the same year [1538]—an exact date has not been preserved—at Rieß in the Fluck valley near Brixen, Martan from Villgraten and Caspar Schuster were beheaded.[118]

On December 1, [1538] Griesinger's wife Anna was interrogated at Hennfels Castle; as was made known 15 days later, she suffered from epilepsy. Besides her, Oswald Schuster and his wife were imprisoned at Hennfels. Schuster had given himself away at Griesinger's execution.[119] He had pushed through the crowd in order to once more shake Griesinger's hand and was thereupon arrested. He managed, though, to escape from the dungeon together with his wife. Dr. Müller made great efforts to convert several Anabaptists imprisoned at Fragenstein and St. Petersberg.[120] Since Anabaptist traces were thought to have been detected also in Rodeneck, Christoph von Wolkenstein was asked to carry out a reconnaissance there. In December 1538, he reported that a year ago Anabaptists headed by Onoferus had indeed settled at Rodeneck but that now the air was totally clear and no sign of any Anabaptists in residence there."[121]

It had been assumed that Griesinger's execution had dealt Anabaptism in the Puster valley and Adige country a fatal blow; however, after barely a few weeks news was bruited that no less a person than the "clothweaver" [i.e. Hans Amon] himself had arrived in Tyrol. Immediately orders were sent out in all directions that he be tracked down, and the *taglia* (reward for capture) of 80 gulden only recently paid out for the apprehension of Griesinger was also promised for the capture of the "clothweaver."[122]

2

INNSBRUCK REGIONAL GOVERNMENT, 1539-1545

"Several Anabaptists imprisoned in Schwaz, namely Georg Keberl, Cristian Heckl, and others have stated that an overseer by the name of Lienhart Seiler, a person of medium stature and wearing a coat (*Wappenrock*) of the color of iron, had resolved to make his way into the Adige country." That is what the Innsbruck authorities wrote to the episcopal regents and councillors in Brixen on August 17, 1539. Lienhart Seiler, "who was to be carefully tracked and, if possible, to be captured and overpowered," was the missioner who after Griesinger's passing was called upon to be active in Tyrol.

Like Griesinger and Lochmaier and the Anabaptists' bishop Amon himself, Lienhart Lanzenstiel, mostly called Seiler (i.e. ropemaker) after the trade he practiced, hailed from Bavaria. In 1529, we find him among the baptism-minded in Krumau. In 1536 and 1537, he and his companion Jörg Vasser were incarcerated in Mödling in Lower Austria. Out of their prison they sent letters, six in all,[1] to the "church of God" in Moravia. In 1539, Seiler was chosen to be a minister of the Gospel[2] and henceforth devoted himself zealously to mission work in Tyrol.

In the meantime, the persecution of the "baptism-minded" folk had been vigorously pursued there. On March 20, the Brixen councillors order a pregnant Anabaptist woman incarcerated at Hennfels to be released until further notice, if someone is willing to stand surety for her.³ In the same days the newly chosen bishop of Brixen, Cardinal Bernhard von Cles, issued a mandate urging "more than before, for everyone to be on alert for Anabaptists and to pounce on them in their hovels."⁴ Rewards were to be granted to persons distinguishing themselves in the persecution of Anabaptists, e.g. the court clerk Hans Schönbiehler on the Michelsburg Castle.⁵

On May 3, King Ferdinand I informs the Innsbruck authorities that it had come to his knowledge that Count Wolf von Montfort and Rothenfels, Vice Governor of the upper Austrian lands, had arrested some Anabaptists who will not let themselves be dissuaded from their erring stance. However, since they might have apostatized more because of their simplicity of mind and through being misled than through premeditated malice, it would be best to delay their punishment and rather let them fast for a time and receive instruction from erudite persons; only if they remain obdurate should they be dealt with in accordance with the mandates. Two days later the government issued "strict orders for the eradication of the Anabaptist sect to all administrative offices in the country." Suitable spies and "moles" were to be recruited.⁶

In order to prevent the influx of Moravian Anabaptists, on May 23, 1539, the Innsbruck authorities ordered the administrators of the Ortenburg County to stop any Anabaptists who, coming from Moravia, might want to again sneak via Lienz into the Puster valley and the other parts of Tyrol, as to prevent their entry. The same directive went to the *Zollner* (customs officer) Max Kampf on the Lueg (pass or mountain).⁷

On June 3, 1539, the Anabaptist woman Ursula Hellrigl, whose name will crop up frequently in the days to come, is mentioned for the first time. The Innsbruck authorities inform the king about an eighteen-year old peasant girl from the upper Inn valley, who, "deeply entangled" [in the sect], has by now been lying for five *Quatembers* (quarterly ember days) in the St. Petersberg prison by St. Peter's Mountain. Out of consideration for her sex and youth an attempt had been made to bring her back to the right way through the services of Dr. Gallus Müller. She was not well-read in Scripture, it was said, but based her stand on the presumed piety of those sharing her religion, in contrast to the mean and frivolous world all around, and it had not been possible to shift her away from her error. Her mother, also an Anabaptist, had died in prison. One of her three brothers named Claus, had been in Moravia but had now turned away (from Anabaptism). This brother, it was said, was now requesting that his sister be released.[8] The king felt inclined to respond to the request but had misgivings about letting a non-recanting Anabaptist go free; as it would serve to strengthen injudicious persons in their erring attitude.[9]

To put an end to any further abetment the Anabaptists might receive, particularly where they have their huts close to discrete houses, on June 13, 1539, Ferdinand I issued a severe general mandate:[10] A close watch was to be kept, more diligently than heretofore, by day and by night, for Anabaptists, so as to pounce on and overpower them in their huts. The Innsbruck authorities, as they let the regents and councillors in Brixen know, had just recently sent out special mandates,[11] and Brixen followed the example thus given without delay.[12]

The first news about Lanzenstiel's presence in Tyrol was followed on by a further announcement August 20: Hans Tugentlich, administrator of the principality at Itter, reported that an Anabaptist by the name of Hans Wiener had provided information "about an overseer called Linhart Seiler from Bavaria and that this man had spoken of wanting to go with Hans Schwarz and the latter's wife to the Adige region, to Meran and Switzerland.[13] Copies of this note were immediately sent to all administrators of principalities; yet Seiler (Lanzenstiel) could not be apprehended.

The general mandate of June 12, 1539, was followed on September 3,[14] by Ferdinand I's order to abbreviate the mandates issued against the Anabaptists. For plausible reasons the articles dealing with the Anabaptists' opinions were to be omitted. As for the rest, the mandates were to be strictly carried out. As regards the *taglia* and the number of men making up the "roving patrols," the previous directions were to remain in force. Even though there had as yet been no instance of the sect's invading the bishopric of Trent, a close watch should nevertheless be kept. "If it is suggested that an appendix to the mandate should grant non-recanting Anabaptists a time period in which they can sell their property and move out of the country, and that if still encountered there after that time limit, they be prosecuted according to the mandates, that is not something we have come to see as suitable."

"Given that this insurrectionist sect is again manifesting itself so very much and that the eradication is proving so costly, we herewith command that the Anabaptists' property be used to cover whatever expenses their eradication and prosecution might entail. Whether this still leaves part of their property for the upbringing of their children is something to be considered in each individual case."

"The overseers of the sect and any that have apostatized for a second time are to be prosecuted in strict accordance with the mandates. As regards the others, a separate report is to be first submitted about each of them—unless they are sent to Andrea Doria for service on his galleys."

"In the areas of Lower Austria, too, we have issued orders to be on guard against any Anabaptists trying to sneak in from Moravia, seeing that we want to prevent them from again taking root in our princely county of Tyrol."

A report the Brixen councillors sent to the Innsbruck authorities on September 15, 1539, shows that the Anabaptists were still having adherents also among the area's aristocracy.[15] It relates that Agnes, née von Trautmannsdorf and widow of the St. Petersberg administrator Jörg of Waltenhofen, had joined the Anabaptists together with her young daughter. The authorities confiscated her property and ordered her to be searched for, "lest that widow make her way out of the country and to Moravia."

By way of a postscript to this report the Brixen councillors let the Innsbruck government have more pleasant news: "A day ago in the Lüsen judicial district overseer Lienhart's wife has been arrested as well as others, and have been brought here as prisoners." They are to be proceeded against with suitable punishment.[16]

The case of Agnes of Waltenhofen created a sensation. There was a grave concern that many other persons might follow her example, hence in order to eradicate the Anabaptists in the judicial districts of

Michelsburg, Schöneck and Lüsen a number of lansquenets were recruited immediately.

In order to bring about a close cooperation between the Innsbruck government and the bishop of Brixen and his secular councillors, on September 17, 1539, Ferdinand I sent a special order to Innsbruck.[17] Eleven days later he writes: "We have been informed that a large number of Anabaptist persons—several hundred of them—have made their way into our princely county of Tyrol, especially into the Brixen bishopric, and are intending to remain there."[18] A search patrol carried out on October 5, in the mountains near Ober-Vintl proved unsuccessful.[19] It became known, though, that a number of Anabaptists had held a meeting at Lüsen. The overseer had not been among them, it was said. He had gone with the Waltenhofen lady, the widow of the St. Petersberg administrator, and with Niclas Niderhofer to the countess in Styria in order to get her, too, to join them on their way. On their return the overseer was planning to have a wonderful meeting, it had been heard.

In recognition of Dr. Gallus Müller's outstanding merits chiefly as a converter of Anabaptists, he was the government's first proposal for filling the "Tyrol" benefice (*Pfarre Tyrol*). Dr. Gall, however, declined the offer, pleading that he was a weak, old man, that the "Tyrol" benefice included a lot of rural outposts and that an assistant priest was hard to come by.[20]

Seeing that the Anabaptists were spreading more and more in the Brixen bishopric, the Innsbruck government sent His Royal Majesty's Counsellor, Sir Caspar Kunigl of Ehrenburg, to Brixen in order to take counsel with the prince bishop on how the increase of the sect might be stopped. The result of the deliberation was a sizeable memorandum drawn up on October 17, 1539, in the presence of Sir Caspar Kunigl. It bears the title: "Presentation of the reasons that allowed the Anabaptists to take such a hold on this princely county of Tyrol that it has not been possible so far to eradicate them in spite of all possible zeal on the part of some authorities."[21]

The introduction to the memorandum points out that the common man in Tyrol evinces such an extraordinary attachment to the Anabaptists that he, even if not a member himself, will yet aid and abet them in every possible way: he accommodates and shelters them, provides them with food and drink and will not denounce or stop them.

When the authorities plan a raid on Anabaptists, these are liable to receive warning, and though the man in the street knows where they are, he will deny having seen any. Though he may not let them be in his own house, he will yet allow them to stay close by, and when they move to and fro and do all manner of things, he will not denounce them and still less the camps and meetings where they are to be found—indeed, he will even supply them with what victuals they require. When facing Anabaptists in court, judges and jurors are liable to treat them too leniently and not in accordance with the mandates; they are too often spared interrogation under torture, and the mandates are "either misunderstood or disputed."

Until now, says the memorandum, the overseers and ringleaders as well as other Anabaptists have had their confessions read out while publicly present, and they have mostly behaved as if they faced death willingly and as though it was a special joy to them to die for the sake of righteousness and God's word and that has moved many simple-minded persons to join this sect.

The memorandum also regards the alleviation that His Majesty the King has granted with respect to the Anabaptists' confiscated goods as inadvisable. It may lead many to reason that even if he now joins the sect, it will not mean that his house and goods are lost to his family. Although it is well-known that most Anabaptists are now sojourning chiefly in Moravia and Lower Austria and that they make their way there via Styria and Carinthia as well as down the Inn river, the fact is that nobody gets challenged either on the mountain passes or in towns, in public houses or on the riverboats; without let or hindrance people can travel from this country to Moravia with lots of goods and chattels and with little children.

Whereas it had formerly been easy to recognize Anabaptists, as they would not return your greeting nor carry arms, now it is hard to distinguish them from other people in that way.

How is this situation to be confronted? Three "informed opinions" are being presented. The first one demands that the present jurors be replaced by a committee drawn from all the regional estates, which would take on the jurymen's duties. A general tax in the amount of about 5,000 gulden should be levied, an able man be appointed to head up the campaign and be assisted by four or six reputable assessors. A provost marshal should be appointed and with some lansquenets should carry out patrols in the different parts of Tyrol and be also at the service of the bishops of Trent and Brixen.

The mandate with respect to the goods left behind by Anabaptists had to be revoked, and the previous mandates be put back in force. Over against one well-to-do Anabaptist there are always fifteen that do not own anything and whose trial costs are a financial burden on the country. The goods and chattels of the prosperous ones are to be confiscated without further ado. That would scare people and keep the common man from letting himself so carelessly talked into joining the sect.

Those sentenced to death ought to be hanged or beheaded out in the open street. Their dead bodies should be left lying for several days on the square or street—something apt to strike a bit more terror into the common man's heart.

The memorandum's second "informed opinion" keeps more to the previous practices and calls for them to carry out the promulgated mandates more diligently. The third one demands that the crossings and mountain passes be guarded more carefully and that the judicial districts of Sterzing, Passeyer, Sarnthal, Rodeneck, Gufidaun, Ritten, Taufen, and Altrasen be provided with a number of men for carrying out frequent patrols.

Knowing from experience that certain persons will purchase food in larger quantities from bakers and butchers and then pass it on to the Anabaptists, the food producers concerned are to be asked to immediately report such suspect middlemen to the authorities. The influx from Moravia should be stemmed by a more careful guarding of the roads and mountain passes.

On November 8, 1539, the Innsbruck government replied to the above "counsel" from Brixen. They would not fail, they said, to pass it on to His Majesty and would also leave in place the earlier issued mandates, as far as it seemed necessary and would meet with His Majesty's approval. "That apart, we look forward to hearing from you what you have been able to find out from Peter Troyer's son-in-law (Niderhofer), whom you have put behind bars. It has to be suspected that specific 'practices' are behind it all."[22]

On November 10, 1539, the Innsbruck government informed the King about the consultations in Brixen.[23] They comment that the proposal of levying a general tax in the amount of 5,000 gulden is impracticable, seeing that even the earlier agreed-upon taxes have still not been collected, and that no means have been available to even pay one headman or judge, not to mention four or six in addition to jurors and judges. It would give rise to a great to-do and hullabaloo in the country and do more harm than good. "What we do regard as necessary," the document continues, "is to have Your Majesty's previous mandates renewed and especially the more recent ones, seeing that over a number of years the previously practiced severe punishment of Anabaptist persons, more than 500 of whom have been executed in this country, has proved to be of little avail; on the contrary, it has only served to evermore invigorate and enkindle the Anabaptist sect. It is also a fact that a number of persons in this country, when asked to serve as assessors at Anabaptist trials, have disliked and in some cases refused it, pleading scruples of conscience. We have asked Your Majesty's court preacher, Dr. Gallus Müller, to compose an introduction and exposition for the suggested renewal of the mandate and to point out where that accursed Anabaptist sect comes from, what awful bloodshed it has caused and is bound to go on causing. Seeing that in the Holy Roman Empire no overseer or [any other] Anabaptist is being tolerated, among the orthodox [i.e. Roman Catholics] as well as among the new sectarians [i.e. Protestants], they are banished from every country. Therefore Your Majesty might take into consideration whether it would be good to include the following article in a new issue of the mandate: Any male or female person tainted with the Anabaptist sect in this country who is unwilling to turn away from it must within a fixed period following the promulgation of this mandate sell their goods and chattels and leave the country with his or her spouse and children."

"As regards patrolling and reconnoitring for Anabaptists, a troop of fifteen lansquenets should be assembled for the purpose, and the elected bishops of Brixen and Trent would have to provide as many. A *taja* (reward) should be paid for the capture of overseers and ringleaders and be collected from Anabaptist property. Seeing that the overseers of this sect are for the most part sent into this country from Moravia, we regard it as necessary that in Austria above and below the Enns river, in Styria and Carinthia it be commanded to keep a diligent lookout for overseers and to apprehend them. This is how we hope to uproot, and make an end of, the Anabaptist sect in this country."

"We are forwarding to Your Majesty some special articles, which the Anabaptist overseers keep to themselves and will not tell the common people about and which Dr. Gall has omitted from his addition to the mandate, on account of the offenses and troubles they might cause. May we also remind Your Majesty of our letter inquiring as to whether, in case some able-bodied male Anabaptists are arrested and prove unwilling to recant, your Majesty would intend to send them to Lord Andrea Doria or somebody else to help row the galleys."

On November 29, 1539, a severe mandate against Anabaptists with a number of specified punishments was issued in Vienna. It says, "We intend this to be a renewal of all our previous mandates. From now on and in view of this mandate our administrative bodies, each in its own area, are expected to be well informed about any Anabaptists in evidence there, and these are to be immediately searched for and arrested. Those captured are to be questioned about their doings and intents and their doctrine, and their confession is to be sent to the governor of our Upper Austrian lands. Further instructions are to be expected from him or directly from us. You should also see to it that innkeepers, butchers, and bakers everywhere no longer supply victuals of any kind to Anabaptists and that those who aid and abet them are punished like the Anabaptists. In accordance with earlier mandates the houses where Anabaptists have been clandestinely sheltered are to be torn down, never more to be built, as an everlasting remembrance. Wherever these mandates are not properly obeyed by either the authorities or the subjects, our Upper Austrian government has been directed to have a company of soldiers quartered there and to take forceful action against the Anabaptists. This military detachment is to remain stationed there until the insurrectionist persons are uprooted and any mischief on the part of the overseers is blocked."[24] This mandate was dispatched to the various authorities on December 16, together with a cover letter, in which it said, "We earnestly command you to have these mandates posted on the church doors in your administrative district and to have them publicly read out to the common people in church, on the next Sunday or feast day as well as once a month thereafter.[25]

In that way Ferdinand I in part also responded to the "informed opinions" sent to him on November 10. In addition he had on dispatched a special answer to the regional government in Innsbruck on December 3. In the mandates henceforth to be published all over the country he permitted all those passages to be left out that provided details of Anabaptist doctrines. For the most part he also agreed to the other suggestions the Innsbruck government had brought forward.[26] On December 17, 1539, the prince bishop of Brixen was informed about this.[27]

In the meantime a new prohibition of "Lutheran" books had been issued. Hans Mickh, bookseller from Innsbruck, had openly offered such books for sale at a church council in Sarntheim.[28] In the last days of October the confessions of the imprisoned Anabaptists Niclas Niederhofer and Hans Grübl were sent to Innsbruck.[29] Jörg Köberl, who had already recanted once and had recently been arrested in Schwaz as an Anabaptist, was exiled from the country. But he was allowed to sell his property in the Petersberg judicial district and to take the proceeds with him.[30] On December 1, the Innsbruck government sent in the reply regarding the punishment to be meted out to Hans Grill, Matthes Götzenperger, and Paul Tetscher. The first two had to pay a fine, while the third one, who had no earthly goods, was punished by protracted incarceration. Some other Anabaptists were retained in custody when they could be expected to come up with more detailed testimonies.[31]

Four days later the Prince Bishop of Brixen informs town judge Hans Egli there as follows: "Although at present two persons, Balthasar Venediger and Apollonia Saylerin, have been duly sentenced, which sentence we should also allow to take its rightful course, we nevertheless want to let the sentence of the first-named, because of his friends' pleading, be commuted to execution by the sword and to his being buried in consecrated ground, and as regards Apollonia it is, for various valid reasons, our will that she be drowned."[32]

On December 10, 1539, the bishop of Brixen on his part, too, sent out a mandate fixing a *taglia* for the apprehension of Anabaptists. Whoever delivers an overseer alive, will be paid 100 gulden; whoever will bring one in dead, 50 gulden. The reward for apprehension of an ordinary Anabaptist is 10 gulden. Whoever denounces a supporter of Anabaptists will receive a share in the penance money and in addition 20 gulden.[33] On January 1, 1540, the Innsbruck government followed suit by offering an identical *taglia*.[34]

The forceful actions of the temporal and ecclesiastical authorities checked further expansion of Anabaptism in the country. True, there are Anabaptist trials also during the succeeding years, but they are less frequent and less significant than in the previous years. On February 12, 1540, mention is made of two Anabaptists in the Brixen area, Melchior Raderer and Caspar Schnäfel, about whom no further details are known.[35] What was still a cause of great worry to the authorities was the influx from Moravia. On February 12, 1540, the Innsbruck government informs the authorities in all judicial districts that the Moravian Anabaptists and their overseers have recently once again sent twenty-four of their men to Tyrol in order to convert people to their sect and lead them out of the country.[36]

Among the Anabaptists that were captured at Steinabrunn in Lower Austria on December 6, 1539, and were being sent to the galleys there were three Tyrolese from the Puster valley, who applied for a reprieve. After recanting, they were received back into their native country, where, however, they would still be under police supervision for a time.[37] In June 1540, Count Ludwig of Oettingen interceded for the Anabaptist Caspar Utt, who had done military service under him. Since Utt was unwilling to recant, he was sent "to Doria" to help row his galleys.[38] At the same time it is made known that a young Anabaptist woman has been imprisoned for more than a year in Hall. She had already recanted twice only to "topple over" anew, and at a procession had thrown a cudgel at the church flag. She was transferred to a hospital as "insane" and put in chains.[39]

According to a report by the Klausen town judge in August [1540] a few Anabaptists again made their appearance there. In particular Stoffl from Villach was said to be involved, and also the town secretary's brother was reported to be under suspicion.[40] On August 26, a number of Anabaptists were being interrogated by town judge Hans Egli in Brixen. One of these, Leonhard Raiffer from Lüsen, had been baptized by Lienhart Sailer on June 15, and then sent to Moravia. That is also where Heinz Puehl from Neustift had gone with his whole family. Balzer Inhofer, the report says, had come up again [to Tyrol] in order to take his wife and children down to Moravia. "Schwarz Lindl" from the Puster valley was imprisoned in Kufstein, it is reported. Urban Huetter, too, had returned from Moravia only to take his wife down there. Huetter and Ried had helped set free Anastasius, who had been imprisoned in Brixen. On their way up [to Tyrol] they had been arrested and whipped at Krems, where some shooting was going on, but had been set free again. "By the huts" they had met Christl from Amlach, who had come into the sect just recently, as well as Balthasar Rainer, Oswald Schuster, Leonhard Sailer, Matthes Schöffl, Stoffl Spängler, Ursula Malerin as well as four women and two girls from Klausen. [According to the prisoners] Leonhard Sailer had written to Moravia that no one was to come up from there, for he and all the brothers and sisters still here in this country now want to move down [i.e. to Moravia].

As regards the widow of the Michelsburg administrator (Agnes of Waltenhofen) we learn: "She is in Moravia in Tschäkowitz, where there are about 500 brothers and sisters."

The interrogation [in Brixen] went on until September 2, 1540. One of those questioned stated that there were about 1,000 [Anabaptist] persons in Moravia, not counting women and children. Their overseers, he said, were Hans Tuchmacher [Amon], Lienhart Sailer [Lanzenstiel], Hans Gentner from Swabia, Christoph Gschäl, Peter [Riedemann] from Gmünden (hailing from Silesia but presently in Hesse).[41] It was reported that Stoffl at Villach was getting ready to move to Moravia.[42] In October 1540, an Anabaptist woman also turned up in Gufidaun, Anna Steiner, who, however, claimed to have got into the sect merely through "misapprehension."[43]

There are rare cases like that of Leonhard Arnold, who confesses to having come into the sect twelve years ago through Lienhart Sailer, but having found with them, too, nothing but sectarianism and cleavages, envy and hatred, backbiting and vainglory, he had again separated from them.[44]

During the following months the regional authorities came across Anabaptists in Afy (Afers?),[45] in the judicial district of Ehrenburg, in Heunfels, Imst, Landeck, and in the Ziller valley.[46]

The mandate for the Anabaptists' eradication issued on June 24, 1541, by the Duke of Bavaria was getting known also in Tyrol.[47] On March 29, 1542, a new decree was published concerning the use of the sequestered goods of Anabaptists. In the first place these should serve to defray the costs incurred on account of the Anabaptists. In any case all such goods were to be duly inventoried and administered by the authorities until informed by trustworthy persons that the Anabaptists in question had died. Then the goods were to be released to the heirs.[48]

One of the most eminent personages among the Anabaptists, who as early as 1528, had made an appearance in Tyrol, Ulrich Stadler, had in the meantime died in Butschowitz in Moravia. He hailed from Brixen and for quite a time had been employed in the mining office at Sterzing. As a "minister of the Gospel" he was active in Moravia and far into Poland. Prominent among his writings are the *Entrance into Christianity*,[49] the book "about the living and the written" or about the "inner and the outer word,"[50] his "epistle on original sin," written against Krasnikow and to brother Michael from Ladomir in Podolia,[51] his "epistle about original sin, for and against,"[52] "about community,"[53] also "about exclusion," "about the saints' order and community," and his "epistles to the pilgrims (and) against Krasnikow in Poland."[54] His last years of activity were devoted to uniting the different sects among the Moravian Anabaptists.[55]

A dispatch of July 25, 1542, served notice to the government that the movement from Tyrol to Moravia was far from ceasing. It reported that six Anabaptists from Lüsen intended to make their way to Moravia but had been stopped at Kropfsberg and sent to Brixen by the Archbishop of Salzburg.[56] Not long afterwards there were reports about Anabaptists surfacing at Sterzing, Schwaz, Rattenberg and Freundsberg.[57]

The Anabaptist Georg Liebich gave the Innsbruck government a lot of trouble. In 1538, the church in Moravia had sent him "on account of divine business and reasons" to the "upper country." He was captured in the Inn valley and put "into an evil tower" on the Nellenberg. After being beset by manifold delusions[58] he was banished from the land on April 24, 1544, and made his way to Moravia. His coreligionists regarded the way in which he was saved as so miraculous that the strangest stories circulated about him.[59] His trial had earned the "dispensers of justice" a reprimand from the ruling prince, for on January 26, 1543, the latter wrote to the Innsbruck authorities that he had gathered from their communication that the judges, contrary to all the issued mandates, presume to discern and judge solely according to what they consider right and good—an attitude we will no longer let pass or tolerate. "In future the judges are to stick to the content and direction of the issued mandates and not arrive at any other conclusion."[60]

Christian Lochler and Mathias Legeder[61] managed to flee from the Sterzing judicial district, and Hans Prugger, who was about to be taken to Hungary to serve on the galleys,[62] escaped from Landeck. And from the Steinach judicial district it was reported that Thomas Eppstainer had moved to Moravia; on the other hand two Anabaptists were handed over to the Rattenburg authorities from the Imst district and one from the Oetz valley.[63] On April 12, it was newly commanded to carefully search the riverboats at Hall, for already several Anabaptists had departed for Moravia after Easter, and more were due to follow.[64] The Steinach judge is ordered to search for two Anabaptists who had just arrived from Moravia.[65]

On May 31, the Innsbruck authorities were apprised of the decrees issued by the government in the Upper Alsace, with an accompanying note requesting them to take equivalent measures against the Anabaptists. The reigning prince had sent the following message to Ensisheim: "A large part of the Anabaptists captured in our upper and lower Austrian lands have entered the sect more through simplemindedness and a frivolous disposition than through evil intent or wickedness.

However, once in the sect, they get so hardened that no punishment or other means are able to bring them away from it, and they would rather suffer any torture or even death.[66] This has filled us with horror, and we find it hard to proceed against such poor, misled, and obdurate people using the full severity of the imperial constitutions and of our mandates and to sentence them to capital punishment. That is why from now on service on the galleys will be the punishment meted out to such people; only the overseers will still be dealt with in the old manner. Those Anabaptists that remain obdurate are to be deprived of their property as well as of their children, and the latter are to be given a Christian upbringing in orphanages."

With reference to this letter the Innsbruck authorities on June 21, 1542, sent a report to the king[67] informing him that in Tyrol the judges and those involved in sentencing, when confronted with Anabaptists, feel incompetent to deal with matters concerning men's souls and religion, as they feel too simpleminded and unskilled in such things—a situation that had in fact cropped up just recently in the judicial district of Sonnenburg and at Landeck. Because of this, the regional government suggests that at the next diet His Majesty issue a decree ordering all those still adhering to Anabaptism to leave the country within a certain time period. They might be graciously permitted to sell their goods and chattels. If still found within the country after this time period, they should be regarded as having forfeited their lives and would be shown no mercy. If even after the publication of this edict someone were to go over to the Anabaptists and refuse to leave that sect, he should be proceeded against, in accordance with the mandates and imperial constitutions, with capital punishment and sequestration of property.

It was in those days that Dr. Gall, who had proved so meritorious by his efforts to convert Anabaptists, took up the living in Meran he had been granted.[68] In view of his already bearing the burden of the "Turkish tax," he was excused from having to pay the 80 gulden normally due pro primis fructibus. In this context it is being noted once again that "the burdensome troubles and aberrations instigated by that confounded sect not only in Tyrol but throughout the German nation have had their cause in the great shortage of priests, so that it is mostly impossible to obtain able and learned priests for even the most eminent prebends and livings."

On July 28, 1543, there is news of more recent migrations to Moravia. Ursula from Wangen is reported to have moved there; her property has been impounded.[69] And there is a report from Klausen to the effect that Martin Legeder, a citizen there, has left together with his wife and children.[70] The Innsbruck authorities address to the captain and the secular councillors at Brixen a sharp ordinance against the "sect's taking root there anew."[71] The "penitent" Anabaptist Martin Rogg, who has returned from Moravia, is being assured of clemency if he turns away from Anabaptism and denounces the baptism-minded persons in the Steinach judicial district. At the same time the goods of the Anabaptists who have moved from Zams (in the district of Landeck) to Moravia have been impounded.

The Tyrolean government's more lenient way of dealing with the Anabaptists during the preceding years and especially in 1543, is also made abundantly clear by the court files of the following years. It had, of course, taken a long time for the recognition that the severe capital punishments were by themselves insufficient to bring forth a general effect, and it meant a definite step forward for Ferdinand I to openly avow his "dismay" at the ceaseless executions and to declare that he found it hard to proceed against those poor, misguided folk with the whole severity of the imperial and princely mandates. Up to that point the reverse practice had been in force; in Ferdinand's opinion the regional government never proceeded with sufficient zeal against the separatists, and great is the number of royal reprimands dealt out to individual administrators on account of their negligence. Judges and juries had always detested those bloody sentences, and this abhorrence became ever more persistent as time went on. Not only members of the Innsbruck government but also several clergymen demanded emphatically that "instruction be used rather than punishment." In many instances the authorities countenanced the flight of Anabaptists to their fellow believers and relatives in Moravia.

On February 20, 1544, the sheriffs at Schwaz, Rattenberg, Kufstein, the magistrates in Ambras and Hall and the law-agent at Tauer are being notified that the Anabaptist overseers, as soon as they reach the

Inn valley, try to board a riverboat in order to escape to Austria and Moravia,[72] and that fourteen or fifteen of them are reported to be on the way. With life in Moravia offering greater safety, they are reported to be trying to bring as many fellow believers as possible to that country and out of Tyrol. Thus on February 22, 1544, the government of Upper Austria notifies the captain, the legal agents, and councillors in Brixen that in the coming spring the Anabaptists in Moravia intend to send out several persons for the purpose of conducting their adherents down to Moravia.[73] Especially in the pledged fief (*Pfandschaft*) Schöneck, Michelsburg, Utenheim, Heunfels, Matrei, and Kitzbühel a strong movement for emigration is evident.[74]

On April 18, 1544, the government forwarded to the captain and councillors in Brixen a princely mandate of the same date, with the strict injunction to have it published in those places where there are Anabaptists, hence particularly in Schöneck, Michelsburg, Uttenheim, and Heunfels. The mandate complains that "we sense that our earlier mandates and decrees have had little effect among our subjects and have rather been slighted." The command is given to fully stress the apprehension of the overseers.[75] In response to this mandate nightwatches were appointed in these districts. In the districts of Michelsburg and Schöneck "the subjects have failed to show obedience," and it was not much better in the districts of Steinach, Stubai, Sonnenburg, and Bruneck. On April 22, the authorities report that everywhere orders have been issued to "keep a sharp lookout for overseers and agitators arriving from Moravia." "We find, however, that they have been sheltered by the subjects, partly out of compassion and partly through obduracy, and have not been denounced to the authorities, with the result that a lot of simple-minded folk, among whom it is the wealthy that the overseers preferably keep friends with, have let themselves be talked into the seductive sect and into turning their back on this country, after secretly converting anything suitable into cash." There are renewed complaints to the effect that "the justices pass sentence on the Anabaptists as their conscience tells them and not in accordance with the issued edicts." There is a demand that Anabaptists simply be banished from the country; only those who, disregarding this command, are still encountered here should be punished in life and limb. "Then the judges might be expected to not refuse to pass correct sentences." And there is an urgent request for the land to be supplied with suitable priests.[76]

On May 21, 1544, Ferdinand I sent from Speyer his reply to the Innsbruck government:[77] Those found aiding and abetting the Anabaptists are to be fined 50 gulden. As regards the justices' conduct, a new mandate is to be issued in which the authorities and justices are earnestly commanded, on pain of severe disgrace and discipline, to pass sentence in no other way than according to the mandates. As regards a reduced punishment, Ferdinand was not in agreement with the government's opinion. What they suggest would most likely move many persons as yet untainted by the sect to join it and "turn their back on their homes and their native country."

That the authorities were well informed when they reported that many Anabaptists were intending to migrate to Moravia, was demonstrated by the fact that in June 1544, three of them were stopped in Hall at the very moment when they were about to board a riverboat.[78] On the other hand, at the same time, three Anabaptists, Michael Meysl, Jakob Prunner, and Martin Mayr came back to their home area in Steinach and in return for their promise to recant were granted a reprieve.[79] On June 16, 1544, Innsbruck informs the legal counsellor in Lüsen that in his district are "several Anabaptist overseers who have infiltrated the land."[80] This was also the case in Heunfels and in the Weitenthal. In the last-named locality night-watches were set up against the Anabaptists.[81] Among the overseers mentioned in the above report was Michel Madschidl from Lüsen, called "little Michel," who at the beginning of August was traveling about in the Oetz valley.[82] On September 4, it was reported that he had spent the night in a woods by the Isarco (Eisack) river behind Sterzing. Two other overseers, Hänsl Metzger and Paul Fleischhacker are reported to be knocking about in the area of Rottenburg, Sonnenburg, and Steinach.[83]

In the first days of September (1544), fourteen Anabaptists together with some women, who intended to make their way to Krems in order to travel on to Moravia, were stopped in Wasserburg[84] and arrested. Most of them were from the Brixen domain, one from

Bruneck. The judge in Kufstein was made to understand that the boatmen involved should also have been arrested. Contrary to the latest decrees, according to which the property left behind by Anabaptists was to go to their relatives, on September 6, 1544, the regent and councillors in Brixen ordered "the house of Martin Zimmermann from Weitenthal, who with wife and child had gone to the Anabaptists and had left the country, to be burned to the ground, as an example to others and to let the neighbors know that this would happen also to them if they got involved with that seductive sect."[85]

On November 8, 1544, the Innsbruck government was informed, in Gufidaun "thirteen persons had gone off at nighttime and made their way to the Anabaptist sect."[86]

On the basis of the resolution of the imperial diet of Speyer, on September 10, 1544, Ferdinand I issued a mandate[87] against the Anabaptists, which was to be in force in all his domains. The Innsbruck government was informed by rescript of December 12.[88]

In spite of all these mandates new Anabaptists keep surfacing both individually and in sizeable numbers. Towards the end of the year individual Anabaptists were encountered in the Weiten valley, in Meran, and in the Ehrenburg district.[89]

Dr. Gallus Müller had got into a quarrel with his parishioners in Meran, and before long the strife became so fierce that the citizens threatened to cast their clergyman into a well and that they authored and distributed lampoons against him. That is why on January 10, 1545, the administrative head of the Adige district was asked to put matters in order and to restore peace.[90] The cause of the uproar was in all likelihood the non-German [*welsche,* i.e. speaking Romansh or Italian] priest Peter, who preached several tenets that diverged from the orthodox doctrine and who the people apparently adhered to.[91] It was said that "he did not believe in the Mass, that he despised it and called it an abomination." Gallus Müller, who on April 13, had still requested a reprieve for a converted Anabaptist, Hans Nesis,[92] was yearning to get away from his parish. It was reported that the air in Meran does not agree with him, and he therefore would like to move lower down toward Freiburg and conclude his life there." The real reason was the people's ill-will, who "because of his long-lasting illness had not been edified by him."[93] As regards this matter, the Innsbruck government on December 30, 1544, notified the administrator of the Etsch province that the parish priest Dr. Gall had "on account of his physical weakness" asked for discharge from his parish in Tyrol, but that he was to remain there until a capable and erudite man could be found to replace him. And those conducting themselves inappropriately toward him were to be punished, thus setting "an example to others." As the imperial court in Ghent was not informed about the present situation of the Meran parish priest, Charles V had been considering the possible participation of the Innsbruck preacher Dr. Gall in the religious discussion scheduled for December 14, 1545, between the Catholic and Augsburgian parties.[94]

On July 31, 1545, it was reported that Anabaptists had turned up in the Petersberg judicial district and in Stubai, also that those in Stubai had escaped to Moravia. On the same day the Innsbruck government informed Brixen that once again Anabaptist overseers and agitators had made their way to Tyrol.[95] It was at this time that an Anabaptist from the Etsch (Adige) area, Anderl Koffler, was "condemned to death at Ips on the Danube and was executed by the sword."[96]

The years 1546 and 1547 were comparatively quiet ones, evincing only reports of reprieves granted to individual converted Anabaptists. On January 23, 1546, the Innsbruck government wrote as follows to the councillors of the Cardinal of Augsburg: We have received your letter of January 9, concerning the case of the Anabaptist Pergmüller, who has conducted many people to Moravia. We have turned to Erasmus Offenhauser and the Innsbruck council for information about him and are concerned that he be proceeded against with serious and suitable punishment. Offenhauser's report relates that Pergmüller had wanted to make his cousin drink from a bottle, which might have contained something magic. Also other overseers and ringleaders have made use of such magic. He ought to be questioned about this and a report sent to Innsbruck.[97]

In the following year the government learned that several persons from Telfs, Kilpmais, and Mieders were intending to go to Moravia. It therefore instructed the administrator of the Stubai judicial district to be on guard and prevent them from emigrating.[98]

For a number of years already Ferdinand I had demanded that the Moravian nobility expel the Anabaptists from that country, but had mostly received evasive replies from the nobles, who would not let themselves be deprived of so capable a workforce. In the end they did accede to Ferdinand's more and more urgent demands, and at the *Laetare* [i.e. third Sunday before Easter] diet of 1545 decided that wherever the Anabaptists were living "in communities," they were not to be tolerated and would have to be gone by *Kunigundentag* (September 9).[99] "Community" was one of the Anabaptists' most important tenets, and they were unwilling to give it up. "They thought that no more than four or five should be together in one house, but because of their confession of faith the devout were unable to accept that." The king demanded a general expulsion but it was only after Emperor Charles had vanquished the kingdom he was quarrelling with, and Duke Hans [i.e. Duke Elector John Frederick I of Saxony] had been taken prisoner, that he attained his objects. "Then it was out with us; everywhere the Moravian lords ordered us to leave their estates and move away—both young and old, including the weak and sick ones."[100]

Ferdinand was worried that the Anabaptists would now seek to return to their Tyrolean homeland. That is why on January 19, 1548, from Augsburg he gave strict orders to the Innsbruck government to have the boundaries guarded better than before, so on February 28, the government sent a corresponding directive to the administrations of the various districts.[101] Nevertheless already on June 1, the authorities served notice that Christian Gärber, former innkeeper at the Lenken in the Matrei forest, Hans Metzger from Matrei and Hans Mayer from Feuchten had been spotted in the Steinach and Stubai districts.[102] On the same day the government correspondingly ordered the regents and councillors in Brixen to restore order especially in the pledged fiefs of the Puster valley.[103]

Whereas in November 1536, the ruling prince had given order that the goods of executed or fugitive Anabaptists be passed on to their heirs, on November 6, 1548, the government suggested to the king that this "law be set aside and that Anabaptist property be seized on behalf of the revenue office, given that so far grace and lenience have promoted rather than impeded the Anabaptist cause."[104] On

September 26, the king replied that he had misgivings about agreeing to this proposal. "To extend our overflowing grace to the innocent widows and orphans and friends (relatives) is better than having them pay for somebody else's guilt."[105] While the Innsbruck government was seriously considering whether to proceed more firmly against the Anabaptists, the latter were once more provided with a purposeful leader of the kind they had had in the person of Jakob Hutter.

3

HANS MÄNDL'S ACTIVITY AND TRIAL, 1548-1561

ON NOVEMBER 10, 1548, the Innsbruck government sent a missive to the captain, regents, and councilmen at Brixen informing them that "in the past days the Rodeneck magistrate, Andre Täxler, had arrested two Anabaptists, one of whom is said to be an overseer." The magistrate, said the letter, had been instructed to prosecute both of them in accordance with the mandates of 1544 and 1545; to begin with, though, an attempt should be made to divert them from their error, and this would require an erudite priest.[1] The two Anabaptists were Hans Gregenhofer and Hans Mändl. The last named was one of the outstanding Anabaptists, not only in Tyrol, where he baptized more than 400 persons, but quite generally of that period.

He had been born in Gufidaun and in 1537, he was received by Offrus Griesinger into the church community. He was baptized "near Sterzing in a wooded valley called the *Weißenbach* [white brook]." Already in the first year after his baptism he fell into the beadles' hands and lay for about 26 weeks in prison in Sterzing. "But God helped him get out." In 1544, he was imprisoned in Landeck for 22 weeks and was there interrogated under torture, but in this case, too, he managed to elude trial by escaping.[2] So this was the third time for him to be apprehended. The parish priests of St. Lorenzen and Brixen were given the task to "instruct the two prisoners from Holy Writ and make them turn away from their error,"[3] but they did not achieve their ends. "Both of them want to hold on to their Anabaptism, regardless of what might happen to them."

The two priests learned to their dismay that the magistrate treated the two prisoners much too leniently, that he had told them he had not arrested them on account of their sect but due to their disobedience, in returning to this region in defiance of the mandates.[4] He had comforted them and had promised to let them have a Bible or other books if they wanted them. They had no lack of either food or drink, and if they felt too cold in the prison, he was going to remedy that. How could such a procedure bear fruit for the eradication of the Anabaptists? They knew from actual experience— the two priests said—that as time went on this cursed sect was taking root ever more firmly in the Rodeneck district, that the Anabaptists were gathering in the open air up in the mountains and would hold their meetings there, and when coming down, they would find accommodation with a fellow traveler in Nauders.[5] Brixen without delay reported this to Innsbruck, and the authorities there let the Rodeneck administrator have the required directives.[6] The two priests were told to attend zealously to the conversion of the two prisoners, "given that in this vale of sorrows there can be no loftier and more spiritual work than to direct those erring in faith to the right path."[7] The two erring ones in question, however, managed to escape from their prison. Most likely they went to Moravia, and this was also where in the following year baptism-minded persons from Landeck, Schwaz, and Petersberg made their way.[8] In the year 1550, we come across individual Anabaptists in Taufers, Castelbell, Sterzing,[9] and Terenten,[10] in 1551 in Stubai, "from where Christian Holzmeister has led many persons out of the country,"[11] in 1552 in Klausen, in 1553 in Steinach, where the "overseer" Jakob Zimmermann turned up and in October recanted[12] in Bruneck,[13] in Villnöss and Tarant,[14] Klausen, Gufidaun, Nauders, and Landeck. That is why on September 6, 1553, Ferdinand I issued a mandate to be made public by all sheriffs and administrators.[15] They were strictly commanded to search for the Anabaptist "overseers." A second mandate, issued on September 12, confronts the spreading of heretical books and pictures.

In October 1554, individual Anabaptists arriving from Moravia turned up in the Puster valley.[16] It is mainly against them that Ferdinand I directed the mandate of October 22, 1554.[17] They were also encountered in the Vintschgau, at Schlanders and Castelbell.[18] At Kortsch they held a meeting attended by about 50 persons, among them the overseer Gilg Federspiel, converted in that very year by Klein-Michel.[19] Gilg Federspiel was apprehended together with two other brothers, one of them Hänsel Pürchner; but by leaping upon a wall and descending by holding on to its festoon of vine-branches he managed to save himself.[20] Pürchner, who was subjected to a particularly cruel examination, was beheaded in Schlanders in 1556. "They propped him up with a block of wood against his back and thus beheaded him, for he could not kneel—so terribly had they racked and stretched and tortured him."[21]

The fact that not only poor folk joined the Anabaptists but also well-to-do persons is evidenced by a report of March 28, 1555, relating that two brothers, Remigius and Christoph Heugen from Eyra had sold their goods, but had still left behind property in the value of 12,000 gulden, as they wanted to go to the Anabaptists in Moravia.[22] On May 31, 1555, the Innsbruck government submitted to Count Montfort a report about the interference of the Ehrenberg administrator, Georg Kautz, with the count's rights by carrying off the property of the Anabaptist Hans Tauscher, disregarding the count's officials.[23] In August 1555, several Anabaptists imprisoned at Schöneck escaped from there.[24] In Castelbell once again some "overseers" were being noticed and sought.[25] In this judicial district on June 23, 1556, the goods of nineteen Anabaptists, who had migrated to Moravia, were impounded. A few days later the administrator Christoph von Wolkenstein and other officials were notified that there was an increasing number of Anabaptists in the Puster valley, that whole crowds of them were going out into the woods to there listen to their overseers' sermons, and that something ought to be done about it.[26] At the same time, the ruling prince sharply condemned he confiscation of Anabaptist property by unauthorized persons.[27] The archbishop of Salzburg, the bishop of

Passau and Duke Albrecht of Bavaria were requested to have the mountain passes and waterways carefully guarded, as it had been learned that Anabaptists moving about freely in remote places and were making their way out across the Tauern and other mountain ranges as well as down the Inn, Salza, and Danube rivers.[28] The archbishop of Salzburg replied that "he had already taken appropriate measures in regard to this matter but would nevertheless proceed in accordance with the government's wishes."[29] Anabaptists were trekking to Moravia from Schöneck, Rodeneck, Landeck, and Schlanders.[30] At the beginning of May 1557, the Anabaptist overseer Hans Král from Kitzbühel was apprehended in Taufers and put on trial.[31] He remained in prison for almost two years[32] before regaining his freedom. After this, having been entrusted with the service of the Word, he would make his way into the "upland" (Tyrol) several more times. The Castelbell administrator, who had served notice that about nineteen persons had departed at nighttime to go to the Moravian Anabaptists, on July 23, 1557, received the reply that he should have been more watchful.[33] In the next year these fugitives were followed by still more inhabitants of Castelbell, and also by persons from St. Georgen, Laas, Sterzing, Rattenberg (said to be "downright poisoned with Anabaptists"), Mühlwald and Sonnenburg. A number of these emigrants were arrested at Stein on the Danube and taken to Vienna.[34]

On August 13, 1557, the Anabaptist congregation at Auspitz sent a letter on behalf of all Anabaptists to the citizen Christoph Seyer at Brixen "to be forwarded to him wherever he is." The congregation had received among them an evildoer, Veit Weber, with no knowledge of his crimes: "We have been unaware of his murderous deeds, and it did not occur to us that he was such a rogue. For we find it horrible to even look at such persons, let alone receive them into the congregation of the devout, and if he had given us something, be it much or little, we would not keep it for even one day after finding out about him, but without waiting to be asked, would send it up to Brixen or wherever it belongs, for there is no place for blood money in the house of God."[35]

Soon after, the coadjutor of Feltre complained about the sect's spreading out more and more in the principalities of Delphan (Telfano) and Ifan (Ivano), and his envoy, Pasquale Sanzio, requested help. On

January 1, 1557, the Innsbruck government sent a report about this matter to the ruling prince, also stating that they had not known about this.[36] The king commanded that the matter be closely investigated and that whatever Anabaptists were still found there be done away with.[37]

For a long time already the authorities had been searching for Hans Mändl. On January 19, 1560, the Innsbruck government had Gufidaun, Steinach, and Axams make inquiries whether Mändl owned property in Albeins, whether he had a wife and children, how he conducted himself, etc.[38] The matter drew all the more attention because of the constant complaints reaching the government about the increase of Anabaptism. On February 6, 1560, a large Anabaptist meeting is said to have taken place in a woods named "*an der Hagau*" in the Rattenberg judicial district. On November 12, 1560, the Innsbruck government informed Simon Bosch and other administrators as follows: "We have learned that a short while ago up to a thousand Anabaptists gathered in the Schlanders district, accepted many persons into their seductive sect and also led them away with wives and children as well as a great deal of money."[39]

All the greater was the elation when news was received that on Friday after St. Martin's Day (November 15) Mändl and two companions, Jörg Rack and Eustachius Kotter—had been captured near Rosenheim in Bavaria.[40] Already in the summer of 1556 or 1557, Kotter had been apprehended by guards at a desolate place near a woods and was taken to Neuhaus castle. He escaped from there and soon after he went to the Adige area and to the Vintschgau. He was captured a second time but again managed to escape.[41]

The Kufstein sheriff (*Landrichter*), Georg Kronegger, was given the task of taking the prisoners over from the Bavarian authorities,[42] of which action Duke Albrecht of Bavaria was being informed. The *Ainspännige* (operator of a one-horse vehicle) Bort Schranz conveyed them from Kufstein to Innsbruck.[43] Mändl, being "a minister of the Gospel, who had many times been sent to this country," was put into a deep tower dungeon at Vellenberg, the two others into the *Kräuterturm* in Innsbruck.[44]

Preacher Jörg Schiechl, later parish priest at Eppan, a "capable and erudite priest," was given the task to "examine them on matters of faith and by arguments from Holy Scripture to convince them of their error." Schiechl found them "well versed in Anabaptist doctrine but also totally obdurate in it and not open to his Christian ministration." Hence he counselled the government to proceed against them more earnestly and sharply, "on the basis of the spiritual examination already held to list a number of questions and have the prisoners interrogated about these both with and without torture." On January 2, Mändl was interrogated, using both civil means and torture; likewise for Kotter on January 22, 23, and 24 and Rack on January 26 and 27.[45]

They had several articles placed before them, which they had to answer point by point. To the question whether they believe that one ought to obey the church, they replied, "one ought to indeed hold to the order that the Christian church set up through the Holy Spirit at the time of the Apostles but that the present church in no way adheres to the Apostles' way of life and teaching, hence "they cannot acknowledge it to be the true church." They regard as true Christians and as the true Christian church "they only regard those that walk in accordance with the teaching of their faith and its way of life and therefore serve God in the truth, as the true Christians and Christian church—not the others!" The next questions deal with the "twelve articles of our true Christian faith"; to them they want to hold firmly, as well as to the forgiveness of sins. They were also asked if John is right in saying that no man on earth is without sin (here it should be remembered that the Anabaptists were said to hold that they alone were without sin), if they believe in original sin, what they think of baptism, if they had been rebaptized, and who had made them do it. Rack (Jörg Mayer) replied to this question by saying that "before coming to that faith, he had heard that someone called Jakob Hutter had been burned alive here in Innsbruck, and that when taking him to Innsbruck, they had gagged him to keep him from proclaiming the truth." "Secondly, he had heard how at Klausen they executed Ulrich Müllner, who was greatly liked by the people but adhered to this faith. Thirdly, he had seen with his own eyes how one of the same faith was burned at the stake at Steinach. All this he had deeply taken to heart and had come to the conclusion that it was only due to a tremendous grace of God that they could remain firm in their faith right until death. This had prompted him to inquire about these people." The prisoners also testified that "last fall it had been 24 years that Mändl had been baptized by Offerus Griesinger [hence in 1537] in a wooded valley two miles below Sterzing called Weißenbach ("white brook"). He was burned at the stake in Brixen in 1538. Kotter had received baptism in the fall of 1540, in a meadow on the Jaufen mountain, and Jörg (Mayer or Rack) was baptized 15 years ago by Leonhard Lanzenstiel."[46]

The next question was whether they consider baptism a sacrament, and this they affirmed. However, they did not regard marriage as a sacrament. Then they were questioned about their clandestine meetings in houses and nooks, where they serve each other bread and wine. When asked if they believe that the Sacrament of the Altar contains the real body of Christ, they denied it. As regards marriage, they do not think a wife obligated to follow an unbelieving husband, nor do they consider it "godly" to marry for the sake of money or out of fleshly lust. The following questions are about keeping the Sabbath and the veneration of images, which they consider idolatry. They say that it is for the sake of the dear brothers here that the church community in Moravia sent them up here and that they know nothing about money and goods siphoned out of this country. Here in this land, they say, they have held their gatherings partly at night, out in the fields but also in towns; but during the day mainly in the woods. They are now being driven out also in Moravia, hence have no permanent place anywhere, being persecuted everywhere. However, they believe, a time will come when they will be repaid a hundredfold for these sufferings. Their faith is no "accursed sect," they say, nor do they have "ringleaders"; Mändl had been appointed a teacher and overseer by his brothers and the whole church community. The last (25th) question was whether they had ever revoked their error and subsequently fallen back into it. They replied that, praise be to God, they found themselves in the right faith, in which they wanted to remain right to the end.

These questions with corresponding replies were remitted to the royal court. However, they were not considered sufficient. From Mändl's first confession (*Urgicht*) it had been gathered that he had baptized close to 400 persons and particularly in the Vintschgau had caused many people, also persons of standing and affluence, to undergo rebaptism and had persuaded them to leave the country. So as to get to the bottom also of these things, they were to be questioned about their activity in the Vintschgau, in Scharl, and the Landeck judicial district, as well as about the amount of money they had taken out of the country, also where they and others had raised the money—about 100 gulden—that the Fischbach sheriff had taken away from them, for what reason they had come from Moravia, what places they had stayed at and what other dodges and designs they had been harboring. They were also to be questioned again about the divinity of Christ and about the sacrament of marriage.[47] The new questions were to be handed to them by Dr. Mathias Alber, imperial counsellor and administrator at Vellenberg. Alber was then to "fix a trial date and as regards the jurymen required for this, before these would sit down on the appointed day to administer the law, he was, on behalf of the authorities, to get them to vow and pledge (and have them confirm this by a solemn oath to God and the saints) that they will judge and pass sentence not according to what they themselves regard as right but strictly in accordance with the issued mandates and ordinances and in no other way."

"In addition, Dr. Alber was to instruct the sheriff that after the jurors had handed down a verdict he was to delay publication until receiving word from the government. For the time being Dr. Alber and the sheriff were to keep this secret from the jurors." "To obviate troublesome annoyances among the ordinary unlettered lay people [the Anabaptists'] confessions were not to be made public as spoken out but only in extracts and without the Anabaptists' arguments."

On February 8, 1560, the Sonnenburg sheriff was ordered to conduct the trial at Innsbruck.[48] The Schwaz preacher, who had been asked to come to Innsbruck for the purpose of "dealing with" the imprisoned Anabaptists there and who had consumed 13 gulden's worth of food at Augustin Fröhlich's inn, had this sum paid out to him on February 14.[49] Three days later the government asked for the trial of the three Anabaptists to be expedited so that His Majesty might soon get a report.[50] The vice chancellor was asked to secretly speed up the trial.

Meanwhile the jurors of the Sonnenburg judicial district had been summoned for February 20, 1560. According to this district's long-established rule the adjoining lower court areas had to provide the jurors; to be exact, the town of Innsbruck had to supply two jurors and Stubai, Ambras, Wilten, and Axams one each. The remainder were obtained from the Sonnenburg district itself. "However, with difficult cases liable to turn up,[51] it is also customary that at the government's special request in addition to the above-mentioned persons several jurors summoned for from the adjacent towns and districts, in this instance two, Augustin Fröhlich and Paulus Kleepüchler, from the town of Innsbruck, Paul Kapferer from Stubai, Christoph Kleyber from Ambras, Hans Hopfner from Wilten, Jakob Pruggner from Axams, as well as from other neighboring towns and districts, to wit Niclas Schütz from Hall, and Thoman Müllner am Gries from Steinach." Another four jurors were recruited from the Sonnenburg judicial district: Caspar Mag, the son of the old district magistrate, Caspar Küechl, Paul Lenz from Götzens, and Ulrich Brym from Hötting. When all these jurors had gathered, Dr. Alber introduced them to the case and to their duty to take an oath.

They were taken aback by this demand and, since evening had fallen they requested a time to consider until next day. When they had reassembled they handed Dr. Alber a written apology setting forth the "reasons why they found it difficult to sit in judgment upon this case and in particular to take an oath."

Alber refused to accept the document and demanded that they reply orally and yield the obedience they owed, whereupon they orally pleaded their inexperience with the imperial constitution, their inability to even understand the Latin words occurring therein and altogether to adjudicate in so important a case.

"In the second place," they pointed out, "they found it onerous to be burdened with a new oath, though they had never reneged on their earlier one."

"Thirdly, they would have to regard a new oath as a diminishment and reprimand as if they had acted contrary to their previous oath."

"Fourthly, at the regional diets it had been decided that if the regional law code does not contain a specific ordinance for the case in question, jurymen were to pass judgment not according to general written laws but in accordance with what they consider right."

"In the fifth place," they maintained, "the case in hand was a spiritual matter involving the Christian faith, on which they were not able to pass judgment and which by rights should be brought before a clerical court of law and not a secular one; for which reason they requested to be excused from adjudicating in this case and in their place to call upon a learned *commissarius* and some erudite and perceptive judges."

Dr. Alber did his best to refute these arguments point by point. He showed that the demanded oath did not involve anything new and that the matter in hand, although not provided for in the general law of the land, on the strength of the mandates issued by His Majesty had nevertheless been promulgated and given the status of a regional law, and that as loyal subjects they were bound to accord it the same respect as they would give to the long-established laws. They had not been called, he told them, to pass judgment upon matters of faith, rather, upon agitators and sectarians such as every Christian was duty-bound to root out. "And in conclusion, they should take into consideration the disfavor and punishment they had to be prepared for on account of their unjustified refusal."

In spite of all this, the jurors insisted on their demand, as evidenced by the government's report. Dr. Alber's reaction was one of "profound displeasure and searching perusal"; he once again summoned the jurors to appear before him. "Here he reprimanded them for their disobedience, trenchantly refuted, point by point, the grounds for their refusal—their incompetent and trifling arguments—and let them know that one would expect them to adhere to the ancient and true church and not to any sectarian error and that they ought to give the government no reason to suspect them of failing in that."

However, all the efforts and dexterity expended on "bringing them to a modicum of obedience" were in vain. On the contrary, they now submitted the "apology" rejected by Dr. Alber to the Innsbruck government itself and requested to be excused from sitting in judgment on this particular case. If this were not possible, they asked to be held to their former oath and to be allowed to pass judgment according to their conscience and discretion, being accountable before God.

In reply to this declaration, the Innsbruck regents, in order to find out who had fomented this business and also to scare the jurymen, asked those willing to obey the mandates to step on one side and the others to stand on the other side. Thereupon three of the jurors: Niclas Schütz from Hall, Paul Kleepüchler from Innsbruck, and Paul Lenz from Götzens, referred to their written apology and stated that they could not be obedient in this matter, whatever God might allow to happen to them. The others asked once again to be excused, pleading that they had until now always been obedient subjects and would continue to be so in the future, but that this was too difficult and weighty a case for them to cope with. Others stated that they wanted to follow the lead of their older fellow jurors. One alone, Christoph Kleyber from Ambras, declared that if it absolutely had to be, he would comply; he was not prepared to quit the country because of this.

Now the government let the matter rest for the time being and decided to let His Majesty have a report. In this assessment of the situation (dated February 27, 1561) the regional authorities state that they cannot counsel or recommend to let these jurors get away unpunished with their refractoriness, even less to release them from the oath they are required to take, but least of all to allow the jurors to pass judgment on the three Anabaptists at their own discretion instead of as prescribed by the mandates.

Meanwhile, says the report, the government had been creditably informed that all the jurors had decided that, if released from the oath, they would not sentence to death any of the three Anabaptists but rather banish them from the land. If by oath sternly and rigorously compelled to pass judgment according to the mandates, they would comply; but in an appendix to the published verdict they would state that they had been forced into it.

"Even a simple-minded person," the report goes on, "can grasp how unfavorable an impression this matter would create among the people; hence the government would like to suggest that His Majesty deign to have an open mandate addressed from the royal court to these twelve jurors, in which they, and in particular the jurors Schütz, Kleepüchler and Lenz, are sternly reprimanded for their continuing disobedience and under threat of punishment are strictly commanded to take the required oath without delay. It would be good if that missive would also state that His Majesty has authorized the government to proceed with punishment against the refractory jurymen. His Majesty might also deign to fix the punishment awaiting the jurors should these unexpectedly remain obdurate. Lastly His Majesty ought to renew the old general mandates,[52] in particular the order that jurors not pass sentence as they themselves deem right but as prescribed by the issued mandates, and this ought to be publicly announced in all His Majesty's patrimonial lands.

Hans Mändl, who had already disputed five or six times with Schiechl in Innsbruck and shortly before the beginning of the year 1561, had been placed into the Liebich tower. In a letter to his fellow sufferers he describes his dungeon as follows: "They have put me into the tower where our dear brother Jörg Liebich has lain for a long time; it is pretty deep—six fathoms [of about 6 ft. each] if I have got it correctly; up high it has a little window, and when the sun gets there, it shines in for a while and sheds light. After New Year the authorities came along with a new demand." Mändl was handed forty-six articles and was required to reply. "I went into torture as undaunted as if there wasn't any. After having a go at me for three days, they put me back into the tower. At times I can hear the worms in the wall; at night the bats fly around and make a whirring sound, and the mice rustle about,[53] but God makes it all light for me to carry. He is with me most faithfully, rendering homey and serviceable for me even those nocturnal spirits he sends forth to spread terror and fright." "They had another try at me for just one day, but this time it was only six articles they asked me about." The questions referred to here are in accord with what has been related above about this matter. Mändl's and his fellow prisoners' confession of faith agrees with Riedemann's confession, which appeared in print four years later.

Ferdinand I did not want to use force to break down the jurors' resistance. His reply is dated March 13 and reads: "We have received your letter plus the appended advice, opinion, and request as regards your dealings with the jurors. As we see it in our privy council here, the matter has taken a totally wrong and in many ways questionable course." The king then pointed out that what he was most concerned about and what did not come out clearly in the government's suggestions was the question whether and with what punishments the jurors were to be proceeded against if they persisted in their obdurate refusal. It ought to be carefully considered if the royal commands suggested in the government's letter would suffice to bring the jurors to heel and if, in case these were deprived of their juryman's status because of their disobedience, those commands might not end up being a laughing stock instead of a threat of punishment. If the resisters were punished by banishment from the country or by imprisonment or fines, it would have to be considered if such punishment has a basis in our land's laws and traditions and if it might not be seen by many as too severe, especially if, as in this case, the jurors happen to be honest and blameless persons in all other respects. Then, too, the king points out, there is the danger that in future nobody will want to hold such an office or take on such a duty. As regards the present case, bearing in mind the three prisoners' testimonies and the torture they endured, it is to be expected that they will hold on to their opinion. As the case has already dragged on for so long, it should be considered carefully if the suggested procedure might not be more likely to cause offense in the world around than to bear good fruit, and His Majesty would like to be shown ways and means to obviate that. The letter goes on to state, "We have thought of a way to avoid all such complications, and that is to quash any further trial and by virtue of imperial and princely authority to have the three obdurate Anabaptists taken off and chained to the galleys." "In that way," the letter says, "we get out of the labyrinth the jurors have landed us in; the evil will not go unpunished, and the common people have less reason to be horrified. This punishment would scare others just as much as if the evildoers were put to death. His Majesty is looking forward to receiving further and more detailed advice."[54]

On March 28, 1561, the Tyrolean authorities submitted to the emperor their "considered opinion" about his letter. The emperor's misgivings were refuted. In the regents' opinion the jurors should not be released from their duty, since that would merely do them a favor. Rather, they ought to be confronted with the "Newly instituted legal code (*Landesordnung*) of Tyrol, VIIIth book, 23rd Title,[55] according to which all judges and jurors called upon to sit in judgment in criminal cases are to pledge themselves by oath to consistently adhere to the text of this legal code. Even though the punishment to be meted out to the Anabaptists is not specified there, His Royal Majesty, it is pointed out, had nevertheless arrived at a unanimous agreement with the electors, princes, and estates of the Holy Roman Empire as regards the uprooting and punishment of Anabaptists, namely that they were to be dealt with by virtue of the constitution promulgated in 1529, and this has been given legal validity also in the Austrian patrimonial dominions (Tyrolean Legal Code [*Landgerichtsordnung*], Book VIII, Title 23. Title 23).[56] From the aforesaid, the letter goes on, His Majesty might be pleased to gather that there would in fact be legal authority for banishing the disobedient jurors from the country, not only on the strength of written laws but also on that of the Tyrolean *Landesordnung*. When they see that the royal court is in dead earnest, they will not refuse binding themselves by oath to pass judgment according to the mandates, especially since the Innsbruck burgomaster and council are not pleased with their fellow citizens' disobedience. Hence the Innsbruck authorities request that His Majesty issue a mandate declaring that the government has authority to proceed with punishment befitting the individual offense against these and any future disobedient jurors—be it by banishment from the country, by depriving them of their office and their civic rights, or by incarcerating them for a time.

The Tyrolean government also felt it had to advise against the proposed galley punishment for Anabaptists, as it was to be expected that such a mitigation of their punishment would only increase their defiance. It would in future be impossible to preserve the land from the poisonous Anabaptists, since these, tolerated as they are in Moravia, are continually infiltrating into Tyrol, especially in summer when they move up into the mountains and it is impossible to apprehend them.[57]

These remonstrations had the effect that the emperor by an ordinance dated in Vienna, April 7, 1561, reprimanded the twelve jurors and ordered them to "adjudicate in future not according to what they considered right but in accordance with the imperial constitution and the promulgated mandates." They are also told that His Majesty had authorized the (Tyrolean) government to "proceed with punishment and disgrace against those persisting in their opposition." Thus the Innsbruck government was granted power to take action against those persisting in their disobedience, be it by banishment, dismissal from office, loss of civic rights or temporary imprisonment.[58]

On May 16, 1561, the Sonnenburg district magistrate (sheriff) was ordered to summon the jurors drafted for adjudicating in the trial of Mändl and his consorts to present themselves the following Friday (May 19, 1561). After arrival in Innsbruck they had the recently issued mandates read out and the case once more explained to them, and they were faced with the question, what attitude and judgment one might expect from them. Each of them was asked individually if he was going to obey His Majesty's mandates. The answer was to be yes or no.

Schütz, Kleepüchler, and Lenz urgently pleaded to not only be excused from taking the oath but also to be totally relieved of jury duty. "Regardless of all warnings and admonition they protested that they could not burden their conscience with such a case and would rather endure any punishment on that account. The other jurors yielded and took the oath. Since the three could in no way be shifted from their position, they were put into prison."

Lenz reversed his stand already the following day, Schütz on May 30, and Kleepüchler on May 31. They were released from prison. Information obtained about their churchly behavior brought to light that until now they had conscientiously complied with all the ordinances of their religion, that Lenz had been refractory more due to simplicity of mind than because of an evil heart. So they were exempt from punishment.

On May 18, 1561, one day before the above events with the jurors took place, Hans Mändl wrote from his prison an epistle to the elders of the Moravian church community,[59] letting them know that things were well with him, but that any day now he expected to be led out to be slaughtered, given that now, on the Monday before Whitsun (May

19, 1561) the jurors had been summoned anew, which led him to think that God was about to end his (and his fellow prisoners') predicament, "whether this mean life or death for us, on either land or sea, or by lifelong imprisonment. The emperor is said to have often referred in writing to his power to send us to the galleys without a trial. So there is good reason for you to be mindful of what may be in store for us now, this being the third time for them to go into our case with the jurors. As regards what they did with us: they spent four days on me, and there were about 60 points I had to answer, both under torture and without. But God has been with me in everything. They may still expect us to change our minds; however, with God's help I will go into death joyfully, having opened my heart to you in everything. Hence will I in God's love take leave of you."

The authorities made still another attempt to get the three prisoners to change their minds. On June 14, they reported to the emperor,[60] "We have not omitted to attempt once again with all diligence, through the priest of Hall and other clerics and on the grounds of Holy Scripture, to convert the three prisoners, or at any rate the two, Rack and Kotter, from their error. But since this has proved totally fruitless with all three of them, the tenth of this month (June) has been set as the date for their execution. The district magistrate has supplied us with the sentence as formulated by the jurors as well as with the extracts from their testimonies and confessions that will be publicly read out in front of the people. As specified in the sentence, Hans Mändl, being an overseer and teacher of the sect, is to be burned alive, the other two to be beheaded and subsequently also burned." "On the tenth of this month the above sentence has been carried out and all three of them have been put to death."[61]

Like Mändl, so also Jörg Rack and Eustachius Kotter, and these two jointly, had sent an epistle to the church community in Moravia on June 5. "We want to let you know," they write, "that we are to be executed on the Tuesday after Corpus Christi and that we shall fulfill our promise to God. We do it with joy and are not sad, for this day is holy to the Lord. We also take leave from you in the name of our brother Mändl. He is not with us, but is here in Innsbruck. We cannot send messages or write to him, for we hear they don't want anybody to visit him." On the day this letter was written Kotter was so sick that Rack thought the executioner would come too late for him.[62]

The sentence was carried out in the way described. From among the fellow believers of the condemned men the following were present: Leonhard Dax, formerly a priest in Tschengels, who, as the authorities reported on May 28, 1558, had at that time joined the "seductive sect of the Anabaptists,"[63] as well as Stoffel Schneider and Hansl Král from Kitzbühel.[64] The two first-named brothers were able to hear the condemned men, undaunted and manly, witness to divine truth in presence of a large crowd of people whom they exhorted to repent. Brother Dax shook hands with them on their way to the place of execution, and that gave them great joy.[65] On the execution place their confessions and indictments were read out. The condemned men reproached the government representatives and jurors with shedding innocent blood. These excused themselves by pleading they had to obey the emperor's mandates. "O blind world," Mändl retorted, "everybody ought to judge according to his own heart and conscience; you, however, judge in line with the emperor's mandates!"

"What do we care about those imperial mandates?" added Eustachius Kotter. "Read out our confession of faith, based on Holy Scripture!"

Mändl made a long speech to the people, urging them to repent and follow the truth of Christ. "What I have taught and avowed is the divine truth," he told them. The magistrate said to him, "Now Hans, let this be enough," but he continued talking until he was nearly hoarse. The brothers went on speaking to the people right to their death; "they were not cut short but given ample opportunity to speak."

Eustachius, who "was weak in the flesh," was beheaded first; then Jörg Rack turned toward the executioner and cried joyfully, "Here do I forsake wife and child, house and home, life and limb for the sake of faith and truth!" Then he knelt down and held out his head for the mortal blow. Hans Mändl was tied to a ladder and cast alive into the flames together with the two beheaded corpses.

In addition to his epistles Mändl left behind four Christian songs;[66] Kotter and Rack both authored three songs.[67]

On June 27, 1561, the relatives of Jörg Mayer (i.e. Rack) requested to have the latter's estate given over to them.[68] On August 11, the chamber of finance asked the Sonnenburg sheriff for an account of what the execution of the three Anabaptists had cost.[69]

The censured jurors were not further molested; however, the three mainly involved were placed under police supervision. In addition, Kleepüchler had to endure many reproaches from enraged fellow citizens. Paul Lenz from Götzens was the one most deeply affected by the three Anabaptists' death, with the result that he became one himself before long. When it became known that in Götzens several persons were about to join the Anabaptists, at the beginning of September 1561, sheriff (district magistrate) Sauerwein went there himself in order to investigate the matter. He came too late, though: Paul Lenz had already departed for Moravia, to be followed there by his wife and children. Hence his property was all they could get hold of.[70]

4

HANSL KRÄL'S ELECTION, 1561-1578

IN HANS MÄNDL'S TRIAL, while the emperor was inclined to refrain from applying the death penalty to captured Anabaptists, the regional (Tyrolean) government insisted on execution. It may be assumed that they took that course because they were preoccupied with further Anabaptist trials. In the same year (1561) Anabaptists were discovered in Georg of Freundsberg's judicial district,[1] in the Rattenberg district, in Landeck and Sterzing; it became known that people from Imst had fled to Moravia,[2] and that Anabaptists were gathering in the Kitzbühel principality.[3] In addition, the authorities were under the fresh impression of the Anabaptist movement presently manifesting itself all over "Outer Austria" (*Vorderösterreich*). On July 5, 1561, Ferdinand I issued a special mandate against this movement, 60 copies of which were forwarded to the Innsbruck authorities.[4]

The terror that the execution of Mändl and his companions was intended to strike among the Anabaptists did not last long, if it had any effect at all among people who were still queuing up for a "martyr's death." Before long there were fresh reports of Anabaptists gathering in Amtholz and at Uttenheim.[5] In Amtholz, Gregori Pruner from Neunhäusern, an "Anabaptist consort and agitator, was arrested together with some people he had gathered." On July 11, 1561, he stood before honorable Rolf Sölln the Younger, town judge of Bruneck and magistrate at Amtholz. Pruner's testimony shows how many people in Tyrol were still holding to a baptism of faith. "We meet with persons from Lüsen, Taufers, Kitzbühel, Terenten, Sillian, Sterzing, and other places[6] and are made aware of the close relationship the Tyrolean Anabaptists in Moravia kept up with their native country. They return there in the summer, when wind and weather are favorable and they can camp out in the open, in woods and fields. Hansl Král from Kitzbühel is now their leader,[7] who preaches to them, baptizes them following the sermon, and provides those trekking to Moravia with money and food. As a witness of his three companions' courageous death in Innsbruck, he had sent an account of their passing to the Moravian church community and was now engaged in upholding the hesitant ones in the "upland" (*Oberland*)." "Not for even one hour are we safe from their bloodthirsty hands. Day and night they are on the prowl to get hold of us. For they will not allow people to be snatched from the devil's clutches and led to a devout life. With God's help, though, we will not let this be denied to us."

On August 1, 1561, the prince bishop of Brixen issued yet another mandate for the eradication of the Anabaptists.[8] The Innsbruck authorities sent to Rattenberg an order for the interrogation of the Anabaptist Peter Zell who had been arrested there.[9] Soon afterwards they sent the following directive to the coadjutor, captain, regent, and councillors in Brixen: "Regrettably, in this princely county of Tyrol the incorporated branch churches are but very poorly provided for, and the subjects are suffering great want and lack not only as regards the dispensation of the blessed sacrament but also the proclamation of the word of God, and this partly accounts for the fact that the Anabaptist sects are spreading the way they do. Only just recently once again several persons from this land are said to have sold their goods and chattels and to have gone with wife and child to join the Anabaptists. Hence we ask you to enjoin the parish priests to be more diligent in having not only their parish churches, but also the branches incorporated with them, provided with more able and suitable persons than heretofore—persons that instruct and teach the people and exhort them to be on guard against that seductive Anabaptist sect."[10]

In the following year (1562) it was mainly the two "overseers" Leonhard Dax and Hansl Kräl that the authorities were after. Both of them had at nighttime been sighted in Horlacher's house at Götzens.[11] News about these Anabaptists' appearances there was received from Schuls and the Münster valley, from Schwaz, Scharl, from the Oetz and Puster valleys and Stubai.[12]

At the beginning of August 1563, the administrators of Castelbell and Schlanders reported that several individuals from their districts had been on their way to the Anabaptists; some had been apprehended, others had escaped. On the whole an increase of the sect was being noted.[13] The Innsbruck government requested the issuing of new mandates, in which persons denouncing an Anabaptist would be promised a third of all the property confiscated from that person. Also the "taja" of an overseer was to be "increased to 40 gulden." The requested mandate was issued on October 2, 1563.[14]

In order to impede the flight of Anabaptists, several of whom in the following year moved away from Kitzbühel (most of them well-to-do persons) and Scharl, as well as from Sterzing, the bargemen and fishermen along the Inn river were ordered to be on the lookout for Anabaptists being ferried out of the country.[15]

On June 5, 1565, the Kropfsberg administrator informed the archbishop of Salzburg that four Anabaptists had recently come into the Ziller valley and were sojourning at places where they think they remain unnoticed, that they already had brought several persons over to their opinion and had sent them out of the country. The administrator reported, Kilian Adamer from Fügen, had been denounced to him as a prime suspect; he had arrested him, and Kilian had confessed that he had intended to leave the country but that his wife had not been in agreement. The administrator had succeeded in bringing him back to the right doctrine. The man called Schneider ("tailor"—being either the man's name or description of his trade) who had moved away from there (Lüsen) was reported to have done a lot of teaching and preaching, to have sent out letters and things like that; he could read and write and knew the gospels and the prophets, it was said.[16]

On July 6, the same administrator reports that a total of nineteen persons had made their way out of the country, of whom only four had been non-Tyroleans. Of the Tyrolese in the group, only one had been a married property-owner; all the others had been single and fairly young and had left no property behind.[17]

Under these circumstances the Innsbruck government considered it appropriate to ask Archduke Ferdinand II, who had meanwhile [in 1564] taken over the government, that at his next meeting with King Maximilian II [1564-1576] in Vienna he prevail on that monarch to command that Tyrolean subjects no longer be accommodated in Moravia. Ferdinand II considered this a praiseworthy undertaking.[18]

On September 18, four Anabaptists on their way to Moravia were apprehended in Wasserburg. They hailed from Kitzbühel and from Bavaria were extradited to Tyrol.[19]

The following year (1566) there took place in Innsbruck the trial of Niclas Geyerpüchler, who together with seven companions had been arrested in the Kling judicial district. He was sentenced to death, beheaded, and his corpse was burned.[20] From now on it was a rare case for executions to take place. There is no doubt that the Anabaptists themselves were becoming more cautious; on the other hand the authorities were looking for other means than terror to leave an imprint on the people. By trying hard to supply all parishes with clerics as far as possible and by selecting the most suitable from among these and posting them in the separatists' home areas they achieved much better results than by the old method, which had proved rather unfruitful.[21]

In the meantime on September 16, 1566, Archduke Ferdinand II had issued a mandate in which, at the outset of his "happy and blessed government, if God wills it" he expresses a firm will to "uphold the ancient, true, catholic religion, to let no apostasy come in nor allow any new doctrine and sect to take root."[22] In the following year in addition to this mandate an earlier one of Ferdinand I's—that of July 5, 1561—was republished;[23] it was similarly republished also by the bishop of Brixen. Generally speaking, under Ferdinand II's rule there was no lack at all of earnest commands and punishment threats against the Anabaptists; the mandate of August 12, 1567, was followed by others dated October 16, 1576,[24] October 8, 1578,[25] February 1, 1581,[26] and July 20, 1591.[27] With their commands to proceed with stern punishments against overseers, recidivists, and those failing to have their children baptized, pretty well all these decrees reflect Ferdinand I's mandates of the years 1542-1545.

In 1545, even recidivists, provided they truly converted, had had the prospect of a reprieve held out to them. In a renewal of that mandate Archduke Ferdinand II expects the jurors to let themselves be guided by it when casting their vote. And everybody is asked to be on the lookout for persons wanting to sell their property in order to migrate to Moravia with the proceeds. The river boatmen are once again forbidden to transport fugitive Anabaptists.

In spite of all these ordinances the movement of baptism-minded persons showed no sign of abating also in the following years. As late as 1567, we hear of Anabaptists at Axams, in the Ziller valley, at Fügen, Rattenberg, Brixen, Götzens, Kropfsberg, Glurus, in the Wipp valley and Imst. In Fügen an Anabaptist insulted the parish priest in the pulpit in front of all the people,[28] and the administrator of Glurus, who had himself "succumbed to Anabaptism," escaped the death penalty only due to the intercession of several clerical and secular persons. On January 19, 1568, the above-mentioned Fügen Anabaptist had to defend himself with respect to twenty-three articles and was then transferred from the jurisdiction of the archbishop of Salzburg to that of the Tyrolean government. On October 29, 1569, the latter informed the Schöneck administrator that three Anabaptists were "gadding about" in the Schöneck area.[29] On November 23, the same government reported that in the Puster valley Anabaptism was getting more and more aggravating as time went on.[30] In Gufidaun things were no better.

In the meantime the Anabaptists' situation on Austrian soil had changed drastically. In Moravia it was with reluctance that the landed nobility had obeyed the mandates requiring the Anabaptists' expulsion. Since Maximilian II's accession to the throne a more lenient outlook had been gaining ground. Significantly the Anabaptists' annals date the "golden age" of their brotherly community from the year 1565. "In the year 1567," the *Geschichtsbücher* explains, "some of the Moravian lords, on whose lands we dwell, earnestly pleaded and remonstrated with King Maximilian to allow the brethren referred to as Anabaptists to remain in the land and to ply their industries and trades.³¹ It was only for one year that this was granted: however, God let us have a livelihood, and we could remain where we were, unburdened." The manorial lords were not satisfied with a concession valid for one year only. They remonstrated with the emperor about the disadvantages the land would suffer by being deprived of so efficient a work force as represented by so many of the Anabaptists. One year was not sufficient, they represented, to send them all away. Not knowing where they could possibly go, they would rather let themselves be killed than vacate the land. Maximilian replied that he wanted to consider the matter.

The more freely the baptism-minded folk could move about in Moravia, the more the treks from Tyrol to the promised land of religious liberty increased. Severe ordinances making it unlawful to sell one's real estate and leave the country without the government's foreknowledge remained unheeded. As early as October 28, 1570, the Innsbruck authorities inform Baron Kunigl of having learned from his letter of October 23, that from the Schöneck judicial district twelve persons, young as well as old and both male and female servants, had gone off to the Anabaptists and been guided out of the country by two overseers, these being specially intent on gaining younger converts.³² In the following year sizable numbers of Anabaptists surfaced in Uttenheim; here overseer Jörg Koffler brought about numerous conversions.³³ In 1573, David Hasel was successfully active as a Anabaptist missionary south of the Brenner Pass.³⁴ In 1574, Jakob Planer, engaged in similar work, kept traveling about in the Vintschgau.³⁵ In June of the same year Hans Plattner from Passeyer was arrested in the Rattenberg judicial district and put to death at Rothholz.³⁶ He is known as the author of the song:

> Help. Lord in this great need,
> See, Lord, the grievous pain!

In this year (1574) the Tyrolean government published a fixed form of the creed that Anabaptist persons were to affirm by oath when recanting—indeed even when simply suspected of being Anabaptists.³⁷

On March 19, 1574, there is a report from the Imst area alleging that a miller named Matthes Redler was in contact with Anabaptists.[38] Some persons from Irtzen were said to be intending to visit the Anabaptists in Austria. A letter from Moravian Anabaptists found its way to Hartl Schneller in Landeck.[39] For the purpose of getting hold of an inheritance the Anabaptist Hans Kuhn, recently returned from Moravia, was "gadding about" in the area of Hall.[40] In October 1577, Ferdinand I's mandates of 1542 and 1544, with respect to property left behind by executed or fugitive Anabaptists were abrogated by a new mandate issued by Ferdinand II, and the older ordinances with respect to the sequestration of Anabaptist property were reestablished.[41] But already Ferdinand I had emphasized that this was of little use for the eradication of the Anabaptists. These would simply abandon their goods and chattels. Quite apart from the religious viewpoint, the remarkably low food prices prevailing in Moravia attracted a lot of people.[42] Only one year after the issue of the new mandate the magistrate at Stein, Michael Windt, informed the government[43] that Friedrich Pertulo, called Lochmann, resident of Völlern, had gone with his wife and eight children to join the Anabaptists, leaving behind two properties; also that he had persuaded two other local residents to undertake the move, but that these had been apprehended and were now being crossexamined by two priests. The government replied to the magistrate as follows: As it had been learned that there had been frequent gatherings in Lochmann's house, a sharp lookout should be kept in the hope of possibly capturing some Anabaptist overseer in that area. On July 5 [1578] the magistrates (sheriffs) at Matrei and Stein are informed that at Whitsun two such overseers had been in the Stein district, had been agitating the subjects and trying to get them to move away. One of them was Jakob Wurmbs, a native of Mals in the Vintschgau and a shoemaker by trade, the other Adam from Matrei, a tailor.[44] The following day the sheriffs of Meran and Sterzing are informed that Anabaptist overseers when entering the country will read and preach to the subjects, will agitate them and lead them away. They are reported to find shelter in both the diocese of Meran and the judicial district of Sterzing. There ought to be a special lookout for those aiding and abetting them.[45]

On July 9 [1578] Archduke Ferdinand II approached Duke Albrecht of Bavaria about the following matter. A short time ago a peasant (farmer) who had been living in "our Steinach domain" but was in the process of journeying with his wife and four small children to the Anabaptists in Moravia was apprehended by the authorities in Oetting. It is requested that they be handed over to the Tyrolean authorities.[46] The Kufstein authorities are ordered to pick up that peasant. In addition, the riverboat captain in Hall, who had allowed that party to come on his boat, was to be put in prison. To prevent such things from happening in the future, all authorities along the Inn river are by special sealed orders to be instructed to see to it that in future no unknown suspect person "be accepted without a proper discharge, passport, order, and papers documenting where the person in question comes from and is bound for." The farmer or peasant concerned was called Adam Stixner and hailed from Lafiss. Two baptism-minded persons traveling with him escaped in Oetting. He himself declared himself ready for recantation.[47] Clemens Schwärzl, the master of the riverboat in question, was for a time confined in the *Kräuterturm* prison in Innsbruck, but was then reprieved by the reigning prince. He had to promise, though, in future to "refrain from transporting strange and suspect persons unless they produce a regular passport or permit."[48] On July 16 [1578] was issued a general prohibition against transporting Anabaptists on the Inn river,[49] and on October 8, 1578, a new general mandate, linking up with the earlier ordinances against Anabaptists, was issued against them.[50]

In every administrative district it was to be read out from the pulpit by priests and pastors, as well as by the court clerks at the legal tribunal.[51] A similar mandate was on October 30, 1578, issued by Bishop Johann Thomas of Brixen.[52] How little it bore fruit is made evident by his feeling obliged to issue yet another mandate only half a year later.[53] Once again Anabaptist overseers are infiltrating the Brixen diocese; traveling back and forth, they cause many people to fall away, with the result that many persons, pretending they have purchased real estate in Austria and Moravia, sell their goods and chattels and move away to Moravia. This is being reported especially from the Taufers and Uttenheim municipalities.

What made the baptism-minded Tyroleans even more inclined to move to Moravia was the fact that Peter Walpot, head overseer of the burgeoning Anabaptist community there, which he was leading with outstanding ability, was himself a Tyrolean. At twenty-four years old, he had been elected a minister of the Word in 1550, and was one of the three founding elders of the church community; in 1565, he was chosen chief elder, "from whose lips gracious words were wont to flow."[54] When he died in 1578, yet another Tyrolean was chosen—Hans Kräl, who had already made a name for himself by his intrepid missionary journeys into the "upland."

5
ANABAPTISTS IN THE BREGENZ FOREST

THE SEVERE ORDINANCES that the Zurich authorities, urged on by Zwingli and his adherents, had issued in 1525 and 1526 against all the baptism-minded had totally squashed the promising beginnings of an Anabaptist church there. In the other Swiss cantons the Anabaptists were persecuted with still greater severity. Only in Appenzell were they able to maintain themselves and even there led a quite precarious existence. Ever since April 30, 1560, when the five Catholic towns had decided in Luzern to make the eradication of the Appenzell Anabaptists a subject for discussion at their next meeting, the brethren in Appenzell started to look for help to the Moravian communities. Repeatedly teachers had been sent to them from there,[1] and they had also come to complete doctrinal agreement with them. Emigration from there to Moravia began in 1579. The authorities understandably looked at this with great disfavor. They proceeded to impound the emigrants' property and would only hand it back if the emigrants returned and recanted.

The emigration to Moravia was particularly strong in 1585 and 1586, as the *Geschichtsbücher* bears witness: "In this year 1585, so many people arrived from Switzerland that at several places the gates had to be closed, as it was impossible to receive and accept them all." And as regards the following year it is recorded: "In this year 1586, a great many people have come to the church community from Switzerland."

But it was by no means only the Swiss that arrived with these treks. A considerable number of them hailed from the inner or rear section of the large Bregenz forest, in particular from the Au parish.[2] An artisan who had spent a considerable time in Switzerland and had gotten to know the Anabaptists there, praised them after his return. In the spinning-rooms at evening he would tell about their way of life and persuaded many to accept their teaching. In spite of all their efforts the authorities did not manage to completely eradicate the separatists; in the end they issued a mandate declaring that the Anabaptists must either return to the Catholic doctrine or leave the country. Most of them chose the latter course.[3] In 1577, three Anabaptists were put into prison: Hans Berwig, Jakob Seiffrit, and Hans Sailer, son of Conrad. They swore to keep the peace and Hans Berwig was sentenced to pay a fine of 200 gulden, and the other two paid fines of 100 gulden each. It seems that soon after his "oath of peace" Jakob Seiffrit relapsed, for already in 1578, we find him again in prison along the Egg river. He escaped from there, and the prefecture brought the matter to the attention of the regional government. Arrested anew, Seiffrit swore a second time to "keep the peace,"[4] but managed again to escape. On June 25, 1579, Archduke Ferdinand sent the following sharp reprimand to the "administrators and officials at Feldkirch": "It is very burdensome to hear of subjects' falling away from their religion, and it would have been the supplicants' and in particular your own constant duty to take appropriate and timely measures and not to just look on and let things slide. We are highly displeased with your negligence and lack of zeal and herewith earnestly command you to see to it that those named in the enclosures and other religiously suspect persons are diligently questioned about who incited them to join that sect, so that these instigators can be proceeded against with appropriate punishment. Those who in spite of exhortation and instruction will not turn away from their erring stance[5] are to be sternly enjoined to sell their goods and chattels and within one month, six weeks or two months (according as they find opportunity to dispose of their goods) to move away from the above-mentioned village of Au and from all our other principalities and patrimonial domains and not to re-enter any of them without our foreknowledge."

"But particularly concerning Jakob Seyfritt among those persons: for having twice broken the oath to keep the peace he was ordered to swear for religious reasons, and for having publicly contradicted the priest preaching in church we earnestly command you to put Seyfritt on trial for his crimes and have him sentenced, but that you do not carry out the sentence but rather report it to us and wait for further instructions from us."

Seyfritt was re-arrested on November 3, 1579, and together with his wife was sentenced to death by the sword. He was granted a reprieve by the Archduke and was banished from the country; she was sentenced to lifelong imprisonment, and their goods and chattels were confiscated.[6]

In accordance with the reigning prince's mandate a great number of baptism-minded folk left the country. On March 15, 1581, the magistrate and council of the inner Bregenz Forest notified the Innsbruck government that forty Anabaptists with their wives and children had set out for Moravia and that still many more were getting ready to leave. They report a number of sectarian writings had been taken from them, and ask for directions as to what to do with these people. On April 7, the Innsbruck government informed the archduke[7] that they had ordered the books in question to be taken from their owners and to be burned in the presence of the parish priest, that the escapees' goods were to be dealt with in accordance with the ordinance of October 16, 1577, hence to be confiscated, and that the bishop of Constance was to be requested to furnish erudite priests for the purpose of leading the erring ones back to the right path. The authorities considered Jakob Seyfritt to have been the heart and soul of the whole movement, so he was to be specially searched for, apprehended, and his arrest to be reported. On May 30, the archduke made a corresponding decision, adding that the above Anabaptists were to be prosecuted as prescribed by the mandates, if instruction were to prove useless. However, before carrying out the sentence, the reigning prince's decision was to be obtained. Nevertheless individual Anabaptists did escape to Moravia also in 1582, and in 1583, the religious stir was greater than ever before in the four domains situated in front of the Arlberg (*Vorarlberg*). Melchior Platzer, who had been an apothecary (pharmacist) and then a schoolmaster among the brethren in Moravia played a part in that. True, in the following year individual participants in the 1582 exodus to Moravia returned in a penitent mood, begged to be reaccepted and offered to turn away from their error and do penance;[8] but they were far outnumbered by a great host only too ready to shake their homeland's dust off their feet.

On June 12, 1583, the Feldkirch administrator (*Hubmeister*), Georg of Altmannshausen, served notice that an Anabaptist, Melchior Platzer, had been arrested and imprisoned at Feldkirch, had been instructed by the officials and the parish priest there and called upon to desist, "he has, however, not the least intention to give way and has also confessed to having been sent out by his superior (Hans Kräl) for the purpose of winning more people for him, and that only a few weeks before he had in fact converted to his faith, and already conducted away, sixteen persons, young and old, from the Bregenz Forest."[9]

The *Hubmeister* asked for a directive on how to handle this matter. In the reply he is referred to the decree of May 30, 1581: Platzer was to be diligently examined with respect to the questions placed before him, but if he won't listen to reason, the mandates issued against the likes of him were to be applied. As regards his own property and that of the other Anabaptists, the authorities were to proceed in line with the mandate of October 10, 1577, and with Ferdinand I's mandates of the year 1528. "However, seeing that those mandates are rather severe and in violation of the imperial constitution and were already rescinded as long ago as 1542 and 1544, by His Imperial Majesty himself, it had then been decreed that the Anabaptists' goods and chattels, both mobile and immobile, were to be accurately listed and stored and, at the authorities' discretion, be handed over to the Anabaptist owners' children for their use. This arrangement was to be adhered to.

On October 4, 1583, the Innsbruck government notified His Serene Princely Highness[10] that the Cardinal of Austria would inform them about Melchior Platzer's reply to the questions put before him. The Feldkirch officials report that all persuasive powers and arguments had proved fruitless with Platzer, but that he had audibly complained about severe dullness and weakness in his head on account of his long-lasting imprisonment in the tower and had asked to be transferred from the deep, dark dungeon to another prison where he could see the light of day, to be handed the questions there in written form and to be allowed to answer them in his own handwriting and by an avowal of his own. He had said he hoped to reply to the questions in a way likely to prove him guiltless in the eyes of whoever might read it.

In the government's opinion "his confession does not show him to be deficient or ailing as far as his mind is concerned, seeing that until now he had not let himself be turned away by either kindness or threats or any other Christian, godly expostulation (*Fürwahrung*)." He was not to be handed the questions in writing, since "as a schoolmaster and agitator of the sect he is unlikely to let himself be disabused." Out of Christian compassion, though, his confinement was to be mitigated, and he was once more to be instructed by clerical persons. If this still left him obdurate, justice was to take its course. "However," continue the Innsbruck authorities, "since the Feldkirch officials request a more formal instruction in this case, which they regard as too difficult for them, Your Serene Princely Highness might deign to point the warden (Vogt) and other officials to the decree of August 14, to have Platzer's confinement alleviated and order him to be 'worked on' by the priest, and, should this, too, prove unfruitful, to order the officials to pass sentence in line with the Holy Empire's criminal code and with the mandate of July 5, 1561. For this, though, a jurist ought to be drawn in, and what is considered the right sentence should then also be carried out. And since Platzer appeals to the authority of his 'superior' Hans Goral (Kräl) from Kitzbichl, one ought to be on guard also for the latter."[11]

The attempts to convert Platzer remained fruitless. The *Geschichtsbücher* relates that when the instruction by Catholic clerics proved of no use, the authorities called in the help of Lutheran pastors, but that is hardly credible, nor is the report that Platzer was offered reprieve and unhindered departure if only he would request this and swear to forever stay out of this land and jurisdiction. He might quite well have accepted both these conditions if not compelled to recant. After being taken from Rankweil Castle, where he had originally been incarcerated, to Feldkirch and being kept imprisoned there for 26 weeks, he was taken back to his first prison and there handed over to Count Hannibal of Hohenems, whom "the prince in Innsbruck had authorized to deal with him." On November 6, 1583, Platzer was beheaded.

Only eight days later also his "superior" Hansl Kräl passed away at Neumühl in Moravia.

Whole crowds of baptism-minded folk were now trekking from the Bregenz Forest to Moravia. In 1585, from Au alone 37 persons migrated, leaving behind property worth 1415 gulden.

To combat the spreading of Anabaptism in Reutte, as early as July 18, 1584, in a letter to the Ehrenburg administrator, Johann of Winkelhofen,[12] Ferdinand II asked him to deny entry into Tyrol to the Anabaptists on the move at its borders. Many of these were still lingering in the Bregenz area. Marx Sitticus, later to renounce his episcopacy at Constance to live in Rome as a cardinal, had entrusted Jakob Müller, a student of the German college in Rome, with paying a visit of inspection to the town and diocese of Constance. This was carried out so successfully that it caused Archduke Ferdinand to request that the bishop send Müller on an inspection visit also to Bregenz, seeing that "Anabaptists were furiously intruding there" or rather were trying to get the simpleminded to move to Moravia. Müller accepted the task and succeeded in making most of the would-be emigrants return to the bosom of the Catholic church.[13] Even more successful were the Jesuits who in 1598, were sent to the Bregenz area. Most Anabaptists there abjured their separatist confession, and only the few who would not be converted were obliged to emigrate; most likely they all made their way to Moravia. However, two decades later Anabaptism was still not totally extinguished in the Bregenz area: on May 24, 1618, Jost Wilhelm, a "devout, God-fearing man also blessed with temporal goods, in a village *an der Eck*, two miles from Bregenz, was put to death by the sword."[14] He was followed soon after by Christine Brünnerin, who had "set out for Moravia in order to get away like the patriarch Abraham from the idolatrous Chaldeans." She died at the same place on August 8 of the same year. Only around 1630, did the last vestiges of Anabaptism disappear in and around Au.[15]

6

ANABAPTISTS IN TYROL, 1579-1599

WHILE THE RELIGIOUS movement was in full swing in the area around Bregenz, urgent complaints about the rampant increase of Anabaptists or about their emigration to Moravia were coming in also from the various parts of Tyrol. Even before August 13, 1580, the parish priest at Taufers informs the bishop of Brixen, and the latter the Innsbruck government, that various overseers of the Anabaptist sect are stirring up the subjects and that in the last four years several persons have gone off to Moravia.[1] This was specially noticed at Kematen, "where the Klockner woman shelters and accommodates Anabaptists," and in the Uttenheim judicial district.[2] As a result of these observations the mandate of October 8, 1578, was republished on February 1, 1581, with increased threats of punishment in all towns and judicial districts.[3] "In defiance of all mandates," says a governmental missive to the burgomaster and council of Hall on February 21, 1581, "about a fortnight ago several Anabaptists on their way to Moravia boarded a riverboat at Hall *an der Länd*, and there ought to have been more diligence and watchfulness. From the Rattenberg judicial district departed for Moravia the sister of Lienhard Niederdorfer at Ried with two sons and one daughter[4] from Alt-Rasen, Gregor Schmötzl with wife and children, and from the Thauer district Georg Schwedlinger and Hans

Schweizer (from Schlitters), who had both been arrested but escaped during the night of May 24-25.[5]

Significant is the mandate issued by Bishop Johann Thomas on August 23, 1582, which laments the fact that the Anabaptist sect is gaining ground in the Puster valley, that its overseers and preachers rove about quite publicly and freely and lead away a lot of people. People are commanded[6] to "diligently heed the herewith renewed mandates." The following case throws light on the regional government's manner of dealing with the sequestered goods of fugitive Anabaptists: In 1582, Georg Pögerer with his wife and five children had moved from Imst to Moravia. Their estate had been sold for 203 gulden and these had been pocketed by the Innsbruck Chamber (of finance). After the wife's death in 1588, her brothers filed an application for 190 gulden of the inheritance. On November 22, 1588, their request was rejected on the ground that there were still children of the deceased who might raise a claim to the estate.

Repeatedly the government had reason to complain about the excessive lenience of the jurors.[7] There were also complaints about the Anabaptists' being given assistance. On July 20, 1583, the Schlanders administrator reports that the chamber messenger Gotthard Prandtner, whose parents and siblings had made off to the Anabaptists, for several years had been receiving letters from Moravia that he was meant to deliver to the senders' relatives and friends. The directive thereupon given was to "pay that messenger an inspection visit and take into custody any suspect letters he might have."[8]

On May 26, 1584, Andre Pürchner, a tilemaker (*Ziegler*) from Sterzing, was arrested in Latsch on the Adige (Etsch) river.[9] On June 5, he was taken to Goldrain in the judicial district of Schlanders and "was three times racked and tortured."[10] "He would not let himself be turned away from his erring stance." Administrator Franz Händl is asked to question him about five Anabaptist overseers reported to be presently in this country: Zuckenhaimer, Veit Uhrmacher from the Vintschgau (said to have a red beard, to have been a preacher at Nikolsburg for three years, and to have already been imprisoned in Salzburg); Gilles, a Rhinelander; Crämer, and Peter from Titmaning. The report that the Innsbruck government submitted to the reigning prince on August 20, 1584, relates that Pürchner, who had in no way let himself be converted, had been sentenced to be pilloried, to be driven with rods out of the village of Schlanders and to be forever banished from the patrimonial domains of His Serene Princely Highness. The councillors of the Innsbruck government had differing opinions about this sentence. While some of them thought that, once passed, the sentence ought to be carried out, the majority was of the opinion that the "sentence, being somewhat disjointed and not fully of one piece" and also not in line with the mandate of August 12, 1561, ought to be rescinded and the jurymen be exhorted to return a verdict in conformity with the above-mentioned mandate, and "not otherwise." This then did take place, and Pürchner was sentenced to death by the sword. Right to the last moment, when "the executioner was already drawing back the sword for the blow," efforts were made to get Pürchner to recant; however, "he was not willing and with laughter in his mouth finished his earthly course on October 10."[11]

In order to capture the above-named overseers, numerous missives were sent to the various administrators in the land and to the secular councillors in Brixen.[12] In a letter of July 31, 1584, to Prince Bishop Johann Thomas, in addition to the above-named Anabaptist overseers a sixth one is mentioned, "Bastl Schmidt from Brauneggen," who quite likely may have gone to his relatives there.[13] A few days later the Kropfsberg administrator Wilhelm Gartner is notified that Anabaptists are gadding about at Ried in the Ziller valley, some of whom are named: Georg Alpacher, a shoemaker; Christian Gartner from Kupach in the Ziller valley; Georg Schaichnagl, and one woman, the "old Niederdorfer."[14]

In May of the following year (1585) Oswald Traut from the Oetz valley and Hans Weber from the Pitz valley were captured; the first one escaped before recantation; the second one recanted.[15] Soon afterward we hear about two apprehended Anabaptists: Mathias Platner from Unterperfuss and Paul Gänsler, the latter arrested in Schlanders. Of greater significance was the arrest made on May 6, 1585, by the Lienz magistrate, Jost Tausch[16] called Aichele, by apprehending these four: Jakob Platzer from Prad in the Vintschgau, Ruprecht Sier "from the Laubach," Leonhard Mareez from Tschengele, and Caspar

Rauchenpüchler. Already the following day they were subjected to intense interrogation, the results of which were forwarded to the Innsbruck government.[17] Platzer refused to name the houses where he had been given shelter, except the inns. Ruprecht Sier maintained that he had only wanted to visit his father and his friends and then return home. He would betray nobody nor swear an oath; he would rather surrender his life. This was also the evidence given by Leonhard Mareez. Rauchenpüchler testified that he had already been "up" here three years ago and had been traveling about; he had had nobody with him, he said. But if somebody wanted to go with him, he would not advise him against it.

A second interrogation took place on June 1. Platzer testified that the previous summer some untold number of Anabaptists had journeyed up to Tyrol. His people had given him no direction as to where to lodge; they had only been told that, once in Tyrol, they were to stay in the woods by day and night and avoid getting arrested. But a brother had given him a piece of paper or guide, he said, on how "by inquiry to find his way from one place to the next." Mareez had definitely not been told to gather people [for Moravia]; however, if he happened to meet somebody [eager to go], they would be pleased. Caspar Rauchenpüchler stated that "he had been sent out by his brothers just as Christ had sent out his apostles, namely to meet people eager to learn about the truth and the right way and to live it, and to instruct such people."

Mareez recanted on July 3. Ruprecht Sier managed to escape on Ascension Day [40th day after Easter]. On July 5, Platzer, too, declared himself ready for recantation, stating that what had pleased him was the way of life of the Anabaptists, not their faith. "Only the wife and child he had been 'saddled with' right after his arrival, had made him stay," he said. Somewhat later Rauchenpüchler, too, let himself be converted.[18]

Meanwhile on July 1, Ferdinand II had issued a mandate for Tyrol and Outer Austria, which, referring back to the mandate of 1566, ordained stern measures against the Anabaptists and demanded greater zeal from the authorities.[19] Nevertheless we learn already on August 3 [1585] that Thoman Mark with his wife and six children and

Bartl Pegner with his wife and one child (who had been living in the Pengler Woods in the Lech valley) as well as Hans Weber from Wenns ("regardless of his written promise to keep the peace") have gone over to Anabaptism.[20]

As early as 1584, overseer Wastl Schmid, called Segesenschmid (or "Sensenschmid" i.e. scythe smith) had come to public notice in the Braunau area; in the following year he lay in prison in Bern.[21] On April 16, 1587, the Innsbruck government notifies Prince bishop Johann Thomas that this Wastl Schmid was once again surfacing, together with another Anabaptist called Zuckenhamer and that both of these should be reconnoitered.[22] Similar missives were sent to the authorities in Hall, the Adige area, Kufstein, Kitzbühel, the Inn valley, Rotenburg, Rattenberg, Steinach, Altrasen, Taufers, Ehrenberg, and Kropfsberg. Already on February 28 [1587] the Bavarian government had called attention to Sensenschmid and Zuckenhamer.[23]

It appears that the Gufidaun administrator Maierhofer's wife, who was known to be attached to the new doctrine, was more inclined towards the Anabaptists than to the Lutherans. In 1582, she had been expelled on account of her "disgusting religion" and her unwillingness to desist in spite of being repeatedly instructed by the Prince's father confessor Antoni Klesel and the bishop of Brixen. As she had reappeared in her home area, the Innsbruck government asked His Princely Serenity if she was to be tolerated in the county. What the government suggested was expulsion lest this case present a bad example and offense.[24] However, due to intercession on her behalf from Brixen she was soon afterward granted a reprieve.

Of much greater significance was the movement among the baptism-minded folk in Tyrol in the year 1588.[25] On August 4, Christoph von Wolkenstein, writing from Rodeneck, lets Brixen know that "a few days ago the administrator of the Lienz judicial district had arrested and imprisoned the Anabaptist Martin Gruber as well as six young persons of both sexes, whom he was about to take with him to Moravia, that Gruber had testified that some of his brethren are still in Tyrol but were intending to return to Moravia around either St. Lawrence's or St. Bartholomew's Day [i.e.August 27]. The minutes of Gruber's interrogation of August 1, were included with the letter.[26]

Gruber hailed from Graun on the Mals Heath (*Malser Haide*) and had been with the Anabaptists for twenty years. He testified that Ambrosi Resch—the brother who left behind an interesting chronicle of the Anabaptists[27] —had made him take that step, and that Klein Hänsl (Hans Mändl), who had been put to death at Innsbruck, had baptized him. This was the third time for him to come "up" [i.e. to Tyrol], and he had been accompanied by somebody called Georg Mühlwalder. The latter had been the reason for his being sent up here to conduct people down (i.e. to Moravia). Apart from him, he stated, yet another overseer was up here [in Tyrol]: Wastl Schmid from Stubai, as well as a brother named "Hänsl" (Zuckenhamer). On the way to Tyrol they had lodged with the innkeeper at Leisach, with Klettenhammer in the Heunfels judicial district, in the barn by the inn at Neunhäusern, with the innkeeper in St. Georgen, at Mühlbach "where Gall had an elderly female relative (*mumb*)," and with Schaller near the church in Natz. Also, the four Anabaptists previously imprisoned at Lienz, enabled the miller (Mareez) to be reaccepted into the brotherhood but he had since then passed away, and that the other three—the locksmith, the cabinetmaker, and Riepl (Ruprecht)—had been taken back into the brotherhood after undergoing penance.[28]

On August 12, 1588, the Innsbruck government notified Prince Bishop Johann Thomas at Brixen as follows: "Your princely grace will doubtless remember what Your Grace wrote on July 31, 1584, and then on April 16, 1587, as regards several Anabaptist male persons and overseers of the sect, in particular about a certain Bastl Schmidt or Segesenschmidt. Now, however, in addition to that Bastl Schmidt the following persons are said to be here in the country: two from the Puster valley, one called Matthes, the other Gall; also somebody named Martin from the Oetz valley, and still another one: Martin Gruber from Graun on the Malser Haide.[29] Your Princely Grace will surely take measures to have these Anabaptists apprehended."[30] Warrants of arrest were issued against Matthes and Gall, both being *Pusterers* (i.e. from the Puster valley).[31] Matthes hailed from "near Klausen," Gall from "*an der Vintl*." Christoph von Wolkenstein was similarly notified. Bastl Schmidt, already mentioned several times in the court files, was also referred to as Anfang[32] and was a scythe smith by trade. He hailed from Stubai, according to other sources from Bruneck; he was one of the most intrepid Anabaptist apostles, who from 1584 to 1588 came to Tyrol every year and, though encircled by constables and diligently pursued, managed every time to return safely to Moravia.[33]

On the same August 12, 1588, eighteen suspected Anabaptists were being interrogated at Rode-neck.[34] Joachim Paumbgarther from Natz stated that he had not seen, let alone accommodate, any Anabaptist for thirty years. Many years ago when still in service in the Puster valley, he had repeatedly been "approached about going to Moravia but had not been willing," he said. He had heard of Anabaptists staying with Gebhardt in Natz but had not set eyes on them. And when the Anabaptists had tried to mislead him, he had put up resistance.

Christian Gebhardt testified that he had relatives in Moravia, who had several times written to him. His mother's brother, he said, had moved away from the Neustift and through an Anabaptist had sent him a letter requesting that he obtain for him the 100 gulden which Planer in the Neustift was owing him. His other relatives, he said, had moved to Moravia so long ago that he didn't even know them. He was the guardian of Balthasar Mörtzen's daughter Christina, but she had moved away without his knowing where; it was only through Cässl Walder, who had come up from Moravia, that he had learned of her being there. She had asked Cässl to bring back to her whatever was still there of her property.

Five weeks ago, Christian Gebhardt went on to testify, two men had come to his house at nighttime, and he had been aware that they were Anabaptists; they had asked him for the remainder of his ward Christina's property. He had replied that he had not yet done penance (*gerait*), and if some of her property was still around, he could not let them have it without the authorities' permission. He had allowed the two men to spend the night in his house. The following day he had left the house, and when he returned at midday, his wife told him that somebody was walking about on the floor above. When he had a look, he found the two Anabaptists, who pleaded with him not to be wrathful toward them; they had been too late but wanted to leave the following night; they didn't ask for anything to eat, as they still had some bread. Nevertheless he had carried a bowl of soup up to them at midday. He had never listened, he said, to Anabaptism being preached, let alone allowed this in his house. It was out of pure mercy that he had given them shelter. As to the persons who had left from Natz he only knew what his wife had told him. The woman at the Schallen farm who relayed this information had told her that her children had gone to the Anabaptists because they get so little to eat here.

Joachim Huber at Natz testified that he had not sheltered any Anabaptists. But on St. Vitus Day, when he had sent his son Hänsl to Sterzing for some money, the other son, Georg, had come and said, "Father, let me have some money!" But he did not give him anything. The following day his wife had told him that Georg had run away. He had also heard that the Anabaptist Gall Weiß had been in Natz and had taken with him two of the day-laborer Trina's children. Fifteen years ago a man called David (Hasel) had tried to make him an Anabaptist, but he had refused as he "did not feel attracted to their faith." He would be happy if his son were brought back.

Christina Pöcker(in) testifies that at the count's well in Natz she had heard of Anabaptists having been with Paumbgarter. And she had seen some Anabaptists at Kranewitten. This is also the evidence given by Agatha Mörtz(in).

Katharina Padrutscher(in), wife of the young innkeeper in Natz, tells that during the recent hay harvest Balthasar Schaller in Natz had come to her house with a short letter as well as a *Pixl* full of *Treujappes*"[35] and had asked her to read the letter. She had inquired where he had got it from, and Schaller had replied that when on his way to Räss[36] he had heard whispering among the bushes, and when he got closer, he came upon Gall Weiß and Wärtl, both of them Anabaptists, and Gall had given him the letter. And when Trina had read it, it became clear to her that this was the Gall that years ago had wanted to marry her. And she said to Schaller, "Well, and do I now have to pay him for the *Treujappes*?" And Schaller had said, "Why don't you reward him by giving him shelter?" So she had found Gall quarters with the tailor Saitner, whose house belonged to her father, and there she had sent him two pieces of meat. And when she had come into the tailor's garden, his wife had shouted to her from the window, "Trina, Gall is back!" And then she had thought he might regard the *Treujappes* as not yet paid for, and she took him a *Puschen Krapfen*. And when she got there, Schaller had just left, and Gall had told her that she was deeply enmeshed in sin and would be doomed to hellfire if she remained like that. Thereupon she had said that God was bound to take pity on her and let her find blessedness, but that she was in our[37] land. And when Gall had gone, the tailor's wife had commented that Gall was such a fine, gracious, and gentle man, that she hoped he would soon come back, as she felt bored without him. She herself, Trina, had had no liking at all for what Gall represented and had not agreed with it. Helena, wife of Sigmund Mesner in Räss, confesses to having let Gall take the children away "because they are starving so badly." If Mesner and his sister had not intervened, the children would in fact have gone. She actually felt sorry about it afterward.

The testimonies of Katharina Fischer, Melchior Gätscher, and Margaretha Schaller from Natz are irrelevant. Of greater importance are those of Anna Kaltenhauser, surviving daughter of Hans Kaltenhauser. She states that for a long time already and when her father was still alive, Anabaptists had found accommodation and shelter with Kaltenhauser in Räss and had brought her father letters from Stockner in Moravia. On Schaller's *Heu Tillen* in Natz the Anabaptists had tried to persuade her, her brother Stoffl, Sigi (Sigmund) Mesner and his wife, as well as the Geständler woman at Schaller's place to go with them to Moravia. She had been willing to go to Moravia, but not to the Anabaptists. Her brother Stoffl, she said, had gone off with the Anabaptists; she had accompanied him as far as Schabs and had given him 7½ gulden worth of old sixpence coins to take along to exchange.

Apollonia Carusin had given permission for her two children, Lex and Eva, to be taken away because she couldn't do anything good for them and they had to go so hungry. The Anabaptists had promised that the children would be well brought up "down there." If she had the right faith, she, too, would follow the children. However, no sooner had the children left with the Anabaptists than she felt great remorse and grieved deeply about the children. She would never do this again and felt ever so sorry about it.

Anna Troger(in), wife of Wolfgang Wolfgruber, burgher at

Mühlbach, had recently at 11 o'clock in the night taken in three Anabaptists, one of them her cousin, Gall Weiß by name, as well as six children they had led away from Natz and Räss, and that she had sheltered them for two days and two nights. When Margaretha Sober(in), Kaltenhauser's sister, came to Mühlbach and inquired if the children taken away from her were there, Anna Troger(in) had asked whether she felt sad about her children, and Margaretha had answered that it did not affect her all that much but that it caused great grief to their father and that she, too, would never do such a thing again. Her husband testified the same.

Ambrosi Kaltenhauser testifies that while his father was still alive one brother and one sister had gone off to join the Anabaptists. His brother Stoffl had told him he wanted to go with the Anabaptists to Moravia and have a look at what his brothers and sisters were doing there.

Martin Fletscher, who lived at the Schaller farm was also accosted by Anabaptists. He had right away felt sorry for the children and was glad to see them back.

Balthasar Tauber, in spite of the fact that his father and siblings were in Moravia and wanted him there, too, had not felt inclined to go and join them there, but at Stoffl Kaltenhauser's request he had accompanied him as far as Schabs. Christine, whose husband had gone off to war, had told him that she, too, wanted to send a little daughter to the Anabaptists—a statement he had neither lauded nor taken exception to. Insignificant is Balthasar Schaller's testimony that he felt no desire to go and listen to the Anabaptists' teaching.

These testimonies cast a more revealing light on the Anabaptists' working methods in Tyrol than could be achieved by detailed accounts. What made such news all the more unwelcome to the authorities was the fact that during the preceding years they had done their very best to combat the spread of Anabaptism by means of commands and prohibitions. Nor had the assistance provided by the Jesuits proved effective. Only by closing off the well from which Tyrolese Anabaptism drew ever fresh nourishment could a complete elimination of all baptism-minded folk in Tyrol even be considered. There was still a long way to go before reaching that point.

In the meantime the authorities were informed that soon after Pentecost of 1588, Anabaptists and their overseers had turned up in Sack below Sterzing. Hence on August 13, 1588, they ordered the local district magistrate to question the innkeeper at Sack. On February 15, 1589, the Innsbruck government informed Imst, Nanders, Glurus and Mals, Castelbell, Landeck, and Schlanders that somebody by the name of Hans Ganser from the Vintschgau was "gadding about" in the upper Inn valley, especially at Imst, and was engaged in "catching fish" there. He is said to belong to the new "Hutterian" Anabaptist sect, and an effort should be made to apprehend him.

In the following year [1590], on the evening of St. James' Day, the government succeeded in apprehending at Lorenzen in the Puster valley one of the most active Anabaptists: brother Georg Wenger. In Lorenzen where he was imprisoned for 33 days, he was interrogated three times. When asked to name the people who had sheltered him, he replied, "We do not even betray our enemies, so how could we betray those who do good to us?" On Monday after St. Bartholomew's Day [August 27] he was taken to Michelsburg castle and was there most horribly tortured.[38] Taken to Brixen, he was put into a vermin-ridden dungeon and chained up in there. The scorpions—he wrote—were crawling about on the wall by his head and bed and so horrified him that he had to keep his head covered. He lay imprisoned in Brixen for ten weeks. From all sides great efforts were made to "direct him once more to the right church," but he said, "I have not turned away from the right doctrine and church and that is how I want to remain." From Brixen he was again taken to Lorenzen and from there to Michelsburg. He was to be executed on March 1, 1591, but the death of the Prince Bishop of Brixen four days previously interfered with that. Thus it was only on August 5, 1591, that Georg met his death at the place of execution at Lorenzen. "A lot of people had gathered and some were in tears. He told them they ought to weep about themselves."[39] Seventeen days prior Jakob Platzer had been arrested at Sillian on the Drau river. He remained more steadfast than six years ago at Lienz and, as he "would not deviate," he was beheaded on August 7, 1591.[40]

At the very same time yet another overseer" turned up in the Uttenheim principality or domain.[41] Under these circumstances Ferdinand II had as early as July 20, 1591, sent a new mandate against the Anabaptists to all regional authorities. In the versions sent to Taufers, Uttenheim, and Sarnthal the following additional sentence was included: "Only a few days ago eight persons, male and female, slipped away from the Heunfels principality; two male persons together with the leader and overseer were apprehended, but two more such persons are reported to have gone to the Sarn valley." In addition the Rattenberg administrator was notified that several Anabaptist persons had made their way to the Ziller valley and to Pfarrmünster.[42]

On October 6, 1592, in a letter to court attorney Matthäus Schlechter at Imst the government regrets to learn that the Anabaptist Georg Pintlechner from the Kitzbühel principality will not be turned from his error; if he remains obdurate, he is to be dealt with according to the mandates.[43] A letter from the Innsbruck government to the chief administrator of the Etsch (Adige) area makes it clear that the sect was taking fresh root in the area along the Adige river and in the Vintschgau.[44] Three years later, on August 11, 1595, the government informs this head administrator as well as the administrators at Nanders and Schlanders that once again some Anabaptist male persons, whose names are not known, are making their way into the county of Tyrol and especially the Vintschgau.[45] Indeed, at the very turn of the century we are informed that the population is now even exposed to the impact of printed writings of an Anabaptist trend. On May 28, 1599, the Innsbruck authorities inform the "urban and rural magistrate" Jakob Vogler in Sterzing that they have received his report of May 14, according to which Anabaptist books had been found with Jakob Gasser, called Hansemann, innkeeper at Mittewald, and that he as well as his father are said to have sheltered and accommodated Anabaptists. The magistrate is ordered to immediately go to Mittewald, ask for the aforementioned books and writings, describe them and submit the list. If found guilty, Gasser was to be dealt with in line with the mandate of August 12, 1567.[46]

The Gasser affair dragged on for more than two and a half years.[47] On November 6, 1599, the "urban and rural" magistrate served notice that not long ago Gasser had gone off at nighttime with an Anabaptist by the name of Säxl but had come back a few days later.[48] Investigation brought to light that Gasser had indeed intended to become an Anabaptist. With this in mind he had taken with him 90 gulden and gone off towards Vintl. He asserts, though, that he only did this due to a lack of common sense and that "he quite generally had no misgivings about the Catholic religion." In spite of this asseveration the government considered it necessary to make an example of him; hence it decreed a court trial for Gasser in accordance with the regional ordinances of Tyrol and the other mandates concerned, but the sentence arrived at was to be sent to the government for confirmation.

7

EXTINCTION OF TYROLEAN ANABAPTISM, 1600-1626

THE "GOLDEN AGE" of the brotherly community in Moravia had lasted 27 years—from 1565 to 1592. The Anabaptists' annals date the "return of tribulation" starting in 1592. The situation of the Moravian Anabaptists was indeed getting more difficult than previously. "Their opponents loudly complained about the brethren's inordinate increase in numbers and that their practice of trades and crafts was very detrimental to the towns and villages. That is why the authorities have decided to forbid us to establish new communities but to allow the manorial lords to go on availing themselves of the brethren's labor."[1] Already "at Lent time" of the year 1601, a mandate of Rudolf II[2] decreed that "the manorial lords in Austria send the brethren away. This mandate, instigated by the Jesuits, did not last long, but nonetheless the lords, fearful and scared, dismissed our millers and others in their service'. The church community in Moravia suffered great harm from the troops frequently passing through; some of the land's grandees no longer proved as favorably inclined as formerly toward the brethren; they also had to bear a heavier burden of taxes than the other subjects. Before long the worsening of their situation in Moravia also showed itself in their relations to the "upland." The accessions from Tyrol grew ever weaker as the years went by and ceased completely once catastrophe hit the Moravian church community in 1622.

In 1602, we still hear about a number of persons making their way to Moravia. On November 14 of that year the "urban and rural" sheriff at Rattenberg informs the Innsbruck government that he had arrested the sixty-year-old Schwellinger from Alpbach as well as the unmarried daughter of old Unterberger from Steinberg and a servant boy of Unterberger's. The sheriff also reports that Altperger had absconded with a daughter, a boy, a male servant and a girl as well as several hundred gulden. Schwellinger had "joined the sect already thirty years ago and had let himself be baptized together with his wife." On November 21, 1602,[3] the government ordered a painstaking judicial investigation of the case. Even if Schwellinger were to convert, he should still be proceeded against with and without torture, seeing that he had already journeyed from the Moravian Anabaptists to Tyrol twelve times. They should try to find out how he had gone about his journeys, how he had made his way from one night's lodging to the next, etc. As Schwellinger had already confessed to having conducted Christian Gartner from Kapfing, a poor girl whose name was still to be ascertained, and Martin Rainer, innkeeper at Brugg, along with his wife down to Moravia, it ought to be ascertained just when this had taken place. Since Schwellinger had himself testified that he had been in the Puster valley and from there had gone to the Ziller valley, to Alpbach and to the Wildschönau, he ought to be interrogated about his activity at those places.

Shortly afterward Schwellinger made a successful escape, which earned the magistrate a sharp reprimand.[4] On the same day (November 16, 1602) the Innsbruck authorities inform the Rodeneck magistrate that they are greatly concerned about a certain Bartelmä Weingartner, a peasant residing at Mühlbach, not far from Brixen, who was intending to move to Moravia. They ask the magistrate to obtain precise information about this.[5] What concerned the authorities even more was Säxl from Aich in the Rodeneck judicial district, who was mentioned previously. As they write to Sterzing on January 24, 1603,[6] in the previous year Säxl had misled into that confounded Anabaptism a day laborer with his wife and two children, then a woman, three children, and a servant girl, had taken them on secluded paths via Pütsch to Rattenberg and from there on an Inn river barge to Moravia. These people, the government had learned, had then "run away" and made their way back to Tyrol. That is why Säxl and other Anabaptist persons should be diligently searched for.

In 1604, on orders from Brixen a number of persons whose religious stand was under suspicion, were being closely scrutinized; such an examination was carried out in Heunfels, Michelsburg, Nieder-Vintl, Lüsen, Klausen, and Tiers.[7] In the market town Sillian (in the Heunfels district) houses and storage containers were being searched without warning, and "suspect books were said to have been found." Martin Mayer and his wife, Christoph Scharlinger, and Caspar Troyer were said to be under suspicion as regards their religion.

In the Michelsburg district Niclas Stainer or Ziegler at St. Georgen is said to own suspect books. A short while ago he is reported to have said in Bruneck that it "was not possible for the Trinity to be one God," and that "baptism is unnecessary."

"In Nieder-Vintl several persons are not at all clear as regards rebaptism, hence it would be good for the pastors to take greater care."

"Maierhofer in Lüsen ought to be more closely examined as regards his religion." "Several persons in Klausen are said to show opposition to the Catholic religion in their actions and behavior; there are also various sectarian books about, which the parish priest is aware of."

The following years provide but little material with information as to the occurrence and distribution of Anabaptists in Tyrol; which in any case, can no longer have been extensive. It seems that just about everybody in any way connected with Anabaptism had moved away. By that time the Anabaptists were exposed to manifold ills also in Moravia. The frequent troops marching through, heavy taxation, and many other calamities laid heavy burdens upon the church community. Finally on September 28, 1622, a decree was issued in Brünn declaring that "if still found in Moravia four weeks after the date indicated any persons adhering to the Hutterian brotherhood, both male and female, will be liable to severe corporal and capital punishment." So the church community left behind its twenty-four large household-communities: Neumühl, Schäckowitz, Kobelitz, Tracht, Pausram, Prybitz, Poherlitz,

Nusslau, Austerlitz, Dämerschitz, Gerspitz, Nicolsburg, Nemtschitz, Oleckwitz, Stigonitz, Wischenau, Teikowitz, Schermakowitz, Mascowitz, Altenmarkt, Göding, Schaidowitz, Urschitz and Gostl, all of them accommodating many people of Tyrolean descent. The church community moved away from a "land in which they had been living for 80 years in honesty and modesty, doing nobody any harm, but for their faithful services they earned great ingratitude from the Lord Cardinal (Dietrichstein) and the other noble lords."[8]

Of course, the lords who had once in the hardest times granted asylum to the fugitives from Tyrol, were now facing totally different circumstances.

In the chronicles there is now no single reference to Anabaptists in Tyrol. Though it is documented that individual Anabaptists were still in evidence[9] they no longer held any significance. What did most for the eradication of the separatists was the "reformation of the Catholic Church." From hundreds of confessions one used to hear time and again: "what attracts us is not the Anabaptists' belief but their conduct and devout way of life." At the end of our era the clerical situation in the land—the life and discipline of the clergy—had undergone a change for the better, and that took away the most prominent reasons that had caused "the common people to take off into Anabaptism."

NOTES

FOREWORD

1. "Zur Geschichte der Wiedertäufer in Mähren", in *Zeitschrift für allgemeine Geschichte, Kultur-, Literatur- und Kunstgeschichte* I (1884) 438-457.
2. "Die Stadt Waldshut und die vorderösterreichische Regierung in den Jahren 1523-26," in *Archiv für osterreichischer Geschichte* LXXVII (Vienna, 1891); "Deutschböhmische Wiedertäufer," in *Mitteilungen der Vereins für Geschichte der Deutschen in Böhmen* XXX (1892); *Doctor Balthasar Hubmaier und die Anfänge der Wiedertaufe in Mähren* (Brno, 1893) VIII, 217; "Wiedertäufer in Steiermark," in *Mitteilungen der Historischen Verein für Steiermark* XLII (1894) 118-45; "Der Kommunismus der Huterischen Brüder in Mähren im 16. und 17. Jahrhundert," in *Zeitschrift für Sozial- und Wirtschaftsgeschichte* III (1895) 61-92; "Der Communismus der mährischen Wiedertäufer im 16. und 17. Jahrhundert. Beiträge zu ihrer Geschichte, Lehre und Verfassung," in *Archiv für österrreichische Geschichte* LXXXI (1895) 135-322.
3. "Studien zu Pilgram Marbeck," in *Gedenkschrift zum 400-jährigen Jubiläum der Mennoniten oder Taufgesinnten, 1525 bis 1925*, 134-178; *Pilgram Marbecks Antwort auf Kaspar Schwenkfelds Beurteilung des Buches der Bundesbezeugung von 1542, Quellen und Forschungen zur Geschichte der Oberdeutschen Taufgesinnten im 16. Jahrhundert*, J. Loserth, ed. (Vienna and Leipzig, 1929) XII, 592 pp.
4. See Claus-Peter Clasen, *Anabaptism: A Social History, 1525–1618: Switzerland, Austria, Moravia, South and Central Germany* (Ithaca, NY: Cornell University Press, 1972), Appendix D, 337; *Idem*, "Executions of Anabaptists, 1525–1618: A Research Report," *Mennonite Quarterly Review* 47, 1973, 115–152. In Tyrol, at least two hundred men and women were executed as Anabaptists between 1527 and 1530, with the total in subsequent years reaching about 600, indicating a disproportionately high rate of execution compared to the rest of Europe.
5. On the broader context of Protestantism in Austria, see Grete Mecenseffy, *Geschichte des Protestantismus in Osterreich* (Graz: Böhlau, 1956).
6. Many of these have been edited by Grete Mecenseffy in volumes of the Anabaptist sources in the series, *Quellen zur Geschichte der Täufer (QGT), vol. 11: Osterreich, vol. 1, Quellen und Forschungen zur Reformationsgeschichte, 31.* Gütersloh, 1964.; *QGT, vol. 13: Osterreich, vol. 2.* 1973; *QGT, vol. 14: Osterreich, vol. 3* 1983.

1. JAKOB STRAUSS AND URBANUS RHEGIUS IN HALL

1. True, in his preface to *Der Widertöufferen ursprung, fürgang* (Zurich 1560), Bullinger denies that connection; however, in a later passage he does raise the question: "How does it come about that the Anabaptists are not sent to, nor preach at, those places where the Gospel has never yet been proclaimed? Why do they

worm their way in only at localities where it has already been proclaimed to the people with much toil and labor and where the church has been reformed and put in order? It is at such places where honest folk are well content that the Anabaptists cause trouble, discord, and confusion."

2. Cf. Ferdinand I's mandate of November 6, Nuremberg 1522 (signed by the Archduke at Salamanca) in the Innsbruck Statthaltereiarchiv. In fol. 56 the prince demands "that you issue a strict mandate against any further Lutheran preaching and also order all printers and merchants to cease printing and selling such books." Cf. also the order to the town council of Rattenberg on the Inn with respect to "Lutheran teachings," Nuremberg, November 17, 1522 (ibid., "From His Grace" fol. 56 and that council's reply of December 1 (ibid., fol. 455).
3. S. Ruf, "Dr. Jakob Strauss und Dr. Urban Rhegius," *Archiv für Geschichte und Alterthum Tirols* II, 67-81; F. Waldner, "Dr. Jakob Strauss in Hall und seine Predigt vom grünen Donnerstag (April 17) 1522, ein Beitrag zur Geschichte der Reformation in Tirol," XXVI *Ferdinandeum*, 1-19.
4. As to more details about his activity in Schwaz see ibid., 8.
5. "They were put into prison by Bishop Sebastian of Brixen (Angerer's Chronicle) but were set free by the peasants and have done great harm to the town of Brixen and to other localities." *Brixen und seine Umgebung in der Reformationsperiode 1520-1525*," XII. Program of the Brixen highschool, 13. Buchholx in his *Geschichte Ferdinands I* (II, 356) in error calls one of these monks "Christoph Söll." This assistant of Bucer's in Straßburg, born in Bruneck, was only five years old at that time. Cf. Rörich, *Mitteilungen* III, 231.
6. Franz Schweyger, *Chronik der Stadt Hall 1303-1572* (Innsbruck: Schönherr, 1867).
7. "In 1522 two priests brought Mr. Strauss a summons and strongly disputed with him, for which reason the citizens chased them as well as other priests into the Lord's house." From the chronicle of Hall in the Ferdinandeum; copy in v. Beck's collection. Cf. Waldner, loc. cit., 11.
8. Cf. Waldner, loc. cit.
9. Cf. Waldner, loc. cit., 16.
10. *Eyn ver stendig trostlich leer uber das wert. Sankt Paulus. Der mensch sol sich selbs probieren, und allso von dem brott essen und von dem kelch trinken.* Zu Hall im Inntal von Doctor Jacob Strauss gepredigett. MDXXII.
11. In the Floss Library in Bonn; newly printed by Waldner, 17-39.
12. See Waldner pp. 15-18. For the sake of completeness I also quote Schellhorn's *Ergötzl.* II, 241; Weller's Report 2703; Strickler: *Neuer Versuch eines Literaturverzeichnisses*, Nr. 97. Cf.also Strobel, J. *Strauss, Leben und Schriften,* Misc. III, 1-14.
13. G. L. Schmidt, *Justus Menius, der Reformator Thüringens* (1867).
14. Statthaltereiarchiv Innsbruck. Lib. Causarum Domini I, fol. 30.
15. Cf. Article *Urbanus Rhegius* in vol XXVIII of the *Allgemeine deutsche Biographie*, 374-378.
16. Report of November 9, 1523, Innsbruck Statthaltereiarchiv, Causa Domini 1523-1526, fol. 30.
17. Ibid. Causa Domini, fol. 35. Letter of November 13, 1523.
18. On that occasion Rhegius had gone to meet the prince clad in his priestly vestments and carrying the host. Ruf, loc. cit., 77.
19. On December 23, 1523. Bibliothek Bremen, Cl. VI fasc. V, 1019.
20. Imprecise copy in v. Beck's collection.

NOTES 231

21. *Ain Summa christlicher leer, wie sy Urbanus Rhegius zu Hall im Intal vor etlichen Jaren gepredigt hat,* Published in Augsburg on March 17, 1527. Vol. 875 in Munich. Copy in Beck's collection.
22. *Von der Vollkommenheit und Frucht des Leidens Christi,* gepredigt durch Dr. Urbanum Rhegium, Prediger zu Hall im Inntal, 1522. (O. O. und J.)
23. *Ein Sermon von der Kirchweihe, Gepredigt zu Hall im Intal, Urb. Regii Deutsche Schriften,* 1562; in fol. IV,, 34-38. [Loserth lists this sermon a second time as item #4, and provides the following bibliographic citation: Cit. Zapf, Aug. Bib. II, 667-8.]
24. *Sermon vom dritten Gebot, wie man christlich feyern soll mit Anzeigung etlicher Misbräuche, Gepredigt zu Hall im Intal,* Ibid. 38-45.
25. *Von Reue, Beichte, Busse. Beschluss, zu Hall im Inntal gepredigt durch Urban Regium.* Weller, Repert. Typ. 3623 cites an edition of 1523.
26. *Velit R.V. operam dare ut mandato Ser. mi principis habitacio in illo oppido illi interdicatur.* Original in the Imperial and Royal House, Court and State Archives. Corr. Land. Bishopric of Trent.
27. Schweyger, *Chronik,* 79.
28. Statthaltereiarchiv Innsbruck, Causa Domini, Copy in von Beck's collection.
29. Statthaltereiarchiv Innsbruck, Causa Domini, Lib. I, fol. 85.
30. Orig. at Brixen, *Lade* 112 No. 6. Lit. A; Sinnacher, *Beiträge zur Geschichte der bischöflichen Kirche Säben und Brixen in Tyrol* VII, 194.
31. Statthaltereiarchiv Innsbruck, Causa Domini. Cf. Schönherr, *Das Lutherthum im Kloster Stams im Jahre 1524,* Archiv für Geschichte und Alterthumskunde Tirols II, 82-91.
32. Ab regimine an Martin Steinhauer, administrator of the bailiwick of Bludenz and Sonnenberg, Innsbruck Statthaltereiarchiv. Causa Domini I, anno 1524.
33. Report of May 5, ibid.
34. Innsbruck Statthaltereiarchiv. Causa Domini.
35. Ibid. Causa Domini.
36. Ibid. I, 119.
37. Ibid. Causa Domini. I. 1524.
38. Ibid. I, 112, 113.
39. Ibid. 217-220.
40. Details about this in Schönherr, *Das Lutherthum im Kloster Stams.*
41. "Brixen und seine Umgebung in der Reformationsperiode 1520-1525," XII. *Programm des Brixner Obergymnasiums,* 14.
42. Innsbruck Statthaltereiarchiv, Causa Domini, 128.
43. Ibid.
44. Mandate issued in our city of Vienna on the first day of the month of September anno 1524; and inserted with it the Regensburg mandate of July 6, 1524. As regards the other resolutions of the Regensburg meeting see Baumgarten's History of Charles V, II, 390.
45. Innsbrucker acten, Causa Domini.
46. Ibid.
47. Ibid. Causa Domini I, 148. Note in von Beck's collection.
48. Innsbruck Statthaltereiarchiv, Causa Domini, 323.
49. Ibid. folio 208.
50. Ibid. dated April 1, 1525.

51. Original in the Imperial and Royal House, Court, and State Archives in Vienna (k. k. Haus-, Hof- und Staatsarchiv zu Wien).
52. Innsbruck Statthaltereiarchiv, Causa Domini, 278.
53. Ibid.
54. Ibid., 314.
55. Copy in the k. k. Haus-, Hof- und Staatsarchiv zu Wien. Regest. in von Beck's collection.
56. Original in the correspondence of Cardinal and Prince Bishop Bernhard of Trent in the Imperial and Royal Household, Court, and State Archives in Vienna. Copy in Beck's collection.
57. Dated June 5, 1526. Statthaltereiarchiv Innsbruck, Causa Domini, 357.
58. Ibid.
59. Egger: *Geschichte Tirols*, II, 86. Sinnacher: *Beiträge zur Geschichte der bischöflichen Kirche Säben und Brixen in Tirol* VII, 195.
60. See Stampfer, *Geschichte von Meran*, 69. Cf. Ibid., 395.
61. The report in question is to be found in the archives of the Brixen *Hochstift*. Also cf. Sinnacher VII, 246/7. J. v. Kripp, *Ein Beitrag zur Geschichte der Wiedertäufer in Tirol*, 27.

2. THE RISE OF ANABAPTISM IN TYROL

1. Wiedertäuferacten in Augsburg, veröffentlicht von Meyer in der *Zeitschrift des historischen Vereins für Schwaben*, 1874.
2. His appointment as mining magistrate, dated Innsbruck, April 20, 1525, in the Innsbruck Statthaltereiarchiv. *Bekennen-Buch* 1525, fol. 81. For the city of Strasbourg he built the water conduits and installations for the rafting of logs in the Kinzig and Ehn (Klingenthatl) valleys—for that age most ingenious constructions —thus making the Since of the Black Forest available to that imperial city in need of lumber. (Beck)
3. Sinnacher VII, 259.v. Kripp, 28. Wolfgang's complete testimony in a copy of v. Beck's collection, taken from the Brixen Protocol 1525-1527, fol 759-761. All together 31 points were listed. A second protocol contains 27 points.
4. Haller Raitbuch. In the *Tiroler Bote* erroneously 1525 instead of 1527.
5. Causa Domini fol. 27, Statthaltereiarchiv Innsbruck.
6. Ibid., Causa Domini II, 31.
7. Report of the Innsbruck authorities of June 26, 1527. Causa Domini II, 36.
8. Cod. Austriacus I, 641, Innsbruck Statthaltereiarchiv. Causa Domini II, 82/3.
9. Archives of the Austrian *Kultusministerium* IV, 3. As may easily be seen, the above figures are not exact.
10. Ibid., IV, 3. Copy in v. Beck's collection.
11. In tergo: "The government wants this command to be carried out and obeyed as much as possible."
12. Innsbruck Statthaltereiarchiv. Causa Domini II, 89. Copy in v. Beck's collection.
13. Dated Innsbruck, November 28, 1527. Statthaltereiarchiv, Causa Domini II, 96.
14. Causa Domini II, 95/2.
15. Ibid.
16. Ibid.

17. Ibid., II, 100.
18. Ibid., 98 and 99.
19. Reg.- Arch. zu Salzburg. Copy in v. Beck's collection. Date: December 9, 1527.
20. Cf. about him v. Beck, *Geschichtsbücher der Wiedertäufer*, 61.
21. Copy in v. Beck's collection.
22. The files concerning Schiemer are in the Statthaltereiarchiv in Innsbruck; extracts from them are in v. Beck's collection. Innsbruck, Causa Domini II, 100/2, 191, 102/2.
23. Statthaltereiarchiv. Causa Domini II, s103-104.
24. De dato 15th December 1527.
25. Causa Domini I, 106. Statthaltereiarchiv Innsbruck.
26. Innsbruck Statthaltereiarchiv, Causa Domini II, 106-107.
27. Causa Domini II, 106-197.
28. Sinnacher VII, 262 and protocol XI, 23, Original at Brixen (L. 102, Nr. 5, A.).
29. Protocol XI, 21-25, 93-95.
30. Dated December 31, 1527. Statthaltereiarchiv, Causa Domini II, 113.
31. Ibid., Causa Domini II, 113.
32. Ex regimine to Augustin von Weinegg and Gabriel Gundrichius (in Bavaria): "We are well pleased by what you have written to Councillor Jakob Kuen regarding the Anabaptists, and we ask you to "make diligent inquiries with the Aurdorf administrator and with the present prisoners about the Anabaptist 'principal' and others more" (as was done with Schiemer on December 19, 1527). Innsbruck Statthaltereiarchiv, Causa Domini II, 116.— The Innsbruck government to both Bavarian princes. Causa Domini II, 116. On January 12, 1528 the district magistrate at Freundsberg was directed to obtain confessions (*Urgichten*) from the Anabaptists at Schwaz and to send these to the dukes of Bavaria. Causa Domini 126/2.
33. Ibid. *Embietenbuch*, fol. 101.
34. Causa Domini II, 117. [Translator's note: The mining magistrate in question was Pilgram Marpeck].
35. Draft (of Schiemer's confession) in v. Beck's collection.
36. See appendix No. 1.
37. In the extant sources words such as these are often very mangled and scarcely recognizable. One has to bear in mind what kind of hands copied these Anabaptist writings. Von Beck's collection contains complete copies of Schiemer's writings.
38. "*entia secunde nitontois*" in Cod. The following Latin words, too, are completely mangled.
39. "That's how it is with these scribes; they have not derived their method from God nor have they been taught by God. It is from the Christians and their books that they have stolen all their knowledge."
40. Original: *Onplatzer*, i.e. *anplatzen,* meaning someone who attacks or arrests.
41. For a list of Schiemer's writings see Beck, *Geschichtsbücher der Wiedertäufer*, 62.
42. Statthaltereiarchiv Innsbruck, Causa Comini II, 122. There is also a note stating that already at that time Linhart Spitzhammer, too, was arrested in Rattenberg as an Anabaptist.
43. What the *Chronicles* report is in accord with Schiemer's confession.

3. INROADS AND STATE COUNTER-MEASURES

1. Schlaffer had given written answers to the questions laid before him, and on December 15, 1527 this account had been sent to Innsbruck.
2. Beck's collection contains copies of Hans Schlaffer's confession and account of faith.
3. Statthaltereiarchiv, Causa Domini II, 128/2.
4. See Beck's *Geschichtsbücher der Wiedertäufer,* 64, for a list of Schlaffer's writings. Copies of them in Beck's collection.
5. Cf. the *Geschichtsbücher,* 62/3.
6. Statthaltereiarchiv Innsbruck, Causa Domini II, 135; *Passauer Akten* C/3. Excerpt in Beck's collection. Causa Domini II, 136, 163, 164.0
7. Causa Domini, 137.
8. Ibid., II, 165.
9. Ibid., II, 199/2. On March 24 the cardinal gave thanks for this information.
10. Governmental report of February 23. Causa Domini II, 168.
11. Printed and found in Beck's collection.
12. Causa Domini II, 178
13. Ibid., II, 182, 183.
14. Ibid., II, 185/2.*Pestarchiv*: "In March 1528 the Swabian League provided 400 horses to punish the Anabaptists'
15. Causa Domini II, 187.
16. Ibid.
17. Cited in the royal edict of March 17, 1528. Innsbruck Statthaltereiarchiv, 'From His Royal Majesty' Lib. II, fol. 164.
18. Causa Domini II, 199.
19. Ibid., 202.
20. Ferdinand I's mandate of April 1, 1528, printed. Cf. the Ofner Edict, Cod. Austr. I, 642. Regents' Archives, Causa Domini II, 211. J. v. Kripp, 29. In the printed copy in Beck's collection the words "Sunday Misericordia Domini" are followed by: "This is still being adhered to, even though the date of Misericordia Domini of the year 1528 is by now long past, on account of the 1529 Ordinance (Abschied) of Speier." An extract is in the *Pestarchiv*. There it says further (XVIII, 39): "On the fourth of April a mandate was issued: specifying that the judicial authorities are to swear that they will pass sentence in accordance with the mandate of April 1, and not otherwise." Cf. Causa Domini II, 212. v. Kripp loc. cit., 38.
21. Statthaltereiarchiv Innsbruck. Cop.-Book; Brixen Documents. Cf. Sinnacher VII, 264-265.
22. Causa Domini II, 207.
23. "Black beard, a full face, tall young person, wearing a red '*flaggen*' on a brimmed (*bramtem*) hat or cap and a dark-blue coat; may also call himself 'Balbierer' (barber)." April 2, Causa Domini II, 203. *Embieten- und Befehlbuch* 1528, fol. 205.
24. Causa Domini II, 206, 207.
25. Ibid., 204, de dato April 2.
26. Causa Domini II, 208.
27. Ibid., II, 212.
28. Causa Domini II, 209.

29. Innsbruck, April 5. Orig. 5 Siegel. Brixen, *Lade* 112, No. 5, Lit. A.
30. Innsbruck, April 7. Causa Domini II, 214.
31. Pestarchiv XVII, 39. Causa Domini II, 216; v. Kripp, 30.
32. Innsbruck, April 24. Causa Domini II, 219. By a decision of May 8 his property was left to his wife and children.
33. *Embietenbuch* (book recording governmental messages and orders), fol. 302.
34. Rescript de dato Deutschbrod, April 4, 1528.
35. From His Royal Majesty L. II, 173; Causa Domini II, 216.
36. Causa Domini II, 224 (May 6, 1529).
37. Ibid., II, 222 (May 9).
38. Causa Domini II, 229.
39. Ibid., II, 422.
40. June 29.
41. Contemporaneous copy in Beck's collection.
42. See also *Geschichtsbücher der Wiedertäufer*, 55.
43. Causa Domini II, 278, 288. This is what the *Geschichtsbücher* (p. 56) relate about Hermann's action: In response to the crowd's jibe, "Just see, how wonderfully your teachers lay down their lives for you now," he had called out, "This is indeed the divine truth, for which I will bear witness with my blood." "They were unable to burn his heart; in the end they cast it into a lake." As regards Hermann as a songwriter see *Geschichtsbücher*, 56.
44. Causa Domini II, 308, 312.
45. Ibid., II, 324, 328.
46. Note about this in the Beck collection.
47. *Katholische Blätter für Tirol* 1868, 13. Cf. also the *Bote für Tirol* 1862, 238 about Anabaptists at Rattenberg etc.
48. Causa Domini II, January 1528. Georgii Registr. Prot. XI, fol. 573. Brixen.

4. NORTH AND SOUTH OF THE BRENNER PASS

1. Causa Domini II, 401-402.
2. Causa Domini II, 422.
3. Von kgl. Majestät des oberösterr. Regiments zu Innsbruck, Wiedertäufer Artikel LII, fol. 400.
4. Statthaltereiarchiv, Innsbruck, Causa Domini II, 349. *Pestarchiv* XVIII, 39 (with glosses). Cf. *Geschichtsbücher*, 90.
5. Statthaltereiarchiv, Innsbruck.
6. Causa Domini II, 350.
7. February 27. Causa Domini II, 351.
8. Brixen. Reg. Pract. 11, fol. 224.
9. Causa Domini II, 358.
10. Ibid., 18 March [1529].
11. 18 March. Speier. Innsbruck Archives, *Geschichte vom Hof*, 1529.
12. Orig. in *Hofkammerarchiv*.
13. Causa Domini II, 370.
14. See *Geschichtsbücher der Wiedertäufer*, 90. Cf. Chronick von Hall. Reg. in Beck's collection.

15. Causa Domini II, 490, 505, 541.
16. *Gew* = country as opposed to town; such as the hamlet Gangs near Münichau, where: the magistrate of Kitzbühel, Jörg Perger, had on April 26 surprised a meeting of Anabaptists and, as mentioned above, had arrested seven of them.
17. Causa Domini II, 395, 402. Official extract in the Pestarchiv.
18. The Government to the administrator of Kitzbühel, 25 June 1529. Causa Domini II, 437.
19. *Geschichtsbücher der Wiedertäufer*, 62-63.
20. Ibid.
21. Causa Domini II, 547.
22. Causa Domini II, 424.
23. Ibid., II, 502, 492.
24. Ibid., II, 527.
25. Cf. the account of the execution of H. Nickhinger, H. Ober and Kath. Streicher in J.v. Kripp, 32.
26. Report by Christoff Philipps of Liechtenstein of December 22, 1529. Orig. paper closed by a seal. Innsbruck Statthaltereiarchiv, Pestarchiv, XVIII, 39; J.v. Kripp, 32. Copy in Beck's collection. There are also notes about the costs of such *Rechtfertigungen* in the Innsbruck Statthaltereiarchiv. On October 23 the Rattenberg customs collector Stephan Wessner has to pay 25 gulden to the district sheriff; 31 gulden were paid out for the *Rechtfertigung* of December 22. *Gemeines Missivenbuch* 1530.
27. Causa Domini II, 566.
28. Letter addressed to the government, Innsbruck, December 25, 1529. Causa Domini II, 566.
29. Government to Peter Braunecker, magistrate at Sonnenburg in December 1529. Causa Domini II, 545. Both executed December 10, 1529, *Hofkammerarchiv*, which also notes the costs of the trial. Innsbruck Archives. *Embieten und Befehlbuch* anno 1529. Cf. *Geschichtsbücher*.
30. Royal decree, Prague, March 16, 1530. Vienna *Hofkammerarchiv*.
31. As regards the conditions on which Jörg von Werth and Michael Resch were granted a reprieve, see enclosures No. 4.
32. Causa Domini II, 1529.
33. Ibid., II, 1529. Report of May 30.
34. Ibid., Report of September 9, Causa Domini II, 533/2.
35. Ibid.
36. Causa Domini II, 350, 374. Missivenbuch 1529.
37. Causa Domini II, 455, 456. Government protocol 11, fol. 870, Brixen. Causa Domini, 468.
38. Register of expenses incurred in connection with the Anabaptists in the Michelsburg judicial district, (more precisely:) "for the 15 Anabaptists taken to Brixen: 1) Gregori Weber together with Wieser and three of his sons arrested on April 27, these five being taken to Brixen... Further, on May 21 were arrested the Koffler woman from Reischach, Caspar Maier Pauln; on May 24 Wilhelm Sämsfeuer at Pflaurenz, Marx in der Au, Hans Vischer at Sonnenburg, Pirchner at Saln, the widow Agnes at Erspan, the Pader woman from S. Laurenzen, the old Wieser woman and her daughter." Excerpt from the original in *Lade* 112, No. 6, Lit. B. Copy in Beck's collection. The confessions (*Urgicht und Bekanntnus*) of these

persons were sent to Innsbruck on June 4. Brixen Archive. Georg. Reg.-Prot. 11, fol. 845.
39. "A great number of people were present, but justice was carried out without mishap." What a good many of the onlookers may well have thought in their hearts is put into words by Jörg Rath, executed at Innsbruck in 1561. He testified "that he had seen with his own eyes how at Stein somebody professing that particular faith was being burned to death, that he had taken that deeply to heart and had come to think that there must be a mighty grace of God with people like that to let them remain so steadfast in their hearts right unto death." (Cod. Gran)
40. Original in *Lade* 112, No. 5, littera A.
41. Innsbruck Statthaltereiarchiv, Causa Domini ad annum 1528, *Embietenbuch*.
42. Reply dated February 25. Causa Domini II, 351.
43. Original: *Einschichten*.
44. Causa Domini II, 562.
45. June 18, 1529. Causa Domini ad annum 1529.
46. *Embieten- und Befehlsbuch* (record of governmental messages and orders), 1529.
47. To supplement the above overview (on p. 478) of the spread of Anabaptists in Tyrol it might here be mentioned that some of these came to notice also in Stubai and in September 1529 were being pursued there. Causa Domini II, ad annum 1529.

5. HUTTER AND PERSECUTION IN TYROL, 1529-30

1. *Geschichtsbücher*, 84. That is also where the opinion is refuted that Hutter hailed from Welsperg in the Puster Valley. There is no ground at all for the assertion of earlier writers, such as Plarre, Meschovius, and even of Hast still (*Geschichte der Wiedertäufer*, 198) to the effect that Hutter was a disciple of Nicolous Storch and a hatter's son and that he, as also more recent researchers maintain, traveled about in Silesia and Bavaria and that he came to Moravia when expelled from Silesia. Gastius and others even confuse him with Hans Hut, who had already died in 1527 at Augsburg.
2. *Geschichtsbücher*, 84-5.
3. Christian Hutter, Leonhard and Peter Gayler, Christian Planer, Georg Esler with his wife, Caspar Schneider, Erhard Schmiedknecht, and Ursula, daughter of Till von Luenz. Report of July 27, 1529. Causa Domini II, 469.
4. Report of June 24, 1529.
5. Report of June 24, 1529. Causa Comini II, 498.
6. Original: *bestäten* = interrogating or instructing
7. Causa Domini II, 550. Given that Gregor Weber had already been put to death in Brixen not long ago [on June 4, 1529], how could he (v. Kripp, 36) now be tried in December 1527 [sic; should read 1529] together with Agnes Hutter?
8. *Geschichtsbücher*, 85.
9. Ibid.
10. *Geschichtsbücher*, 85.
11. As to the whole literature about Jörg from Chur see v. Beck, *Geschichtsbücher der Wiedertäufer*, 79-80.

12. According to v. Beck's (hand-written) biography of Blaurock.
13. Causa Domini II, 358.
14. Causa Domini II, 492.
15. On August 24, 1529.
16. Causa Domini II, 491.
17. *Geschichtsbücher*, 81
18. Causa Domini II, 507. A. Wolf, *Geschichtsbilder aus Österreich* I, 68, 69.
19. See above, 479.
20. See *Geschichtsbücher,* 89.
21. Causa Domini II, 528, 530-532; v. Kripp, 36.
22. *Hofkammerarchiv,* Innsbruck, Causa Domini II, 518, 530.
23. Causa Domini II, 340. "On account of weakness" Tschander was not in the chair.
24. Causa Domini II, 568.
25. *Gemeines Missivenbuch*, 1530; v. Kripp, 36.
26. Causa Domini II, 548.
27. Ibid., III, ad anno 1530, January 23.
28. Innsbruck Statthaltereiarchiv. To His Majesty the King LIV, 18.
29. Causa Domini III, 5.
30. *Geschichtsbücher*, 93.
31. Causa Domini III, 101.
32. The files concerning Partzner are in the Innsbruck Statthaltereiarchiv. Causa Domini III, 10, 16, 141, 143. To His Royal Majesty IV, 52.
33. Statthaltereiarchiv, Causa Domini III, 35, 86. From His Royal Majesty III, 62.
34. Printed. In the Pestarchiv XVIII, 39 it says: On March 2, 1530 was issued a mandate, which among other things decreed that those giving shelter to Anabaptists are to be punished with imprisonment as befits. Causa Domini III, 52. A printed sample and a copy in Beck's collection.
35. Kripp loc. cit. 34, dated August 3. *Embietenbuch* 1530, fol. 186.
36. Order for the eradication of Anabaptists. Lib. Causa Domini, fol 125.
37. The official excerpt from the mandate (Pestarchiv) reads: On July 30, 1530 a mandate was issued to the effect that "anybody providing information leading definitely to the arrest of one or more Anabaptists is to receive between 30 and 40 fl. from the chamber of finances."
38. Lib. Causa Domini, fol. 125.
39. *Embietenbuch,* 20.
40. Sinnacher VII, 283.
41. Date: Prague, February 8, 1530. From His Royal Majesty, Lib. 3, fol. 17-20.
42. Dated February 9, 1530. To His Royal Majesty, *Regiment* III, 50.
43. Causa Domini III, 53, 54.
44. In the manuscript of Kilian Walch at Gran and in Cod. 212 at Pressburg (Bratislava). See *Geschichtsbücher,* 128.
45. Beck's collection contains a copy of a manuscript (originally from Levar) in the Pressburg Lyceum.
46. This is reported in detail in the *Geschichtsbücher der Wiedertäufer,* 91-102.
47. He describes Auspitz as a "rich, precious island, where wine, corn, fish, meat, and all manner of food is more abundant than anywhere in Germany." Reublin's letter of January 26, 1531 to Marpeck in Cornelius, *Geschichte des Münsterschen Aufruhrs* II, 253-259.

6. THE PRINCIPAL MANDATE OF MAY 12, 1532

1. *Geschichtsbücher*, 102.
2. Fontes rer. Austr. I, 487. The number given by Kirchmair is somewhat too high. The above-mentioned report to Ferdinand I speaks of 700, and another report sent eight years later only mentions a figure of 600 persons executed.
3. P. 105.
4. *Hofkammerarchiv* sub "court finances." Copy in Beck's collection.
5. For example, the activities of the above-mentioned Michael Rauch with his one-horse wagon (*Ainspänniger*) led to a quarrel with Salzburg. Here follow some data from "Michael Rauch's register of Anabaptist properties"

    1. Rattenberg district: a) Nickinger's real estate sold for 140 fl.—b) Krenheuser's house and a half-fief (*Halblehen*) is applied for (or claimed?) by a Rattenberg burgher.—c) Sold Obiger's property for 103 gulden. Claimed by his wife and children.—d) On March 27 spent a day at Colfass concerning Schornschlager's property—reverted (to the state). Kufstein (Sept. 19) concerning the confiscated goods of Wolfgang from Elmaw and of Michel from Weissenbach; the inventory notes what is to go to the abandoned children and the heirs: Linhart Hofer left behind two under-age children and a blind father. Michel Weissenbach's two sons left behind three children, Paul Frauenhofer four children, Wolf im Ried eight children, etc.

    3. In the Altrasen district; inventories taken at Gregor Weber's and at Blasi's from Crossen.

    4. In the Schöneck district: Peter Getzenberger, who was executed, left real estate behind. One named Binder has also taken to flight.

    5. In the Bozen district: Sequestered the property abandoned by Simon Koben., as well as that of Rosina, widow of Leonhard Mayer, of Benedikt Gamperer, of Margaret, widow of Gotthard in Sessa, daughter of Mrs. Gamper in the Au, with a sister's share in the farm at Sassen. Jörg Tollinger, who lived for a while in Kurtatsch, has no property. Next follows a list of confiscations:

    6. on the Rittner Horn,
    7. Altenburg,
    8. Kaltern,
    9. Vells.

    Another inventory was taken by Ernst Brandt at Stibling, listing no less than 21 cases, among them Sigmund Schützinger, "fugitive." Georg Vasser has no property of his own. [Translator's Note: Cf. *Chronicle of the Hutterian Brethren* about both Schützinger and Georg Fasser/Vasser.] Copy of this register, in many places hardly readable, in Beck's collection.
6. [Translator's note: Cf. No. 3 in Michael Rauch's register of Anabaptist properties.]
7. Causa Domini III, 224. *Gemeines Befehlbuch* 1531.
8. Causa Domini III, 113; N.F. 602. [Translator's note: About Ulrich Müll(n)er cf. *Chronicle of the Hutterian Brethren*, 376.]
9. Report of March 7. Causa Domini III, 205/2.
10. February 22. Causa Domini III, 199
11. Causa Domini 1531. Report of May 14.
12. Report of September 6.

13. Causa Domini 1531. Report of June 11 and August 7.
14. Report of September 26. Causa Domini III, 188.
15. Report of December 22. *Gemeines Befehluch* ("Common Book of orders" 1531) and Brixen files: Hans Tuchmacher baptizes Lamprecht Gruber and the latter's wife.
16. Causa Domini III, 186.
17. *Gemeines Befehluch* 1531.
18. Causa Domini III, 240.
19. Causa Domini III, 264.
20. The term "Taufgesinnten" is translated here as "baptism-minded folk."
21. *Gemeines Befehlbuch* 1531. Reports of September 9 and December 22, Causa Domini 1531.
22. Causa Domini III, 107.
23. Sinnacher VII, 293.
24. *Embieten- und Befehlsbuch* 1531, fol. 337.
25. To His Royal Majesty, Lib V, fol. 7.
26. *Pestarchiv* XVIII, 39; Kripp, 37.
27. Report of March 9, 1532. To His Royal Majesty V, fol.28/2.
28. Innsbruck Statthaltereiarchiv. Lib. Causa Domini IV, 17 of March 10, 1532. To His Royal Majesty V, fol. 28/2.
29. According to an instruction dated March 15, 1532, the district sheriff (*Landrichter*) Sebastian Hofwirth was to try and ascertain, with or without torture, where Jakob Hutter and other Anabaptists found a refuge in and around Sterzing, who was their overseer and author of the writing with concealed name and character that had recently been found with one arrested Anabaptist and in which a certain Oswald Schuster is pilloried as a horrible traitor and Judas, who in prison had divulged everything he knew, "not only his sisters and brothers but also all non-members who had sheltered them." The sheriff was also to inquire about the key to the secret writing. Causa Domini IV, 20. His epistles make it obvious that the overseer in question was Jakob Hutter.
30. To His Royal Majesty V, 28.
31. Ibid., 37.
32. Printed. Causa Domini IV, 34. Extract in the Pestarchiv: "On May 12 a mandate was issued against those giving shelter to Anabaptists, ordering them to be arrested, to be proceeded against with interrogation and torture, and to be punished in body and property with no mercy shown."
33. In spite of all this, in November 1532 the government received information that in an old mining tunnel near Freundsberg 30-40 Anabaptists had come together for a celebration of the Lord's Supper.
34. Causa Domini IV, 7. Date: February 24, 1532. Copy in Beck's collection.
35. original: *auf dem Bad*
36. Causa Domini IV, 50. A similar reprimand was given to the district magistrate at Sterzing, Andre Flamm. Causa Domini IV, 50/1. Cf. *Schützenzeitung* 1872, No. 25-27.
37. Causa Domini IV, 54.
38. Report of September 28, loc. cit.
39. Report of September 28 to Friedrich Franz von Schneeburg. Causa Domini IV, 54.

40. Hans Amon is said to have been in Tyrol already in 1531 and to have baptized there in various places, particularly on the Rittner Horn. Causa Domini IV, 69.
41. Causa Domini.
42. Füchter lay in prison in May 1532. There he sang songs such as "When bearing the cross we went" and others. At the government's order he was examined under torture and was condemned to death. Causa Domini IV, 37. The jurors had to swear to pass judgment on him as though he were, i.e. to condemn him to death. *Innsbruck Acten.* See *Geschichtsbücher*, 106.
43. Causa Domini IV, 68-69.
44. Causa Domini IV, 86.
45. Original in *Lade* 112, No. 5, Lit. B, Brixen.
46. Causa Domini IV, 104.
47. Ibid., IV, 109.
48. *Geschichtsbücher der Wiedertäufer*, where also Fest's writings are listed.
49. *Geschichtsbücher*, 107-108. Christian and Thomas Häring would later live as ministers of temporal needs in the church in Moravia.
50. Sinnacher VII, 300.
51. *Geschichtsbücher* contain detailed accounts of this (pp. 108 and 109). A man named Wölfl among the captives was gripped by fear, but six other brothers invite Jakob Hutter and Hans Tuchmacher to be witnesses at their wedding feast.
52. Hutter's epistle to the saints of God in the Puster, Adige, and Isar valleys, sent from Moravia by brother Peter Veit. Copy in v. Beck's collection.
53. He was captured in 1533 at Götzenberg.
54. "On Corpus Christi Day [i.e. the Thursday after Trinity Sunday—the Sunday after Pentecost] of the year 1533 they (the Anabaptists) held a joint meeting in the woods above Erenpurg" and there had victuals provided for them from brothers in the neighborhood and Götzenberg." Hutteri interrog.
55. An kgl. Majestät (To His Royal Majesty) LV, 203-205.
56. There was lively traffic to and fro between Tyrol and Moravia. Apart from the two "missives" to the overseers in Moravia seized on Anabaptists earlier on, an identical letter was found on two "brothers" in Kitzbühel. It tells of 500 Anabaptists living in one house at Auspitz and of about 400 in another house, and that they are in constant correspondence with those in Tyrol. The government requests *ut ibi eiciantur.* An kgl. Majestät V, 303.
57. Ordinances containing this information on June 18, 1533 were sent to Sterzing, Gufidaun, to the Rittner Horn, to Rodenegg, Kitzbühel, St. Petersberg, and Lienz, the places, where the Anabaptist overseers were chiefly suspected to be.
58. The government had received information about the number of Anabaptists at Auspitz from the mouth of a prisoner, Offerus Griesinger or Griesstätter, who had recently been captured at Hofgarten. Warrant of arrest against this Anabaptist who had escaped again. Causa Domini IV, 104, 132.
59. Causa Domini IV, 113-114.
60. Ibid., IV, 114-115.
61. This is what occasioned the order of August 16 of "not letting anybody get a passage on river boats without being questioned." Pestarchiv and Lib. Causa Domini IV, 119; VI, 65, 66, 103. Causa Domini IV, 130 "about the church on the *Stamser Joch.*"

62. Prot. XIV, fol. 419. Brixen, to the government September 22, 1533. Brixen, *Lade* 112, No. 5, B, to the bishop of Brixen, September 26.
63. Causa Domini 1533, IV, 131. Governmental report of September 26, 1533 to Steinach, Sterzing, and Freundsberg.
64. An kgl. Majestät V, 238.
65. Causa Domini IV, 130.
66. Ibid., IV, 129.
67. An kgl. Majestät V, 263; Sinnacher VII, 300; Kripp, 38.
68. Von kgl. Majestät IV, 367.
69. Prot. XIV, 593.
70. The government to His Royal Majesty V, 215; August 2, 1533; in the Innsbruck archives and the Court Chamber archives in Vienna. Additional information available in: Court Chamber Archives, Court Finances 16, de dato February 8, 1532; a memorial of the Archbishop of Salzburg ibid., and advice in reply to the complaint of the Cardinal of Salzburg, ibid.
71. Missivenbuch 1533/4. It was specified, though, that fugitive Anabaptists were not to derive any benefit from this arrangement.
72. Causa Domini 1533, fol. 114.
73. The date is derived from the fact that at the interrogation of his daughter on May 24 Gasser is referred to as having been executed at Bozen.
74. Original in Beck's collection.
75. See enclosures No. 8 and 9.
76. Causa Domini.
77. Innsbruck archives. Draft. Copy in Beck's collection.
78. Contemporaneous copy in Beck's collection. Causa Domini IV,105.
79. Report of June 21, 1533. Original in Brixen, *Lade* 112, No. 5, Lit. B.
80. Government protocol XIII fol. 248, 256. Reply de dato July 8, Brixen, Lade 112, No. 5, Lit. B.
81. Original at Brixen Lade 112, No. 5, Lit. B.
82. An kgl. Majestät, Lib. V, fol. 207.
83. Original in Brixen, *Lade* 112, No. 5, Lit. B.
84. According to a note in Beck's collection.
85. Reg. Prot. 14.
86. To judge by the style, the epistle in question might have been by Hutter, given that in the first letter he wrote it says similarly, "We also greet you, each one in particular." Prot. 14, fol. 22.
87. Reg. Prot., fol. 400.
88. Innsbruck archives.
89. Prot(ocol). XIV, fol. 455-459.
90. Brixen, October 21. Gov. Prot. XIV, fol.470.
91. The (Brixen) episcopal register contains under October 24 the false news (on p. 29 in Kripp's book) that the *Vorsteher* Hans Tuchmacher had been among the ten captured at the Götzenberg and had been executed at Michelsburg with the others.
92. November 10, Reg. Prot. XIV, fol.578.
93. Prot(ocol) XIV, folio 565.
94. Innsbruck, December 20. Original at Brixen, *Lade* 112, No. 5, Lit(tera) B. Royal copy thereof to be sent to Sir Caspar. Cf. also Causa Domini IV of December 12.

95. Causa Domini IV, 142, de dato January 10, 1534.

7. "HUTTERIAN BRETHREN" IN MORAVIA

1. Etliche gar schöne und tröstliche Episteln von unserem lieben bruedern und diener Christi Hans Amon. [*Some beautiful and comforting epistles by our dear brother and servant of Christ Hans Amon.*] The first of these is to Leonhart Schmerbacher. Copy in v. Beck's collection.
2. The wording is somewhat unclear: *Wie sich etlich auf seine Zukunft gezogen hinten.*
3. Cod. Poson, 235. Copy Beck's collection.
4. Cod. Amsterdam of 1592, fol. 75-79.
5. Ibid. These disputes are also briefly touched upon in *Geschichtsbücher*, 113.
6. The dates are derived from Hutter's letter of November 1533. At the beginning Hutter there refers to this letter as already the third one he had sent to the brethren in Tyrol. On the Thursday after Simon and Jude (October 30), he says, he had dispatched to them Kunz Maurer and Michael Schuster; "they will give an oral account of what is not contained in the letter and of how things are in the community. The day after the two brothers had left, Peter Voyt arrived with all those you had sent with him. That was a heartfelt, great joy to us, and our hearts leaped with gladness... Just a few days later more brothers and sisters and several children arrived from the Puster and Inn valleys. You know who they are. On the same day our dear brother Klaus arrived from Carinthia and brought seven persons with him. They have all found faith here; praise be to God. Not long after that, brother Stadler arrived with his children, and soon after that Peter Hutter with twenty-four souls, and the day before eighteen souls arrived from Hesse. So we reckon that in the short time of three or four weeks the Lord added over 120 or 130 souls to the church, who were baptized and taken into the brotherhood and whom we have all welcomed and received as the Lord himself." Hutter tells of a strange natural phenomenon he observed jointly with many brothers and sisters. "The Lord alone knows what he had in mind and wanted to show us by it." The epistle concludes with greetings to the dear sisters Gretl Marbeck and Urschi Puchl, both residing in the Rattenberg judicial district, and with the news that Jörg Vasser's wife and Bärbl from Jenbach had been reaccepted into the unity of the church.
7. Cf. *Zeitschrift für historische Theologie* XXIX, 1859.
8. *Geschichtsbücher*, 116.
9. Jakob Hutter's epistle to the prisoners at Hohenwarth. Copy in Beck's collection.

8. THE TRIAL OF THE WOLKENSTEIN FAMILY, 1534

1. The court records concerning administrator Zimmermann are in the Statthaltereiarchiv at Innsbruck, Causa Domini IV, 142, 146-148, 150/2 (here the above-mentioned order) and Brixen, *Lade* 112, No. 5, littera B; No. 6, littera C. In his confession he emphatically denies being an Anabaptist.
2. Brixen, l. c.

3. Causa Domini IV, 142.
4. Ibid.
5. Report of January 25. Prot. XIV, fol. 93.
6. Innsbruck government to Friedrich Füeger in Taufers, 28 January 1534. Causa Domini IV, 197-198, also enclosing instructions for the Innsbruck deputy marshal about how to proceed, and the questions to be asked. Government to Füeger, 30 January 1534. Causa Domini IV, 183/1.
7. Causa Domini IV, 149.
8. Innsbruck Archives.
9. Brixen, Protoc. XIV, fol. 546.
10. Causa Domini IV, 150/2.
11. Original in *Lade* 112, No. 6, lit(tera) C.
12. Brixen, February 22, 1534. Prot. XIV, fol. 765.
13. Contemporaneous copy in Beck's collection. Original in Brixen, *Lade* 112, No. 6, Litt. E.
14. Brixen archives, *Lade* 112, No. 6, Lit. C. About Teutenhofen and Hans von Wolkenstein standing surety for the accused, undated.
15. Brixen Archives. Prot. XIV, fol. 783. Cf. also the report of March 7, Brixen, *Lade* 112, No. 6, Litt. C, in which the government asks for somebody to be newly sent to Taufers in order to convert the prisoners, and Prot. XIV, fol. 823.
16. To His Royal Majesty V, 293/2. March 7.
17. Original at Brixen *Lade* 112, No. 6, Lit. C.
18. A report about this was sent to King Ferdinand: To His Royal Majesty V, 310; see appendix No. 13.
19. Causa Domini IV, 166. Brixen Archives. Original in *Lade* 112, No. 6, Lit. C.
20. Original in Brixen, loc.cit.
21. Innsbruck Archives. From his Royal Majesty IV, 487-488.Contemporaneous copy at Brixen, *Lade* 112. No. 6, Lit. C.
22. Dated July 14, 1535. Causa Domini IV, 192.
23. Decree of May 20.
24. See appendix No. 16.
25. Report of October 6.
26. Reg. Georgii Brixen. Prot. XIV, 1326.
27. From His Royal Majesty IV, 621.
28. Prot. XIV, 729.
29. Ibid., XIV, 767.
30. Causa Domini IV, 153.
31. St. Prot. XIV, 775.
32. *Missivenbuch* 1534. Renewed by mandate from Vienna of November 18, 1536.
33. Original: *um seiner verhandlung abzukommen*. Reg. Prot. No. 18 ad annum 1534.
34. 1534, March 3. Prot. XIV, 785.
35. Causa Domini IV, 155/2.
36. Ibid. IV, 156/2.
37. From His Royal Majesty IV, 312-316.Original in Beck's collection. See appendix No. 12.
38. Causa Domini IV 182. Also printed. In an extract in the Pestarchiv: "On May 9, 1534 a hortatory mandate was issued to the ecclesiastical and secular authorities,

affirming previous mandates against the Anabaptists and decreeing that those sheltering and accommodating them be punished, too."

39. Innsbruck, May 12. Original in Brixen, *Lade* 112, No. 5, Lit. B.
40. *Embietenbuch* 1534, fol. 159.
41. Causa Domini IV, 182/2.
42. Ibid. IV, 184/185.
43. One night in August [1534] a "nook-and-corner preacher" by the name of Wölfl Gayshirt, as well as eleven other persons, men and women, were being spied out and arrested in the house of the weaver Gozmann, but before long were set free again, for which action the district magistrate (sheriff) of Meran on August 26 (Causa Domini IV, 201-202) incurred the displeasure of the government. He was ordered to arrest and interrogate the weaver Gozmann as well as Paul Glaser to find out if they might be tainted with Anabaptism. Since Wölfl had stated that he had spent a night with Burkhart Cramer and there had read in a testament [New Testament?], he, too, was to be interrogated as to whether also he "was involved in the Anabaptist sect." "We have been informed that Wölfl was instrumental in Jakob Hutter's becoming an Anabaptist overseer." Wölfl was to submit a confession and was then to be dealt with in accordance with the mandates. He was reported to have been rebaptized twice—"once with the finger (sic!) and afterwards with water." However, already on September 13 we hear that the authorities were ready to temper justice with mercy in dealing with these people but that they had to pay their feeding expenses, swear to keep the peace, on a Sunday or feast day confess to the priest of Meran and receive Holy Communion. (Causa Domini, loc. cit.).

9. PERSECUTION IN MORAVIA

1. Original in Brixen *Lade* 112, No. 5, Lit. B. Causa Domini IV, 225. April 4, 1535. Contemporaneous copy in Beck's collection. See appendices No.12 and 15. Curiously enough, later on and especially in the year 1540 the Moravian estates pretended to know nothing of a formal diet decision to generally expel the Anabaptists from Moravia and informed the sovereign prince that to the best of their knowledge at that Znaim diet only those nobles actually harboring Anabaptists on their estates had promised to expel them. (Moravian *Pamatkenbuch*) That is why the Anabaptists could, and did, keep on maintaining themselves in Moravia.
2. Cod. 218 in Pressburg. G. J. X. 4 in Gran.
3. Cf. also the *Geschichtsbücher*, 116, 117.
4. See the printed versions in. Beck's *Geschichtsbücher*. None of them is correct, nor is that in Hast, *Wiedertäufer,* 201-204. See appendix No. 17.
5. Innsbruck Statthaltereiarchiv, An kgl. Majestät, V, 487; Das Regiment an den König, 1535, July 28.

10. PERSECUTION IN AUSTRIA AND BEYOND IN 1535

1. Another epistle from dear brother Jacob Hutter, year 1535. Copy in Beck's collection. S. Fischer, *Antwort* J III/2.
2. An kgl. Majestät V, 473. Statthaltereiarchiv Innsbruck, Das Regiment an den Cardinal von Trient, June 29, 1525.
3. Von kgl. Majestät V, 42-43, dated April 4. The same date of April 16 to the regent and councillors at Brixen. Original in Brixen archives, Lade 112, No. 5, Lit. B; Causa Domini IV, 225 of April 10; ibid., IV, 230, 232.
4. Steirisches Landesarchiv.
5. Buchholz IV, 77-478.
6. München, Staatsarchiv.
7. Von kgl. Majestät V, 92.
8. Original in Haus-, Hof- und Staatsarchiv. Correspondenz mit dem Cardinal Bernhard von Trient.
9. An kgl. Majestät V, 484.
10. Brixen archives, *Lade* 112, No. 6, Lit. G. Prot. XIV, fol. 304. His Royal Majesty is being notified.
11. Causa Domini IV, 290, 281.
12. Brixen, Prot. XLV, fol.326; ibid., fol. 324.
13. Lib. Causa Domini IV, 285.
14. The second epistle of Jakob Hutter to the church community in Moravia. Written from the county of Tyrol through Wölflin Zimmermann, anno 1535. In the manuscripts No. 190, 212 and 213 of the Pressburg cathedral chapter; in codex VIII g, 39 at Pest. Copy in Beck's collection. This also contained the Cod. Reslig (?), which is no longer extant elsewhere.
15. In manuscripts No. 190, 212 and 219 at Pressburg and in a manuscript from Levar in the Protestant Lyceum in Pressburg; in the latter Wolfgang Zimmermann is erroneously named as the carrier of the letter. Copy in Beck's collection.
16. In the Pressburg manuscripts No. 190 and 219 and in the Pest manuscript No. V 9. Copy in Beck's collection.
17. In his *Geschichtsbücher*, 121, note Beck reproduces the most telling passage in the letter.
18. P. 122.
19. Causa Domini IV, 294.
20. Brixen, Dec. 4. Brixen tenders an apology to Jörg of Firmian. Prot. XV, fol. 284.
21. "Firmian: capture of overseer Hutter in the judicial district of Gufidaun." Causa Domini IV, 296/1-2.
22. Interrogation of Katharina Hutter on December 3, 1535 at Klausen.
23. December 10, 1535. Causa Domini IV, 296: to the bishop of Brixen. Original at Brixen, *Lade* 112, No. 6, Lit. F.
24. Causa Domini IV, 297/2. Order to Adam Prew to keep the prisoners well guarded at Gufidaun.

11. HUTTER'S TRIAL AND EXECUTION

1. Interrogations of Katharina Hutter.
2. P. 122, Note.
3. Cod. G. J. X., 9 in Gran.
4. Innsbruck Statthaltereiarchiv V, fol. 536.
5. Interrogatoria and questions to be put to Jacob Hutter, the Anabaptist overseer, regarding his activities in the judicial district of Michelsberg. Draft from 1536 in the archives of the Brixen prince bishop; *Lade* 112, No. 6, Lit. F.
6. Innsbruck Statthaltereiarchiv, Lib. Causa Domini IV, 298-299.
7. Innsbruck Statthaltereiarchiv, Von der kgl. Majestät; Lib. V, 1535, fol. 314-316.
8. Pestarchiv, Innsbruck XVIII, 39.
9. Ibid., Causa Domini IV, 299. On January 6 the two beadles are assigned "*6 fl. 43 kr. rheinisch*" as wages; *Embietenbuch*, fol. 448.
10. Causa Domini IV, 311.
11. P. 122.
12. Causa Domini V, 163.
13. Vasser's epistles, Cod. 190, fol. 493-500.
14. I.e. February 24, more correctly on February 25.
15. *Embietenbuch,* fol. 449-450.
16. Causa Domini IV, 307, 335/2, 375.
17. Hutter was also celebrated in songs:
    The church, the Christian Mother,
    so many sons has lost,
    among them Jakob Hutter,
    whom God himself did choose.
    Song by Anabaptist Jörg Bruckmaier, executed 50 years later at Ried in Upper Austria.
18. In Gabriel Kirschner's chronicle: "What took place among the brethren who, driven out of the whole German nation, for the sake of faith, flocked to the land of Moravia to sojourn there, from the year 1528 to the year 1541"—a printed writing that has almost wholly vanished and is presently only known through an extract in Dr. Fischer's *Hutter-Wiedertouf-Taubenkobel* ("Hutter's Anabaptist Dove-Cote"), Ingolstadt 1607, and in Ottius, *Annales Anabaptistici* (Basel 1672).
19. *Gründliche, kurzgefasste Historia von Münster'schen Wiedertäufern* (Munich 1589) in 4th ed.
20. v. Kripp: *Ein Beitrag zur Geschichte der Wiedertäufer in Tirol* (Innsbruck 1857); Adam Wolf: *Gesch. Bilder aus Österreich* I, 72.
21. *Geschichtsbücher der Wiedertäufer,* 41-44.
22. In Cod. VIII, g. 27, fol. 374 at Pest and in Cod. 190, fol.16 of the Pressburg cathedral chapter.
23. In Cod. 234 at Pressburg and Cod. VIII g. 27 at Pest. Copies thereof, as well as of the previous items in Beck's collection.
24. Communications from Calvary's Antiquariat I, Berlin 1870. As regards Hutter's writings, only the above-mentioned epistles have been preserved. Further epistles were intercepted and came to form part of the investigation files, which are no longer extant. Hutter has had erroneously ascribed to him: 1. Riedemann's

"Account" etc. See Gottfried Arnold, *Kirchen- und Ketzerhistorie* 2. *Anschläg und Fürwenden der blinden verkerten Welt und aller Gottlosen gegen die Frommen* ("Plots and dodges of the blind and wrong-headed world and of all the godless against the devout," Cod. G.I. VII, 31. Strigon, ex 1575); 3. *Das verbütschiert mit sieben Siegeln verschlossene Buch*, understood to be either Sebastian Franck's "The book locked with seven seals" or most likely Hans Hut's booklet "About the book and the seven seals, as may be read in the Apocalypse"—a booklet that the [Hutterian] brothers referred to as "the book with the seven seals."

1. POST-HUTTER: OFFRUS GRIESINGER, 1536-1538

1. Cf. G. H. Williams' *Radical Reformation*, 218 for further details about the Mödling prisoners.
2. Before March 31, 1536. See Käls' Epistles.
3. De dato June 18, 1533. Statthaltereiarchiv Innsbruck.
4. Taja is short for taglia, meaning a reward or compensation.
5. Causa Domini IV, 104, 132.
6. *Geschichtsbücher der Wiedertäufer*, 130.
7. Leonhard Seiler and others.
8. Brixen Archives, *Lade* 112, No.11, Littera P.
9. J. v. Beck is inclined to shift this news reported in the *Geschichtsbücher* (p. 131) to the year 1537. It is, however, only the year 1536 that this whole matter fits into. The very fact that Hans Amon's letter refers to "the great sermon brother Jakob preached by his death" speaks for 1536.
10. An unseren gn. Herrn in Brixen, Brixen, April 12. Contemporaneous copy in v. Beck's collection.
11. May 2, 1536.
12. Causa Domini IV, 153, 156.
13. Causa Domini IV, 397/2.
14. Ibid., IV, 398.
15. *Geschichtsbücher*, 131.
16. Brixen Archives: *Lade* 112, No. 11, Litterae C and D.
17. Causa Domini IV, 410.
18. Brixen Archives: *Lade* 112, No. 12, Littera D.
19. *Gesch. vom Hof. 1536*. Innsbruck Archives. Soon afterwards Offenhauser received 10 gulden for the same reason. *Embietenbuch*.
20. Original: "Wir fanden verbrannte und unverbrannte wiedertäuferische,Legenheiten' und ein Heimzeichen nebst einer Behausung..."
21. *Geschichtsbücher*, 131.
22. Brixen Archives. Copy in v. Beck's collection.
23. Contemporaneous copy in v. Beck's collection.
24. Brixen, *Lade* 112, No. 6, littera G.
25. Causa Domini IV, 422.
26. Ibid., 423/2.
27. Brixener Acten.
28. December 16, 1536. Causa Domini IV, 1536.

29. Mandatenbuch, fol. 72.
30. Account given by Christel Kuedegen about himself. Contemporaneous copy in v. Beck's collection.
31. Thus entered in the judicial record of the principality (domain) of Begern.
32. Jörg Ebner had in 1534 been sentenced and executed at Brixen.
33. Original de dato July 6, 1536. Copy in Brixen archives, Lade 112, No. 5, littera B.
34. Brixen, Regist., *Lade* 112, No. 11, littera C.
35. Ibid., *Lade* 112, No. 5, litter C. *Geschichten vom Hof* 1536, fol. 96-97. See addendum No. 1.
36. Ibid., Extract in the Pestarchiv, Lib. Causa Domini IV, 429-430.
37. Ibid., *Lade* 112, No. 11, littera B.
38. Von kgl. Majestät V, fol. 406. Innsbruck Statthaltereiarchiv.
39. Copy in v. Beck's collection.
40. Causa Domini. Extract in v. Beck's collection.
41. Causa Domini V, 36.
42. Ibid., February 18.
43. Innsbruck Statthaltereiarchiv, Von kgl. Majestät VI, 138.
44. According to a contemporaneous copy of the files in question in the Brixen archives (*Lade* 112, No. 11, littera H). Confession of Caspar Huber from Sanct Sigmunden before Christoph Ochs, district magistrate at St. Michelsburg. Caspar stated that he had two years ago moved to Auspitz in Moravia, that he had plied his trade there and had been baptized by Jakob Hutter in the presence of all brothers and sisters, that at present he knew of only two overseers in Moravia, Hans Tuchmacher and one named Christoph, of whom he did not know where he was from [probably Christoph Gschäl]. In the country here [Titol] he was not aware of more than one overseer, Onoferus. According to him Onoferus had a black beard and would wear a coat (*Wappenrock*) of "the new color," a pair of white hosen with a leathern seat (*Gsäß*) and a liver-colored *Schlappel* (slouchhat?). Caspar also stated that Hutter had at God's command baptized him with water and had confronted him with his sins. Item, that Christ had not commanded to break the bread jointly with scoundrels and lechers, nor had he made it into an idol as our monks and priests have done. The brothers duly pay interest and tithes levied on their holdings in Moravia—whatever is not for war purposes. He had come from Moravia about eight days before Christmas (December 18, 1536) together with a certain Kunz, recently sentenced and executed in Bozen. Caspar had been at Bruneck and gone on to the Adige country and had been to the church meeting near Bozen, where several brothers had been arrested. There the peasants had also captured the overseer Onophorus and above Herschwang had fettered him and Hänsl [Unterrainer] with a chain; however, they had all got away. Caspar had then made his way through the Puster Valley to the church gathering up above the Raum Forest (*Raumwald*) near Hirschwang, attended by not many more than 20 persons... This confession of Caspar's was to be compared with that rendered on April 10, 1537 by Martin Peuntner from Vilgraten, imprisoned with Huber at Schöneck. According to him, the brothers hold their church meetings at Weißenbach below Mittewald and in the Schupfen Wood (*Schupfenholz*) above Schöneck. In the past winter, the meetings had been held at Plaas (judicial district of Terlan). Brixen Archives: Lade 112, No.11, littera H.
45. Brixen archives. Cf. also Causa Domini V, 36.

46. Brixen, original sub *Lade* 112, no. 5, littera C.
47. Ibid., and Causa Domini V, 45.
48. Original at Brixen, sub *Lade* 112, no. 11, littera F. As in v. Beck's writings the fact already mentioned above (on p. 132, i.e. Griesinger's arrest) as having taken place on April 23, 1536 is here again referred to as having occurred on April 23 1537—most likely an error. Griesinger's arrest in April 1536 is attested also by other sources.
49. Causa Domini V, 56.
50. Statthaltereiarchiv, Innsbruck. *Embietenbuch*.
51. Tirol, fol. 130.
52. Causa Domini IV, 62. Tirol, L. 4/130.
53. Causa Domini V, 59.
54. Contemporaneous copy in v. Beck's collection.
55. Issued at our royal palace in Prague on the ninth day of the month of May anno 1537, Ferdinandus. Ad mandatum domini Regis proprium Neuner. Original in v. Beck's collection. 10 pages in folia. Excerpt quoted above. Cf. also House, Court, and State Archives Vienna. Salzburg files.
56. Order of May 13 1537 to the governor and counsellors in Brixen. Brixen Archives, Lade 112, No. 5, littera C. A similar order of May 26—same place littera B. Lib. Causarum Domini V, fol. 74, 173, 177, 180, 242 in the Innsbruck Statthaltereiarchiv.
57. Tyrol, fol. 138.
58. Brixen: Lade 112, No. 5, littera C.
59. Brixen Archives.
60. Ibidem, Lade 12, No. 5, littera C. Cf. the document of July 24, according to which Unterrainer gives testimony against many persons in Lüsen. He himself is then dismissed.
61. House-, Court-, and State Archives Vienna.
62. *Geschichtsbücher der Wiedertäufer*, 132.
63. Causa Domini V, 117.
64. Brixen Archives, Original in Lade 12, No. 5, littera C.
65. This report by Griesinger is the basis for the account in the *Geschichtsbücher*. Griesinger's letter speaks of 2,000 persons present, but this might be a writing error.
66. *Geschichtsbücher*, 123. Note 1.
67. Ibidem, Zängerle was the messenger who took Griesinger's second epistle to the church community in Moravia; hence his execution would fall into the year 1538, if not a still later year, seeing that the letter makes mention of the passing of brother Paul Reder, which took place in 1538.
68. Causa Domini V, 114.
69. He is, the writing goes on, "optimaer vitae, constantissimus defensor religionis et caeremoniarum, fundatissimus theologus, quia assidue . . . in contionando inter primos Germaniae" . . . Original in the correspondence of Cardinal Bernhard of Trent.
70. Which "Doctor Urbanus Regius, postea apostata factus, had once held'.
71. He might also have brought about the recantation of the Anabaptist Kneisl, who was granted a reprieve by Ferdinand I on April 18. From His Royal Majesty, VII, 58. Innsbruck Statthaltereiarchiv.

72. Lochmaier's confession is missing.
73. The letter from Innsbruck concludes with an order to Georg Lindenmaier, administrator at Hertenberg, to take over and receive in Hertenberg two Anabaptists and to keep them imprisoned there, as there is no more room at Petersberg. Statthaltereiarchiv, Innsbruck. Causa Domini V, 132.
74. Causa Domini V, 136.
75. Ibidem, V, 135.
76. Council Minutes (*Rathsprotokoll*) III A, 1538, Brixen Archives. Extract in v. Beck's collection.
77. Council. Original in Brixen, council minutes (*Rathsprotokoll*) III. Fol. 17/6 A, 1538. Contemporaneous copy in v. Beck's collection. Cf. enclosure No.3.
78. Brixen Archives: Lade 112, No. 5. littera C.
79. Causa Domini V, 143.
80. *Embietenbuch* (record of miscellaneous government expenses) 1538.
81. Letter of July 1. Brixen, Prot. 16, anno 1538 (Georgii Epp Council minutes (*Rathsprotokoll*) III, 153.
82. 1538, June 26. Causa Domini 142/3.
83. Causa Domini V, 140.
84. Ibid. V, 147.
85. Brixen Archives: council minutes (*Rathsprotokoll*) III, 1538.
86. Its original draft is in the Brixen archives, Lade 112, No. 11, littera D. Cf. also Sinnacher, *Beiträge zur Geschichte der bischöflichen Kirche Säben und Brixen in Tyrol* VII, 325 ff.
87. Causa Domini V, 152: Letter to the king de dato July 25, 1538. Innsbruck Statthaltereiarchiv: To His Royal Majesty VI, fol. 468, 1538.
88. Statthaltereiarchiv: To His Royal Majesty VI, 473. On June 28 Ferdinand I pardoned the son of Gregor Mörl at Pfalzen, who had joined the Anabaptists. From His Royal Majesty VII, ad 1538.
89. From His Royal Majesty VI, 118. Innsbruck Statthaltereiarchiv.
90. Causa Domini V. 158.
91. Brixen: *Rathsprotokoll 16*.
92. J. v. Beck names Ascension Day (May 30) as the date of Griesinger's capture, which is an error—cf. *Geschichtsbücher der Wiedertäufer*, 136. In his notes Beck himself states the correct date.
93. Brixen Archives. *Ratsprotokoll* No. 16/1538.
94. Sept. 2, 1538. Causa Donini V, 160.
95. August 31, Brixen, Council Minutes (*Rathsprotokoll*) II, 1538.
96. Ibidem, report of September 4.
97. See enclosure No. 5.
98. Statthaltereiarchiv Innsbruck. From His Royal Majesty VI, 125.
99. Causa Domini V, 162 and Brixen Archives, Lade 112, No,5, Littera C. To His Royal Majesty VI, 492/2.
100. Causa Domini V:, 163.
101. The peasant uprisings would put such a shoe on a pole as a symbol of their rebellion, or even painted it on flags in Upper Germany.
102. Brixen Archives, original in Lade 112, No. 11, littera F, and Causa Domini V, 161.
103. Sept. 5. Contemporaneous copy in v. Beck's collection.
104. Contemporaneous copy in v. Beck's collection.

105. Sinnacher VII, 324.
106. Brixen Archives: Lade 112, No. 11. litt. F.
107. Statthaltereiarchiv Innsbruck. To His Royal Majesty VI, 493/2. The interrogation questions in the Brixen Archives (Lade 112. No. 11, lit.G do not contain anything special apart from the questions already referred to.
108. Brixen Archives. Council minutes III, 1538.
109. To secretary Sebastian in Linz. Without a copy. Draft in the Brixen Archives, Lade 112, No. 11. Lit. D.
110. Copy, after a Pressburg manuscript, in v. Beck's collection.
111. Griesinger's letters in the Pressburg manuscripts 190, 212,219. Copies in v. Beck's collection.
112. From His Royal Majesty VI, 132. Brixen, Lade 112, No. 11, Lit. F.
113. Causa Domini V, 163/164.
114. The more detailed circumstances of Griesinger's execution in v. Beck, *Geschichtsbücher*, 137 are related according to a report by "Stoffl from Villachen." Brixen Archives, Lade 112, No. 11 ad Lit. G.
115. Sinnacher VII, 325.
116. *Geschichtsbücher*, 137.
117. Hence it is incorrect for Sinnacher to state on p. 227 that Lochmaier had recanted again and had only been punished by expulsion from the country,
118. *Geschichtsbücher,* 135. In the same year Michael Widmann from Reutte was executed at Ehrenberg *Geschichtsbücher,* 140.
119. Brixen Archives: Lade 112, No. 11, Lit. H.
120. 1538, December 12, Causa Domini IV, 1538.
121. Brixen Archives: Lade 12, No. 11, Lit. E.
122. 1538, December 10, Vienna: King Ferdinand directing the vice regent and councillors of the Upper Austrian lands to have the *taja (taglia)* of 80 fl. also offered for the capture of the "clothweaver." Innsbruck Statthaltereiarchiv, From His Royal Majesty VI, 162. Causa Donini V, 173. Brixen Archives: Lade 112, No. 5, Causa Domini V, 180. Lit. D, 1539, January 9. The Innsbruck government informs the Toblach administrator that a taglia of 80 gulden is offered for the capture of the "clothweaver." The rumors turned out to be exaggerated, but it could be taken for certain that Hans Amon, just as he had done after Hutter's death, so now also after Griesinger's execution would not leave the church community in Tyrol orphaned for long, seeing that the church in Moravia was still linked by hundreds of bonds with that in the "Upper Country."

2. INNSBRUCK REGIONAL GOVERNMENT, 1539-1545

1. The *Geschichtsbücher* speak of five letters on p. 130, on p. 217 of six, with the latter number the correct one. The dates they bear are May 8, 11, 13, 19, and 25, and June 1 1536. Cop. after Cod. VII g. 27 in v. Beck's collection.
2. *Geschichtsbücher,* 143.
3. Brixen Archives.
4. Book of mandates in fol. in Brixen Archives. Cf. Sinnacher, *Beiträge* VII, 337.
5. Registr. Georgii et Bernardi. Protoc ad 1539.

6. Original in the Brixen Archives, Lade 112, No. 5, Lit. D.
7. Causa Domini V, 205/6.
8. Innsbruck Statthaltereiarchiv. To His Royal Majesty VII, 30.
9. Ibid. From His Royal Majesty VI, 310. As regards the further fate of this Anabaptist woman cf. *Geschichtsbücher,* 159.
10. See enclosure No. 6. Lib. Causa Domini V, 210.
11. Brixen Archives, Lade 112, No. 5. Lit. D.
12. Sinnacher VII, 344.
13. Causa Domini V, 217 and Brixen Archives: Lade 112, No. 5, Lit. D.
14. Innsbruck Statthaltereiarchiv. Pestarchiv XVIII, 39. Copy. Paper.
15. See enclosure No. 7.
16. Contemporaneous copy in v. Beck's collection.
17. From His Royal Majesty VI, 304.
18. Ibid. 305.Brixen Archives: Lade 12, No. 5, Lit. E. On October 13, 1539 the Innsbruck government asks Christoph, newly elected prince bishop of Brixen, to find ways and means to put an end to this disorder.
19. Original Brixen: Lade 112, No. 11, Llit. I.
20. To His Royal Majesty VI 122.
21. In the appendix we present this remarkable writing in toto; see enclosure No. 8.
22. Brixen Archives: Lade 112, No. 5, Lit. E.
23. Innsbruck Statthaltereiarchiv. To His Royal Majesty VII, 135/6 Copy in v. Beck's collection.
24. Brixen Archives: Lade 112, No. 11, Lit. F. A printed copy is in v. Beck's collection.
25. Contemporaneous copy, written on the above mentioned specimen in v. Beck's collection.
26. Innsbruck Statthaltereiarchiv. From His Royal Majesty VI, 333-335.
27. Brixen Archives, Lade 112, No. 5, Lit. E.
28. Contemporaneous copy in v. Beck's collection. This note is dated the *Erichtag* after Our Lady's day of birth anno 1539.
29. Brixen Archives: Lade 112, No. 11, Lit. H.
30. From His Royal Majesty VI, 331. Report of November 29.
31. Contemporaneous copy in v. Beck's collection.
32. Brixen Archives, Prot. 18 ad 1539. The death of the Seilerin [i.e. Leonhard Lanzenstiel's wife Apollonia] is reported in the *Geschichtsbücher*, 143.
33. No. 39 of the enclosures in *Beilagen des Copeibuches* of the Brixen bishopric. Innsbruck Statthaltereiarchiv.
34. Causa Domini V, 242.
35. Brixen Archives: Lade 112, No. 5, Lit. E.
36. Innsbruck Statthaltereiarchiv. Causa Domini V, 248 and Brixen Archives, Reg. Prot. 18 ad 1540.
37. The raid on Steinabrunn is reported in the *Geschichtsbücher*, 144. The three Tyrolese were Jörg Klatsch, Thoma Hartner, and Nigl Walch. Statthaltereiarchiv. From His Royal Majesty VI, 365/6.
38. Ibid. To His Royal Majesty, VII, 223 and 233. From His Royal Majesty VI, 382.
39. From His Royal Majesty VI, 401.
40. Brixen Archives, *Rathsprotokoll* II.
41. Extract from the manuscript in the Brixen Archives, Lade 112, No. 11, Lit. K.
42. *Rathsprotokoll* III ad 1540.

43. Causa Domini V, 301. Possibly identical with the Anna Steiner mentioned in January 1537.
44. Brixen Archives: Lade 112, no. 5, lit. E.
45. Oath of truce (*Urfecht*) sworn by the woman from Afy on Sunday, July 17 anno, etc. in the XLI. Contemporaneous copy in v. Beck's collection.
46. Causa Domini V, 361, 365.
47. Also Brixen, Lade 112, Lit. H
48. Innsbruck Statthaltereiarchiv. From His Royal Majesty VII, 27.
49. Cod. VIII, g 39 in Pest. Copy in v. Beck's collection.
50. Cod. VIII, g 25 and Cod. Poson, 163. Copy in v. Beck's collection.
51. Cod. VIII, g 39. Copy in v. Beck's collection.
52. Ibid.
53. Ibid.
54. As regards Stadler's activity among the Slovaks cf. *Geschichtsbücher*, 129.
55. Ibidem, 133.
56. Brixen files: Lade 112, no. 12, lit. B.
57. Causa Domini V ad 1542. To His Royal Majesty VII, 461, 491.
58. Details about this in the *Geschichtsbücher*, 158.
59. A brief history of what has occurred with our dear brother Georg Liebich in his imprisonment. Cod. Michanay, fol. 300.
60. Innsbruck Statthaltereiarchiv. From His Royal Majesty VI, 1/2. 7/6.
61. Causa Domini VI, 1/2, 6/7.
62. Ibid., and From His Royal Majesty VII, 115.
63. Causa Domini VI, 11-12.
64. Ibid. 8.
65. Ibid. 14. There were three: Thoman Prem, Stolz, and Gantner.
66. From His Royal Majesty VII, 170 a and 170 b.
67. To His Royal Majesty VIII, 88.
68. Causa Domini VI, 22; report of July 7, 1543. He had actually obtained this living as early as shortly after November 4, 1541. Lib. Tyr. I.
69. Causa Domini VI, 23.
70. Brixen, Lade 112, No. 12, Lit. B.
71. Ibid., Lade 112, No. 5, Lit. E and Causa Domini VII, 39.
72. Causa Domini VI, 65-66.
73. Brixen Archives, original in Lade 112, No. 5, Lit. B.
74. Causa Domini VI, 67, 74. As reported on April 3, 1544 Christian Gärber, called Lenk, with his wife, child, and servant went off to the Anabaptists in Moravia. Causa Domini 76 speaks of emigrants from Kitzbbüchl, and it was no different in the Steinach judicial district. Report of March 26 in Causa Domini 1544, fol. 70.
75. See enclosure No. 9. This mandate was renewed on July 30 of the following year. Lib. Causa Domini VI,142.
76. Innsbruck Statthaltereiarchiv, To His Royal Majesty VIII, 249.
77. Ibidem. From His Royal Majesty VII, 340-342.
78. Causa Domini VI, 87.
79. Ibid. 90. From Moravia also returned Hans Pachet, a tailor from Serfaus, who had once been baptized in the Volder woods and had then gone to Tschäckwitz in

Moravia, also Ruep Viedler and his wife and Martin Schöck, the latter without his wife and child, who had remained behind in Moravia.

80. Contemporaneous copy in v. Beck's collection.
81. Ditto.
82. Causa Domini VI, 98. See *Geschichstbücher,* 153.
83. Causa Domini VI, 106.
84. Ibid. 101, 104.
85. Brixen, Reg. Prot. 22.
86. Contemporaneous report in von Beck's collection.
87. Printed in Innsbruck, Causa Domini VI, 111; See Kripp, 44. Repeated on January 10, 1545. Printed copy in von Beck's collection.
88. From His Royal Majesty VII, 241-243.
89. Causa Domini VI, 120/2.
90. Ibid. 122.
91. Ibid. 127
92. Ibid. ad anno 1545.
93. Governmental report of December 12 to His Royal Majesty. Causa Domini VI, 164
94. Charles V. to Ferdinand I de dato November 2, 1545; Gent, 1545. Original in the Hofkammerarchiv zu Wien. Copy in von Beck's collection.
95. Causa Domini VI, 143 and Brixen Archives: Lade 142, No. 5, Lit F.
96. *Geshichtbücher,* 163. It was also in this same year that the Anabaptist Paumgartner from Natz was put on trial. Brixen Archives, Lade 112.
97. Causa Domini VI, 168.
98. Causa Domini VI, 307.
99. *Geschichtsbücher der Wiedertäufer,* 177.
100. Ibid., 179.
101. From His Royal Majesty, fol. 128 and Causa Domini VI, 331. Pestarchiv XVIII, 39.
102. Contemporaneous copy in v. Beck's collection.
103. Original in Lade 112, No. 5, Lit. F in Brixen Archives.
104. To His Royal Majesty IX, 563.
105. Innsbruck Statthaltereiarchiv.

3. HANS MÄNDL'S ACTIVITY AND TRIAL,
1548-1561

1. Brixen Archives, Lade 112, No. 5, Lit. F. Causa Comini VI, 433.
2. *Geschichtsbücher der Wiedertäufer,* 155.
3. Regents (*Statthalter*) and judges to the Innsbruck government, November 20, 1548. Contemporaneous copy in v. Beck's collection.
4. Ibid.
5. Contemporaneous copy in v. Beck's collection. Report of November 20, 1548.
6. Brixen Archives.
7. Ibid. Lade 112, No. 12, Lit. F.
8. Causa Domini VII, 14, 31, 44.
9. Ibid. 49, 50.
10. Brixen Archives: Lade 112, No. 12, Lit. F.

11. Causa Domini VII, 105, 106.
12. Ibid., 231, 264.
13. Brixen Archives, Lade 12.
14. Causa Domini VII, 265.
15. Ibid., 255/6, 257-259, de dato September 12.
16. Brixen, Lade 112, No. 5, Lit F. Causa Domini VII, 323/4, 325.
17. Causa Domini VII, 326. Copy in v. Beck's collection.
18. Causa Domini VII, 332.
19. i.e. Michael Matschidel—see *Chronicle*, 318.
20. *Geschichtsbücher*, 204.
21. About Pürchner's death a song was written, extant in two revised forms, one by Sigmund Hosaner, the other by Claus Felbinger. Ibid., 205.
22. Causa Domini VII, 352/3.
23. Ibid., 381.
24. Brixen Archives.
25. Causa Domini, fol. 387.
26. Ibid., VIII, 74, 79, and Brixen Archives, Lade 112, No. V. Lit. F.
27. Innsbruck Archives. Georg of Freundsberg had declared the property of the Anabaptist Erhard Gaismayer forfeit. Because of that he was reprimanded on July 16.
28. Causa Domini VIII, 84. Writing September 17, 1556.
29. September 30, 1556. Orig. draft in Salzburg Reg. Arch.
30. Causa Domini VIII, 86, 91, 99, 177, 180, 186, 189, 191.
31. Ibid., 105, 106, 112.
32. As regards his adventures see the *Geschichtsbücher der Wiedertäufer*, 218.[or see *Chronicle* pp.340-347]
33. Causa Domini VIII, 112/2.
34. *Geschichtsbücher*, 219 [cf. *Chronicle*, 364].
35. The original of this interesting item is in v. Beck's collection.
36. To His Royal Majesty, XIV, 245.
37. From His Royal Majesty XII, 303, 330.
38. Causa Domini VIII, 485.
39. Ibid., 481.
40. *Geschichtsbücher*, 222 [*Chronicle*, 372].
41. Cod. VIII, g 39, fol. 67.
42. Causa Domini VIII, 483, 484.
43. Order of November 26, 1560, Causa Domini VIII, 486.
44. The request to not place the prisoners into one and the same prison was on January 26, 1561 forwarded to the Innsbruck government by the *Kammer* (chamber).
45. *Geschichtsbücher*, 222 [*Chronicle*, 373].
46. Mändl's avowal of faith is found in Codices at Pressburg, Gran, and Pest. Copy in v. Beck's collection. It bears the title: "Confession of faith of three men, by name Hans Mändl, Eustachius Kotter, and Jörg Rack, all three of them executed on June 10, 1561 at Innsbruck on the *Schweinanger* (pig meadow) by the *Schießhütten*. First Kotter and Rack were beheaded, following which Mändl was burned alive and the two other corpses were burned with him."

NOTES 257

47. Statthaltereiarchiv Innsbruck. Causa Domini VIII, 506 of February 7, 1561. Instruction to Dr. Alber of February 7; Ibid., VIII, 508/9.
48. Causa Domini VIII, 510/2-511.
49. Innsbruck Archives.
50. Causa Domini VIII, 518/1, 2.
51. From the report to His Royal Majesty XIV, 527-539, February 27, Statthaltereiarchiv Innsbruck.
52. I.e. the mandates of 1528 and 1529, of December 21, 1542, January 28, 1543, and May 21, 1544.
53. An epistle by Klain Hansl ["little Johnny" i.e. Mändl] from prison to his fellow prisoners Hans Rack and Eustachius Kotter. Cf. also *Geschichtsbücher*, 222.
54. Ad mandatum domini electi imperatoris Kobenzl. Innsbruck Statthaltereiarchiv. From His Royal Majesty XIII, 99-100/22. 2 pages, enclosure No. 100. Beck's literary bequest contains a description of this whole matter, and on that the above account is based.
55. It says there: Judges and jurors are to swear an oath to God and the saints that they will diligently attend to all matters brought before them and will consider them to the best of their understanding, that the jurors are to advise and assist the judge as best they can and that in all criminal cases (*über das Bluet und alle schädlichen Sachen*) they will always and in every case adjudicate and pass judgment in accordance with this our legal code and with what this book says and according to the ordinances and mandates we have issued up till now and may still issue in the future, and that they will not let themselves be impeded or led astray by love, friendship, money, gifts, fear, envy, hatred, or anything else liable to twist what is just and right. This they want to be accountable for, here on earth to the princely authority of their land and in the other world to God the Almighty at the last judgment—faithfully, honestly and free from falsehood.
56. Here it says: "Those that unashamedly violate, disobey, and despise our letters, orders, and mandates, will not be tolerated in our land, regardless of who they may be."
57. Innsbruck Statthaltereiarchiv, To His Royal Majesty 1561, fol. 652-656.
58. From His Royal Majesty, XIII, 99-102.
59. Preserved in Cod. VIII, g 39. Copy in v. Beck's collection.
60. Innsbruck Statthaltereiarchiv, To His Royal Majesty XV, 682-688.
61. As regards the date see Beck, *Geschichtsbücher*, 223.
62. Cod. VIII, g 39 and Cod. Michnay. Copy in v. Beck's collection.
63. Causa Domini VIII, 177.
64. *Geschichtsbücher*, 223.
65. Cod. 235, fol. 329, Pressburg. An epistle by Hänsl Kytzbüher (sic) to the sisters in the cotton department, de dato Kitzbühel on St. Vitus Day. Copy in v. Beck's collection. It is on this letter that the account in the *Geschichtsbücher der Wiedertäufer* is based.
66. a. *Dein Wünsch' und Gab' empfangen hab...* Cod. 232, Pressburg.
    b. *O Gott, in Deinem Himmelsthron, Gib mir herfürzubringen . . .* Cod. 203 Pressburg.
    c. *O Vater mein, ein Kindlein, dem . . .* ibid.
    d. *O Gott Vater, in deinem Reich . . .* Ibid.

67. They are found in manuscripts No. 194, 203 and 232 of the Pressburg cathedral chapter.
68. Causa Domini VIII, 545. This led to a lengthy correspondence between them and the government.: August 11 and 27, September 2, 5, and 30. Files in the Innsbruck Statthaltereiarchiv.
69. Ibid.
70. Causa Domini VIII, 567.

4. HANSL KRÄL'S ELECTION, 1561-1578

1. Innsbrucker Acten.
2. Causa Domini VIII, 515, 522 (as regards the Anabaptists in Rattenberg).
3. Causa Domini VIII, 538-539/2; ibid., 543-544, 551.
4. Printed. Causa Domini VII, 551, 553'4.
5. Brixen Archives, Lade 112, No. 6, Lit. H.
6. The interesting confession is in v. Beck's collection. See enclosure No. 11.
7. *Geschichtsbücher*, 218.
8. Brixen Archives, Lade 112, Lit. I.
9. Causa Domini VIII, 566.
10. Causa Domini VIII, 575-576 and Brixen Archives, Lade 112, No. 5, Lit. F.
11. Causa Domini VIII, 618-620.
12. Ibid., 618, 620 691.
13. Statthaltereiarchiv Innsbruck, To His Royal Majesty XV, 954. Report of August 11, 1563.
14. The government's application was agreed to on August 26, 1563. From His Royal Majesty XIII, 588.
15. Causa Domini IX, 165, 197, 245, 274.
16. Draft in v. Beck's collection.
17. Also in Causa Domini IX, 1565.
18. Ferdinand I to the Innsbruck government, July 25, 1565.
19. Causa Domini IX, 298.
20. Everything relating to Geyerspüchler is in the *Geschichtsbücher*, 249, note 3. His "vindication and avowal of faith" in v. Beck's bequest. The order to let criminal justice take its course against him in Causa Domini IX, 508. According to the files of the Innsbruck Archives it was only in 1567, not already in 1566, that Geyerspüchler was executed. The last-named date is found in the *Geschichtsbücher* [But noted as 1567 in the *Hutterian Chronicle*].
21. Kripp, *Ein Beitrag zur Geschichte der Wiedertäufer in Tirol*.
22. Printed copy in v. Beck's collection; republished on July 12, 1567.
23. August 12, 1567. Causa Domini IX, 566.
24. Causa Domini XI, 619.
25. Ibid. XII, 106.
26. Ibid. XIV, 407.
27. Ibid. XIV, 37.
28. Kripp, 48. Hirn, *Erzherzog Ferdinand II. von Tirol*, I, 156.
29. Causa Domini X, 223.

30. Innsbruck Archives, To His Princely Highness V, 712, From His Princely Highness II, 435.
31. *Geschichtsbücher,* 251.
32. Causa Domini X, 388.
33. Brixen Archives.
34. Interrogation of August 12, 1688.
35. Causa Domini XI, 237. Possibly confused in error with Jakob Platzer, executed in 1591 at Silian. Cf. *Geschichtsbücher,* 308.
36. Details in the *Geschichtsbücher,* 266, 267.
37. Causa Domini 1574.
38. Ibid., XI, 391.
39. Ibid., 396.
40. Ibid., 447.
41. Printed. Causa Domini XI, 619.
42. See Kripp, 48.
43. Causa Domini XII, 44-45. The magistrate's report of June 28. The government's reply of July 4, 1578.
44. Causa Domini XII, 45.
45. Ibid., 46.
46. Draft in v. Beck's collection.
47. Causa Domini XII, 86.
48. From His Princely Highness XIV, 70.
49. Innsbruck Archives.
50. Printed. Causa Domini XII, 106.
51. Original: *Ehehaftthätigen*
52. Sinnacher VII, 620.
53. Brixen, Mandatenbuch in fol. 263-264.
54. *Geschichtsbücher,* 271.

5. ANABAPTISTS IN THE BREGENZ FOREST

1. In this sense that Lienhart Langenstiel had been sent to Switzerland in 1539. *Geschichtsbücher,* 143.
2. Bergmann, "Die Wiedertäufer zu Au im inneren Bregenzerwalde und ihre Auswanderung nach Mähren im Jahre 1585," *Sitzungsberichte der Wiener Akademie* I, 106 ff.
3. *Immo eum secularis potestas nefandam sectam tollerare nollet, quidam eam ejerare detrectantes maluerunt clam hinc emigrare quam resipiscere.* Bergmann, loc. cit., 109.
4. Ibid., 113.
5. Contemporaneous copy in v. Beck's collection.
6. Bergmann, l. c.
7. Statthaltereiarchiv Innsbruck, To His Princely Highness XVII, 286.
8. Causa Domini XIX, 447.
9. Ibid., 534.
10. To His Serene Princely Highness XIX 535, 868.
11. Cf. *Geschichtsbücher,* 284, 285 [*Chronicle* pp. 494-496]. The above account of the matter is more complete than the one in the *Geschichtsbücher.*

12. Sinnacher, *Beiträge* VII, 771.
13. Sinnacher, 776; Bergmann, 114. Kripp, 50.
14. *Geschichtsbücher,* 368.
15. Bergmann, 116.

6. ANABAPTISTS IN TYROL, 1579-1599

1. To His Serene Princely Highness XVI, 665.
2. Causa Domini XII, 313.
3. Causa Domini 1581, fol. 407. Printed.
4. Report of May 1, 1581. Causa Domini.
5. Causa Domini XII, 358. Individual Anabaptists departed also from Fügen and Schwaz. Cf. Hirn, *Erzherzog Ferdinand II,* I, 156.
6. Brixen, Mandatenbuch, fol. 163.
7. Instances of this in Hirn, *Erzherzog Ferdinand II,* I, 154/5.
8. Causa Domini XII, 587. Instruction dated August 21.
9. Hirn l.c. 156, reports the execution of an Anabaptist in 1583 at Schlanders. This might refer to Andre Pürchner [executed there in 1584], for the files of 1583 know of no Anabaptist executed 1583 at Schlanders.
10. *Geschichtsbücher,* 290. [*Chronicle,* 497]
11. *Geschichtsbücher,* 290. [*Chronicle* pp. 498-499]
12. Causa Domini XIII, 57. Brixen, Lade 112, No. 5, Lit. G.
13. Causa Domini XIII, 61 and Brixen Archives, Lade 112, No. 5, Lit. G.
14. Causa Domini XIII ad 1584.
15. Causa Domi XIII, 187.
16. Kripp refers to him once as Josef Tauscher.
17. Printed in Kripp, *Ein Beitrag zur Geschichte der Wiedertäufer in Tirol,* 51-60.
18. Kripp, 57. *Geschichtsbücher,* 309.
19. Wörz Archives, fasc. 35.
20. Causa Domini XIII, 231.
21. *Geschichtsbücher,* 296. [*Chronicle,* 503-504]
22. Brixen Archives: Lade 112, No. 5, Lit. G, and Causa Domini XIII, 365.
23. To His Princely Serenity XXIII, 273.
24. To His Princely Serenity XXIII, 273. von Beck does not hesitate to call her an Anabaptist.
25. It is an obvious exaggeration to speak of "1,600 Anabaptists, representing the richest and wealthiest, and the best workers," that Tyrol is said to have lost to Moravia in 1587. Neither the Anabaptists' own history books nor the court files provide any ground for this assumption, which is still found in Hirn, I, 155.
26. Original in Brixen: Lade 112, No. 5, Lit. G.
27. *Geschichtsbücher,* 23.
28. Contemporaneous protocol 1588. Brixen Archives.
29. "Who is presently in prison at Lienz".
30. Original Brixen, Lade 112, No. 5, Lit. G.
31. Enclosure with respect to previous footnote number.
32. *Geschichtsbücher,* 335 [*Chronicle,* 487, 496, 556.].
33. Causa Domini XIII, 469.

34. Contemporaneous "copy of the examination of the persons suspected of Anabaptism" in v. Beck's collection.
35. So in the manuscript. Loserth indicates here he is uncertain of the meaning.
36. Probably Räsen.
37. In the Mòcheno dialect (Trentino), "enkhere" means "our".
38. *Geschichtsbücher*, 307.
39. The notes about his imprisonment in the *Geschichtsbücher* are derived from the letters Wenger wrote to Stoffl Künhuber, Klaus Braidl, and to his wife Aendl in Moravia. They are in Cod. Michnay, fol. 518 ff. [Cf. also *Chronicle*, 517-519].
40. *Geschichtsbücher*, 308-309 [*Chronicle*, 519-520].
41. Brixen Archives, Lade 112, No. 6, Lit. H.
42. Causa Domini XIV (1591-1595), fol. 37/2. Printed.
43. Causa Domini XIV, 117.
44. Ibid., 126.
45. Ibid., 516.
46. Causa Domini 1599-1601, fol. 127.
47. There are reports dated August 2 and 23 about this matter in Causa Domini loc, cit. fol. 388-399.
48. Ibid., fol. 749.

7. EXTINCTION OF TYROLEAN ANABAPTISM, 1600-1626

1. *Geschichtsbücher*, 331.
2. Dated March 23. Ibid., 332.
3. Causa Domini 1602-1614, fol. 157.
4. Causa Domini l. c., fol. 207, 221, 247, 269,
5. Causa Domini, l. c. fol. 206.
6. Causa Domini, fol. 239.
7. The protocol, in a badly damaged state, in v. Beck's collection.
8. *Geschichtsbücher der Wiedertäufer*, 409.
9. October 30, 1627. The Innsbruck government lets Joh. Baptist Gamba, the Rattenberg administrator, know that they had received his report of October 16 concerning some sectarian Anabaptist persons.

INDEX

Proper Names and Places: Page references are provided for names of Anabaptists and select non-Anabaptists and places, but not ancient sources (e.g. Jonah, Jesus, Augustine), unless the name is used as a location (e.g. St. Georgen). In the case of local administrators, their name is invariably connected to their local jurisdiction. The place names of locations of Hutterite settlements in Moravia (for example, those found on pp.227-8), do not appear in the index as separate entries, unless the place name has appeared elsewhere in the preceding pages.

Abson, 14
Adamer, Kilian, 199
Adam (of Matrei), 203
Adige (region, river or valley), 24, 31, 33, 35, 58, 62, 64, 68, 85, 88, 98, 101, 107, 111, 118-9, 129-30, 136-7, 156-9, 175-6, 183, 213, 216, 223, 241 n.52, 249 n.44
Afy/Afers?, 168, 253 n.45
Aischach, Leonard (subcaptain at Säben), 70
Albeins, 64, 183
Alber, Dr. Mathias, 186-8, 256 n.47
Alpacher, Georg, 214
Alpaganer, Hans, 140
Alsaider, Christel (see Häring, Christian)
Altrasen, 163, 212, 216, 239 n.5
Ambras, 65, 172, 187, 189
Amon, Hans (Tuchmacher, 'Clothweaver'), 69-70, 73, 76, 79-82, 88, 90-1, 98, 101, 105, 113-8, 120-1, 128-31, 133, 154, 156-8, 168, 240 n.15, 241 n.51, 242 n.91, 243 n.1, 248 n.9, 249 n.44, 252 n.122
Amtholz, 197-8
Angerer (priest at Innsbruck), 5, 230 n.5
Angst, Bartelme, 23
Appenzell, 16, 206
Arnold, Leonard, 169
Arzl, 13
Aschelberger, 35
Ascherham, Gabriel, 47, 61, 83-8, 121-2, 247 n.18
Au (village), 207, 211, 236, 238-9, 259
Augsburg, 7-8, 10-11, 18, 23, 53, 176-7
Auspitz, 60-1, 66-7, 71, 73, 81, 88, 93, 101, 103, 129, 182, 238 n.47, 241 nn. 56,58, 249 n.44
Austerlitz, 49, 60-1, 103, 228
Axams, 65, 183, 187, 201

Bader, Gilg, 24-5
Basch, Georg, 20
Battenberg, 64
Bavaria, 19, 23, 225, 27, 30, 40, 47, 54, 73, 109, 128, 137, 159, 169, 182-3, 200, 204, 216, 233 n.32, 237 n.1
Beck (d. Sterzing), 67
Benedict, 44, 51, 53
Bern, 216
Berwig, Hans, 207
Binder, Peter, 70, 239 n.5
Blauärmel, Philipp (see Plener)
Blaurock, Georg (Cajacob), 50-1
Bludenz, 11, 13, 231 n.32
Bock (see Pock)
Both, Hans (of Hesse), 88
Bozen, 14, 19, 23, 24, 30-1, 33-4, 36, 38, 43-5, 50-1, 63-4, 76, 79, 110, 112, 119, 129, 136-40, 239 n.5, 242 n.73, 249 n.44
Brandenberg, Friedrich (of Cologne), 68
Brandhuber, Wolfgang, 30
Brandt, Erst, 74, 239
Brandzoll, 112-4
Branten valley, 64
Braun (near Lüsen), 131, 135
Braunegg, 23, 29, 117, 214
Bregenz, 13, 206-9, 211-2
Breitenbach, 41
Breitenberg, 43, 50-1, 53
Breitmichel, Caspar, 85-6, 103
Breitenwang, 11
Brenner Pass, 19, 24, 37, 39, 41-6, 52, 64, 73, 79, 148, 202
Breslau, 109
Brixlegg, 27, 41, 73, 129
Brixen, 4-7, 10-16, 23-9, 33-4, 43, 56, 64, 68, 70-80, 90-101, 109-14, 117-18, 129-39, 143-69, 172-85, 198, 200-4, 212, 214, 216-7, 222, 226-7, 230 n.5, 236 n.38, 246 n.20, 248 n.32
Brixlegg, 27, 34, 41, 73, 129
Brünn, 60, 81, 103, 105, 110, 122, 227
Brünnerin, Christine, 211
Brugg, 41, 226
Bruneck, 13, 43-4, 47-8, 64, 91, 136, 149, 173, 175, 180, 198, 218, 227, 230 n.5, 249 n.44
Bullinger, Heinrich, 3, 99, 239-40 n.1
Burkhard (from Ofen), 61
Butschowitz, 169

Caldirf, 51-2
Calzein, 21, 64

INDEX 265

Carinthia, 19-20, 46-8, 62, 80, 88, 112, 118, 162, 165, 243 n.6
Carneid, 36, 64, 79
Carusin, Apollonia, 220
Caspar (of Freundsberg), 75
Caspar (of Rossitz), 82
Castelbell, 180-3, 199, 222
Charles V (Emperor), 15, 44, 72, 139, 176-7, 177, 209
Christina?, 71
Christoph (Bishop of Stadion), 7
Clara, Abbess at Sonnenburg, 98, 131
Clasen, Veronika, 145
Clausen/Klausen, 17, 19, 24-5, 37, 63
Clement VII (Pope), 15
Cles, Bernard von (Cardinal, Brixen), 158
Colsass, 35
Creuz, 115
Curaeus, 122

Danube, 100, 176, 182
David (from Schweinitz), 60-1, 67, 86
Dax, Leonard, 195, 199
Denck, Hans, 18, 30
Derker, Hansel, 77
Deutsch-Noffen, 37, 43, 52, 53, 64-5
Dominic, St (rule of), 10
Doria, Andrea, 160, 165, 167
Dulfes, 65

Ebner, Georg/Jörg, 134-5, 248 n.32
Eck, Johann, 95, 144
Edicts (and mandates; see also Worms) 7, 10, 13-5, 20-6, 29, 31-4, 45, 48-50, 52, 55-8, 62-79, 94, 99-100, 120, 134-5, 137-8, 145, 147-8, 150, 153, 158-60, 162-75, 179-81, 186, 188-215, 223-25, 230 n.2, 231 n.44, 234 n.17, 238 nn.34,37, 240 n.32, 244 nn.32,38, 245 n.43, 254 n.75, 257 n.56
Egel, Hans, 91, 95
Eggenburg, 89, 101
Eisack, 33, 37, 46, 48, 62, 68, 112, 174
Eisenach, 6
Ehrenberg, 11, 132, 181, 216, 252
Ellen, 115
Ellenbögen, 52
Elm, 98
Engest, Jobst, 38
Enn, 52, 59
Enns, 108, 118, 146, 165

Ensisheim, 170
Eppau, administrator of Altenburg, 54
Eppstainer, Thomas, 170
Erenburg, 109
Erhard, Christoph, 121, 237 n.3
Erspan, 133, 236 n.38
Etsch, see 'Adige'
Eustachius (priest at Kropfberg), 11-2

Fabri, Johann, 7-8, 45
Färber, Caspar, 18
Falkhanej, 76
Falkenstein, 3, 11
Fasser (see Vasser)
Federspiel, Gilg, 181
Ferdinand (Archduke, King, von Habsburg), 11, 13-5, 20, 25, 34, 38, 54, 56-8, 65, 72, 75, 77-8, 93-9, 100, 102, 108-9, 111, 117, 120, 122, 134-5, 138-41, 143-8, 150-4, 158-9, 161-6, 171-2, 174-5, 177, 180, 186, 188-93, 197, 200-1, 203, 207, 209, 211, 215, 230 n.2, 234 n.20, 239 n.2, 244 n.18, 251 n.88, 252 n.122, 255 n.94, 258 n.18
Fest, Ludwig, 70, 241 n.48
Firmian (see Georg, Baron)
Fischer, "Old" and Katharina of Prags, 114, 117, 122, 220, 245 n.1
Flaas, 139-40
Flamm, Andre (district judge at Sterzing), 69, 240 n.36
Flauerling, 42
Fleischhacker, Paul, 174
Fleimser valley, 43, 53
Fletscher, Martin, 221
Fluck valley, 155
Fragenstein, 155
Franz (from Schneeburg), 53, 69, 240 n.39
Francis, St (Franciscans), 6, 10, 55, 141
Frassdorf (Bavaria), 128
Freiburg, 175
Freundsberg, 21-3, 29-30, 64-5, 68, 70, 75, 170, 197, 233 n.32, 240 n.33, 241 n.63, 256 n.27
Frick, Leonard, 30, 51
Froner, 53
Fuchs, Carl, 54
Fuchs, Christoph, 40, 65, 98, 119, 136
Fuchs, Jakob, 34
Fuchs, Rudolf, 14
Fuchsmagen, 5
Füchter, Kunz, 69, 137?, 241 n.42
Füeger, Lord Friedrich, 90-5, 244 n.6
Fuger, Hans, 80

Gänsler, Paul, 214
Gärber, Christian, 177, 254 n.74
Gais, 71
Gaismair, Michael, 16
Gallus/Gall, Dr. (see Müller, Gallus)
Gall (Weiss? of Brixen), 79, 217?, 219-21
Gall, Paul, 115, 217?
Gall (of Puster valley), 217
Gamper, Benedict et al., 51, 53, 239 n.5
Ganser, Hans, 222
Gargatzon, 30
Gartner, Christian, 214, 226
Gartner, Veronica (wife of Leonard), 152
Gartner, Wilhelm, 214
Gasser, Anna, 53, 223 n.73
Gasser, Hans, 31, 45, 76
Gasser, Jakob, 66, 223-4, 242 n.73
Gasteiger, 21
Gebhardt, Christian, 218
Geltinger, Ulrich, 75, 93
Gengel, Blasy, 43
Gentner, Hans, 168
Georg, Baron of Firmian, 50, 64, 75, 78, 113, 121, 136-7, 139, 246 n.20
Georg, Bishop of Brixen, 24, 56, 78, 131-2, 134-5, 139, 151, 212, 222
Germany, 3, 15, 19, 109, 122, 127, 238 n.47, 251 n.101
Geyerpüchler, Niclas, 200
Glaidt, Oswald, 30
Glaser, Hans, 53
Glaser, Paul, 245 n.43
Glaser, Sebastien/Bastl (aka Huebmaier), 89, 143-4
Glasser, Bernhard, 86
Glurns/Glurus, 19, 31, 50, 201, 222
Gobl (Kob), Simon, 51
Göding, 103, 228
Görtz, 62
Gösser, 10
Götzenberg, 71, 73, 77, 79, 109-10, 132-3, 146, 241 n.54, 242 n.91
Götzenperger, Matthes, 166
Götzens, 187, 189, 196, 199, 201
Goral see Kräl, Hans
Goldschmied, Heinrich, 42
Grebner, Josef, 130-1
Gregenhofer, Hans, 179
Greifenburg, 112
Greiffenstein, 138
Gremser, Hänsel, 76

Gretlein, 71
Grienbacher, Christina (of Khiens), 152
Gries, 36, 43, 51, 79, 136, 187
Griesinger, Onofferus/Offrus (see Langer, Anna, wife), 69, 73-4, 88, 101, 127-31, 136, 138, 143, 146, 150-7, 179, 185, 241 n.58, 249 n.48, 250 nn.65,67
Griessbacher, Wilhelm, 82, 102, 110
Grill, Hans, 166
Grison, 16, 57
Gruber/Grueber/Grübl, Hans and Brigitta (from Eggenhof or Asling), 34, 67, 69, 136, 166
Grueber, Lamprecht, 67?, 69, 149, 240 n.15
Gruber, Martin, 216-7
Gruber, Wolfgang, 240 n.15
Grünfelder, Hans, 143
Grünwald, Jörg (from Kitzbühel), 40, 59
Gsäl, Valtan, 71
Gschäl, Christoph, 168, 249 n
Gschöll, Christian, 41, 69
Gufidaun, 19, 24, 35, 37-8, 43, 50, 52, 64-5, 68-9, 71-3, 76-8, 110, 113-4, 121, 129, 136, 143, 148, 163, 168, 175, 179-80, 183, 201, 216, 241 n.57, 246 nn.20,24

Haas, Ruepp, 145
Hagau (see Hegaw)
Hagenauer, Sigmund, 51
Hall, 4-11, 23, 29, 31, 33, 35, 39, 53, 63, 66, 69, 93, 119, 122, 144-5, 149, 167, 170, 172, 174, 187, 189, 194, 203-4, 212, 216, 231 n.21
Hallenstein, Leonard, 30
Halsach, 6
Han, Georg, 59, 153
Hans "the Swabian", 34
Hans (from Langstadt), 34
Hans, son of Terlan sexton, 140
Hansemann (of Mittenwald), 223
Häring, Christian, Christel, Christina, 36, 59, 70-1, 241 n.49
Häring, Thomas, 70, 241 n.49
Hart (Ziller valley), 12
Hasel, David, 201, 219
Hayler, Martin, 120
Heckl, Cristian, 157
Hegaw (Hagau), 73-4
Held, Jörg, 31
Helena (Baroness von Freyberg), 20, 22, 54, 90
Hellrigl, Claus, 159
Hellrigl, Oswald ("old Oswald?"), 143-4, 155, 168, 214, 240
Hellrigl, Ursula, 145, 158

INDEX

Hennfels castle, 155, 157
Herbst, Christoph (administrator at Welsperg), 48-9, 68
Hermann, Thoman (Böhmisch Waidhofen), 35, 235 n.43
Hertenberg, 33-4, 39, 65, 250 n.73
Hetzer, Ludwig, 30
Heugen, Remigius and Christoph, 181
Heunfels, 135, 155, 157, 169, 173, 217, 223, 227
Heyerling, Augustin, 45, 51, 139, 142
Hildebrand (von Spaur), 10
Hirschwang/Herschwang, 109-10, 114-6, 123, 249 n.44
Höllrigl estate, 75
Hoffer, Sigmund, 30
Hofwieser, 42
Hohenberg, 64
Hohenwarth, 89, 129, 243 n.9
Holzkirche, Ursula, 74
Holzmain, Margret (sister of Niclas), 140
Holzmeister, Christian, 180
Horlocher (at Götzens), 199
Huber, Caspar, 137-8, 249 n.44
Huber, Joachim, 219
Hueber, Ruprecht, 79
Hungary, 127, 146, 170
Hungerl, Peter, 67
Hut, Hans, 18, 30, 34, 237 n.1, 247 n.24
Hutter, Agnes, 44, 49, 237 n.7
Hutter, Balthasar, 47-8
Hutter, Christian, 48, 237 n.3
Hutter, Jakob, 37, 43-4, 46-50, 53, 59-62, 64, 66-71, 73-4, 76-89, 101-22, 127-9, 132-3, 153-4, 178, 184, 237 n.1, 240 n.29, 241 n.51, 242 n.86, 243 n.6, 246 nn.14,21, 247 n.17,24, 249 n.44, 252 n.122
Hutter, Katharina (aka 'Traindl', née Purst), 113-5, 121, 153-4, 246 n.22
Hutter, Peter, 83, 85-8, 243 n.6

Ifan/Ivano, 182
Imming, 41
Imst, 13, 64, 143, 169-70, 197, 201, 203, 213, 222-3
Innsbruck, 5, 7, 11-4, 20-25, 31, 37-9, 42, 48, 50-54, 57, 63, 66, 73-4, 78-9, 90-103, 109-13, 116, 118-9, 129-31, 134, 137-9, 144-200, 204, 208-17, 222-3, 226, 234 n.1, 236-7 nn.38-9, 252 n.122, 261 n.9
Innichen, 10
Inn Valley, 4, 6, 8-9, 18, 21, 37, 48, 73, 85, 101, 137, 146-8, 158, 170, 216, 222, 231 n.21

Jakob (of Niederthor), 65
Jauer, 109

Jaufen valley/mountain, 131, 185
Jenbach (Inpach), 63, 243 n.6
Jenosien (Senesigen), 140
Jörg (from Passau), 34

Käls, Hieronymus/Jeronyme, 59, 112, 115, 123, 128
Kaltenhauser, Ambrosi, 221
Kaltenhauser, Anna, 220-1
Kaltenhauser, Stoffl, 220-1
Kaltern, 37, 43, 51, 63, 239 n.5
Karlstadt, Andreas Bodenstein, 16-7
Kautz, Georg, 181
Kautz, Jakob, 30
Keberl, Georg, 157
Kematen, 212
Kentschacher, Georg, 31
Kessler, Heinrich, 65
Kessler, Paul, 79, 112?
Kienz, 44, 116
Kilpmais, 176
Kirchmair, Georg, 29, 62, 239
Kirschner, Gabriel (see Ascherham)
Kirschner, Michael (aka Klesinger, Kürschner), 35, 37-8, 50
Kitzbühel, 15, 21-3, 31-3, 35-7, 39-40, 48, 52-6, 63, 65, 70-1, 75, 77-9, 105, 129, 173, 182, 195, 197-200, 216, 223, 236 n.16, 241 n.56, 257 n.65
Klagenfurt, 47
Klausen (see Clausen)
Klaus (of Carinthia), 88, 243 n.6, 261 n.39? (Braidl)
Kleepüchler, Paulus, 187, 189-90, 193, 196
Klesinger (see Kirschner)
Klingen, 40
Köberl, Jörg, 166
Koffler, Anderl, 176
Koffer, Jörg, 202
Koffler, Philip, 51
Kofler, Hans, 38
Kofler, Lorenz, 136
Kofner, Margareth (daughter of Joachim), 145
Kohl (of Gargatzon), 30
Koller, Hans, 42
Konrad (from Swabia), 4
Kontz?, 71
Kortsch, 181
Kotter, Eustachius, 183-5, 194-5, 256 nn.46,53
Kotter, Jörg (Innsbruck), 63

Krål, Hans (aka Goral, Kitzbüheler), 36, 182, 195, 197-205, 209-11
Kränzler, 107, 130-1
Krain, 20
Kramsach, 41
Kranewitten, 219
Krasknikow, 169
Kraus, Albrecht, 94-5
Krautschlögl, Jörg, 146
Krems, 89, 168, 174
Kniehäusser, Apollonia, 76
Kromau, 103
Kropfberg/Kropsberg, 11-2, 31, 39, 41, 169, 199, 201, 214, 216
Krumau, 157
Kuedegen, Christel, 134, 248 n.30
Künigl, Caspar of Ernburg, 114, 161, 202
Kürschner (see Kirschner)
Kufstein, 14-6, 22-3, 27, 31, 40, 46, 52, 54, 56, 64, 66, 71, 77, 119, 168, 172, 175, 183, 204, 216, 239 n.5
Kuhn, Blasius, 63, 83, 85-6
Kuhn, Cyprian, 145
Kuhn, Hans, 203
Kuhn, Veit, 145
Kuna of Kunstadt-Lukow, 104
Kuppfer, Jakob, 45
Kurtatsch, 36-7, 43, 50, 239 n.5

Laas, 182
Lakstatt, 40
Landeck, 169-72, 179-82, 186, 197, 203, 222
Landsperger, Christoff (priest at Hall), 39, 69
Langegger/Langecker, Hans, 50
Langenmantel, 10
Langer, Anna (wife of O. Griesinger), 130, 136, 155
Langer, Mathias, 33-7
Lanz, Peter, 80
Lanzenstiel, Lienhart (aka Seiler/Sailer), 128, 157, 159, 168-9, 185, 207, 248 n.7
Leder, Stephan, 33
Lederer, Hans, 11
Legeder, Mathias, 170, 172
Leifers, 37, 43, 50-1
Lenz, Paul, 187, 189-90, 193, 196
Liebich, Georg, 170, 254 n.59
Liechtenstein, Lords von, 23, 41, 64, 79, 98, 236 n.26
Liendl, Thomas, 93
Lienz, 78, 129, 158, 214, 216-7, 222, 241 n.57, 260 n.29

Linz, 30, 73, 101, 152
Lipa, Johann, 103, 106
Lochler, Christian, 170
Lochmaier, Bärbl (wife of Leonhard), 151
Lochmaier, Leonhard, 143, 145-6, 149-55, 157, 250 n.72, 252 n.117
Lochmann (see Pertulo)
Lower Austria (*Niederösterreich*), 20, 23, 31, 35, 99, 105, 157, 160, 162, 167
Luckner Valentin, 73, 77
Ludwig (Count of Oettingen, Bavaria), 109, 167
Ludwig (of Emrshofen), 17
Lüsen, 24, 68, 110, 116, 123, 130-3, 135, 138, 143, 160-1, 168, 174, 198-9, 227, 250 n.60
Luther, 7, 12-3, 15-6, 30, 34
Lutheran(s), 3, 5-7, 10-18, 20-21, 63, 79, 91, 102, 144, 166, 210, 216, 230 n.2

Madschidl, Michael, 174
Mändl, Hans, 179-97, 217
Maidenberg, 105
Maier, Wolfgang, 41
Maier, Peter, 112
Maierhofer, Balthasar, 76, 227?
Maierhofer, Margaretha, 76, 216, 227?
Maierhofer, N., 31
Mair, Lienhard, 115
Maler, Annele, 39
Malerin, Ursula, 168
Mals, 19, 41, 44, 203, 217, 222
Mareez, Leonhard, 214-5, 217
Maria, Queen (at Brussels), 135
Maria-Saal, Abbey (see Brünn)
Mark, Anna (daughter of Jos), 145
Mark, Thoman, 215
Marpeck, Egidi, 35
Marpeck, Pilgrim, 18-9, 60, 233 n.34, 238 n.47
Marton (of Herschwang), 115
Matl, Lutz, 11
Matrei, 173, 177, 203
Matschidel, Klein-Michel, 181
Matten (priest at Bludenz), 13
Matthes (of Puster valley), 217-8
Maurer, Hansel, 77
Maurer, Kunz, 243 n.6
Mayer, Hans, 70, 131, 177
Mayer, Jörg (aka Rock), 116, 184-5, 195
Mayer, Martin and wife, 174, 227
Mayer, Rosina (widow of Leohard), 239 n.5

INDEX

Mayer, Walser, 62
Mayerhofer, N., 24, 64?
Mayerhofer, Caspar, 53, 64?
Maximillian, Emperor, 42, 75
Maximillian II, King, 200-2
Mayr/Mayer, Hansl, 132, 177
Mayr, Martin, 174
Meissau, 89
Meran, 4, 16, 31, 50, 159, 171, 175-6, 203, 249 n.43
Meschevius, 122
Mesner, Helena and Sigmund, 220
Messerschmied, Mathias (also B.), 10, 24
Metsburg, 43
Metzger, Hans, 174, 177
Meysl, Michael, 174
Michelsberg, 36, 38, 43-4, 49, 69, 79, 98, 114, 121, 147, 246 n.5
Mickh, Hans (Innsbruck bookseller), 166
Mieders, 176
Mils, 39
Mitler, Michael (from Schwabthal), 34
Mödling, 120, 128-31, 157, 248 n.1
Mölten, 43-4
Mörtzen, Baltasar (Christina, daughter of), 218
Montfort, Count Wolf von, 78, 158
Moos, 43-4, 47, 49
Moravia (region, estates, lords), 34, 39, 47, 49-50, 53, 59-60, 62, 65-7, 70-3, 76-89, 93, 98, 101-22, 128-34, 137-40, 143, 146, 154-5, 157-63, 165, 167-82, 185-6, 192-221, 225-7, 237 n.1, 241 nn.49,52,56, 245 n.1, 246 n.14, 247 n.18, 249 n.44, 250 n.67, 252 n.122, 254 nn.74,79, 260 n.25, 261 n.39
Moser, Jakob, 30, 139-42
Mühlbach bridge, 147-8
Mühlwald, 182, 217
Mühlwalder, Georg, 217
Müller, Dr. Gallus), 117-9, 140, 143-5, 148-54, 158, 161, 164-5, 171, 175-6
Müller, Jakob, 211
Müller/Müllner, Ulrich (from Clausen), 24-5, 63, 98, 184
Müllner, Jörg, 116
Müllner, Thoman, 187
Münichau, 20, 22, 33, 54, 236 n.16
Münster (Westphalia), 98-9
Münsterthal (Val Müstair, Graubünden), 199
Mürz, 108

Näss, Hans, 145
Nanders, 144, 222-3

Natz, 217-21, 255 n.96
Nauders, 180
Nauk, Martin, 53
Nesis, Hans, 175
Netherlands, 102, 151
Neuhaus an der Ache, 80, 90-1, 139, 183
Neumarkt, 43, 50-2
Nickhinger, H., 41, 236 n.25
Nickinger, Leopold, 41, 239 n.5
Niederdorfer, Lienhard (sister of), 212, 214?
Niederhofer/Niderhofer, Niclas and wife, 116, 132-3, 161, 164, 166
Niedermayer, Apollonia, 30
Nieder-Vientl/Vintl, 16, 147-8
Nielauer (of Vilnöss), 116
Nortzen, Linhard, 14
Nuremberg, 8, 10, 13, 30, 230 n.2

Ober (of Herschwang), 115
Oberecker, Hans (of Affers), 128
Oberlahn, 33
Oberpannin, 33
Ober-Vintl, 161
Ochsenhauser, Wolfgang, 15-6
Ochsentreiber, Urschl, 39
Oder river, 63
Oetting, 167, 204
Oetz valley, 36, 42, 143, 145, 149, 170, 174, 199, 214, 217
Ofen, 20, 61
Offenhauser, Erasmus, 91, 95, 113, 131, 139, 176
Onach, 114
Onofrius (husband of Helena von Freyberg), 54
Oswald, the "Old" (see Hellrigl?)

Partzner/Partener, Jakob, 40, 53-4, 65, 238 n.32
Passau, 34, 108-9, 182
Passeyer, 131, 133, 163, 202
Pauhofer, Thomas (and sister), 136
Paul (from Kitzbühel, see Paul Kessler?), 22
Paumann, Jörg, 11
Paumgarten, Martin, 14-5
Paumkirchen, 12
Pegner, Bartl (wife and children), 216
Pediller, Christian, 79
Penon, 50
Pergmüller, 176

Pertulo, Friedrich (wife and eight children), 203
Peter, priest in Adige, 174
Peytelstein, 43, 48, 68
Peringer, Heinrich, 79
Petersberg, 33-4, 42, 52, 64, 75, 78, 129, 144-5, 149-50, 155, 158, 161, 166, 176, 180, 241 n.57, 250 n.73
Peutinger, 18
Pfaffenberg, 33
Pflaurenz, 43, 236 n.38
Pfitsch valley, 65, 147
Pfunderer Mountain, 3
Pintlechner, Georg, 223
Pirger, Hans, 42
Pitz valley, 146, 214
Planer, Andre, 47-8, 67
Planer, Christian, 237 n.3
Planer, Jakob, 202, 218?
Platner, Mathias, 214
Plattner, Hans, 202
Plattner, Virgil, 33
Platzer, Jakob, 214-5, 222, 258 n.35
Platzer, Melchior, 209-11
Plener, Philipp (Blauärmel), 61-2, 83, 85-8, 122
Pock/Bock, Ludwig, 79, 136, 139
Podolia, 169
Pöcker(in), Christina, 219, 221?
Pögerer, Georg, 213
Pögli, Hans, 11
Poland, 39, 127, 169
Polt, Paul, 41
Prader, 116
Prags, 47, 114, 117
Prague, 74, 137
Prandtner, Gotthard, 213
Prefels, 36
Prenz, Georg, 146
Prew, Adam, 121, 246 n.24
Prezin, Gertrud, Elsbeth, 76
Preu, Hans (administrator at Gufidaun), 50-1
Prugg, 64
Prugger, Hans, 170
Pruner, Gregori, 197-8
Prunner, Jakob, 174
Puch (near Rattenberg), 41
Puchl, Caspar (wife of – Urschi?), 76, 215 (Rauchenpüchler?), 243 n.6
Puchler, Vincenz, 76-7

Püchl (town in Passau), 33
Pürchner, Andre, 213-4, 260 n.9
Pürchner, Hans, 181, 256 n.21
Puster valley, 43, 45, 47-8, 52, 62, 68, 70, 73-4, 77, 79-80, 85, 88, 91, 98, 110-13, 118-9, 128, 133, 137, 140, 142-3, 146, 148-9, 156, 158, 167-8, 177, 181, 199, 201, 213, 217-8, 222, 226, 237 n.1, 241 n.52, 243 n.6, 249 n.44

Raderer, Melchior, 167
Räsen/Räss, 110, 219
Raiffer, Leonard, 168
Rainer/Unterrainer, Hans/Balthasar/Martin, 140, 143, 168, 226
Rankweil castle, 211
Ratfeld, 41
Rattenberg, 11-2, 14-5, 18-9, 21-3, 25, 27-8, 31-3, 35, 40-2, 48, 52- 56, 63-6, 68, 71, 73, 77, 79, 129, 146, 149, 170, 172, 182-3, 197-8, 201-2, 212, 216, 226-7, 230 n.2, 233 n.42, 235 n.47, 236 n.26, 239 n.5, 243 n.6, 258 n.2
Rauch, Michael, 56, 239 nn.5,6
Rauchenbüchler, Caspar, 214-5
Redler, Matthes, 203
Regensburg, 13-4, 30, 140, 231 n.44
Rehlinger, 10
Reinhardt (Barefoot monk), 23, 41
Resch, Ambrosi, 217
Resch, Michael, 42, 236 n.31
Reublin, Wilhelm, 60-1, 238 n.47
Reutte, 11, 22, 42, 211, 252 n.118
Rhegius, Urbanus, 7-10, 19
Rheinland, 60, 213
Ridau, 65
Riedemann, Peter, 122, 168, 190
Rieder, Stephan, 70
Rindler, Cyprian, 143
Ritten, 36-7, 43, 45, 50, 78, 129, 139, 163
Rittner Horn, 31, 34, 36, 43, 76, 239 n.5, 240 n.40, 241 n.57
Rodeneck/Rodenegg, 51, 66, 68, 71-3, 78, 110, 121, 129, 136, 147, 155, 163, 179-80, 182, 216, 226, 241 n.57
Rogg, Martin, 172
Rotenburg, 14, 21, 65
Roth, Hans, 22
Rottenburg, 27, 30-1, 146, 174
Rothholz, 21, 129, 202
Ruemer, Paul, 79, 115
Ruepel, 71
Rumler, Jörg
Rumler, Justina, 78

INDEX

Rundler bridge, 147-8
Rungen, Ulrich, 42
Rychard, Wolfgang, 7
Sailer (see Lanzenstiel)
St. Andreasberg, 110
St. Clara monestary (Brixen), 131
St. Gall, 16
St. Georgen, 65, 112, 182, 217, 227
St. Lienhart, 110
St. Lorenzen, 44, 47, 70, 93, 138, 149, 179, 222
St. Pilgrim's, 36
Salern, 97
Salzburg, 15, 19, 21-3, 31, 35, 39-41, 75, 77, 122, 128, 140, 169, 181-2, 199, 201, 213, 239 n.5, 242 n.70
Sarn valley (Sarnthal), 19, 64, 68, 76, 128, 140, 163, 223
Sarntheim/Serntheim, 43-4, 134, 166
Sattler, Hans, 76
Saylerin, Apollonia, 166-7, 253 n.32
Säxl (of Aich), 223, 226-7
Saxony, 6, 17, 35, 177
Schackowitz/Tschakowitz, 103-6, 168, 227, 254 n.79
Schaichnagl, Georg, 214
Schaller, Balthasar, 217, 219-21
Scharl, 186, 199
Scharlinger, Christoph, 227
Schefter, Matthäus, 140
Schlesinger, 93
Schiemer, Leonard, 21, 23, 25-8, 233 nn.22,32,35
Schilling, Peter, 64
Schilling, Thomas, 48
Schlaffer, Hans, 22, 29-30
Schlatten/Schleitheim, 122
Schlanders, 50, 181-3, 199, 213-4, 222-3, 260 n.9
Schlegel, Adam, 61
Schmerbacher, Leonard, 81-3, 243 n.1
Schmidt, Bastl/Wastl, 214, 216-7
Schmidt, Caspar, 64
Schmidt, Christl, 111
Schmidt, Linhard, 80
Schmötzl, Gregor (wife and children), 212
Schmyren, Hansin, 69
Schnäfel, Caspar, 167
Schneider, Caspar, 237 n.3
Schneider, Gilg, 131, 138, 151-2? 161-2?, 199?
Schneider, Hans, 30
Schneider, Stoffel, 195, 199?

Schneider, Valten, 76, 161-2?, 199?
Schneiderknecht, Vincenz, 79
Schneller, Hartl, 203
Schöffl, Matthes, 168
Schöneck, 43-4, 64, 109-10, 112, 116, 121, 129, 132-3, 135, 143, 146, 149-51, 161, 173, 181-2, 201-2, 239 n.5, 249 n.44
Schröffl, Georg, 69
Schütz, Niclas, 187, 189-90, 193
Schützinger (Simon/Sigmund), 49, 60-2, 81-7, 121, 239 n.5
Schuls, 199
Schuster, Caspar, 67, 74, 155
Schuster, Michael, 243 n.6
Schuster, Oswald (and wife), 155, 168, 240 n.29
Schwärzl, Clemens, 204
Schwarz, Hans, 159
Schwaz, 4, 10-1, 16, 21-3, 29-34, 41, 52-5, 63-6, 70, 73, 75, 79, 98, 144, 146, 157, 166, 170, 172, 180, 186, 199, 230, 233 n.32, 260 n.5
Schwedlinger, Georg, 212
Schweidnitz (see also David of Schweinitz), 109
Schweighofer, Hans, 35
Schweizer, Hans (from Schlitters), 212-3
Schweyger, Franz (*Chronik der Stadt Hall*), 4, 7, 39
Segesenschmid (see Schmid, Bastl)
Seifenseider, Michel (of Wallern), 128
Seiffrit/Seyfritt, Jakob, 207-8
Seiler, Leonard (see Lanzenstiel)
Seilerin (see Saylerin)
Seligmann, Stephan, 4
Senesigen (see Jenosien)
Sensenschmid (see Schmidt, Bastl)
Sepach, 33
Serntheim (see Sarntheim)
Seyer, Christoph, 182
Sier, Ruprecht, 214-5
Silesia, 47, 62, 109, 168, 237 n.1
Sillian, 74, 198, 222, 227
Singer, Hans, 13
Spängler, Stoffl, 168
Sober(in), Margaretha, 221
Sonnenberg, 11, 38, 42, 65
Speier, 15, 38, 234 n.20
Spital, 48
Stabmüller, Wilhelm, 38
Stadler, Ulrich, 39, 43, 88, 154, 169, 243 n.6, 254 n.54
Steiner, Niclas (aka Ziegler), 227
Stams, 10-13, 34, 63, 73

INDEX

Steffan (of Braunegg, priest), 117
Steier, 108
Steinabrunn, 105, 167, 253 n.37
Steinach, 53, 65, 73, 101, 170, 172-4, 177, 180, 183, 187, 204, 216, 241 n.63, 254 n.74
Stein, 14, 33, 182, 203, 237 n.39
Steiner, Adam, 41
Steiner, Anna, 112, 116, 168, 253 n.43
Steiner, Hans, 136
Steinfelder, 42
Steinheis, 64
Stephan (Augustinian in Rotenburg), 14
Sterzing, 4, 15-6, 24, 30-1, 35, 39, 42-4, 63-9, 71-3, 76-8, 98, 107, 110-13, 129-33, 136-7, 148-9, 163, 170, 174, 179-80, 182, 185, 197-9, 203, 219, 222-3, 226, 240 nn.29,36, 241 nn.57,63
Steurowitz, 60, 103
Stixner, Adam (of Lafiss), 204
Stoffel (of Villach)?, 71?, 168, 220-1
Stoss, Anton, 35
Strauss, Jakob, 7-17, 230 n.7
Streicher, Hans, 41
Streicher, Kath., 236 n.25
Stubai, 173, 176-7, 180, 187, 199, 217-8, 237 n.47
Styria, 20, 118, 161-2, 165
Swabia (Swabians, League of), 4, 32, 34, 60, 62, 100, 168, 232 n.1, 234 n.14
Switzerland, 3, 10, 19, 50, 159, 206-7, 259 n.1

Täxler, Andre, 179
Tagwerker, Peter Urban, 140
Tarant, 180
Tauber, Balthasar, 221
Tauer, 33, 42, 65, 115, 172, 182
Taufers, 13, 19-20, 43, 64, 73, 91-5, 110, 115, 180, 182, 198, 204, 212, 216, 223, 244 nn.6,15
Tauscher, Hans, 181
Tauscher/Tausch, Josef/Jost, 260 n.16
Telfs/Telfe/Telfano, 34, 144, 176, 182
Terenten, 132, 180, 198
Terlan, 76, 136, 140, 249 n.44
Teutenhofen, Michael von, 90, 93-7, 244 n.14
Teutsch-Noffen (see Deutsch-Noffen)
Tetscher, Paul, 166
Teys, 64
Thal, Balthasar, 70
Thaler, Christian, 67, 144
Thaya river, 105
Tiers, 50, 227
Tischler (from Brirlegg or Brixlegg), 27

Toblach, 43, 48, 252 n.122
Tonauer (of Schwaz), 55
Tonig (near Lüsen), 131, 135
Tracht, 104, 227
Traindl (see Hutter, Katharina)
Tramin, 24, 43, 50-1
Trapp, Jakob, 19
Traut, Oswald, 214
Trens, 115-6
Trent (bishop, cardinal), 10, 14-5, 31, 52, 103, 109, 135, 139, 142, 144, 151, 159, 163, 165, 232 n.56
Triefe, 22
Troger(in), Anna (wife of Wolfgang Wolfgruber), 220-1
Troier, Anna, 132
Troier/Troyer, Caspar, 227
Troier/Troyer, Peter, 132, 164, 164
Troier/Troyer, Paul, 147, 151
Trotter, Nicolaus, 98
Truer, 29
Tschakowitz (see Schackowitz)
Turk(s), 9, 171

Uhl, Georg, 145
Ulrich of Spaur, 52
Ulrich, Duke of Württemberg, 106
Umhausen, 42
Unterrainer (see Rainer)
Untervientel, 76
Upper Austria (*Oberösterreich*), 15, 20-1, 26, 73, 135, 146, 151-2, 173, 247 n.17
Ursala (of Wangen), 172
Utt, Caspar, 167
Uttenheim, 135, 173, 197, 202, 204, 212, 222-3

Valmereis, 131
Vasser, Jörg (aka Fasser), 22, 31, 33-4, 84-5, 120-1, 157, 239 n.5, 243 n.6, 247 n.13
Vels, 35-6, 239 n.5
Venediger, Balthasar, 166
Venice, 52
Vest, Balthasar, 42
Vienna, 20, 38, 59, 102-3, 109, 118, 122, 128, 165, 182, 193, 200, 231 n.44, 244 n.32, 252 n.122
Vientl on the Eisack (Isarco), also Untervientl, 33, 76
Villander, 17, 43, 143
Villgraten, 10, 155
Villnöss, 64, 70
Vintschgau, 33, 181, 183, 186, 203, 213-4, 222-3

INDEX 281

Vinsterwalder, Hans, 21, 31, 33
Vintler, Johann, 24
Vöklabruck, 21, 23
Völs, 37, 43, 50, 142
Vomp, 73
Voyt, Peter, 88, 243 n.6

Wälsch-Noffen, 64
Wärtl (of Natz), 219
Walder, Cässl, 218
Waldner, Michael, 98, 115
Walpot, Peter, 205
Waltenhofen, Agnes (Trautmannsdorf, widow), 160-1
Waltenhofer, 5
Wangen, 36, 43-4, 172
Wasserburg, 73, 79, 174, 200
Weber, Georg, 43
Weber, Gregori (from Pflaurenz), 48, 53?, 236 n.38, 237 n.7, 239 n.5
Weber, Hans, 214, 216
Weber, Veit, 182
Weiss, Gall, 219, 221
Weissenbach, 131, 179, 185, 239 n.5, 249 n.44
Weitenthal, 174-5
Wellenburg, 42
Welsperg/Welsberg, 47-8, 66, 68, 70, 237 n.1
Welser, 10
Wenger, Georg, 222, 261 n.39
Wenns, 42, 216
Werd, Jörg von (Werth), 42, 236 n.31
Widmann, Beatus, 14, 144
Widmann, Michael, 252 n.118
Wiedemann, Jakob, 30, 49, 60
Wiener, Hans, 159
Wilhelm, Duke of Bavaria, 54, 73, 109
Wilhelm, Jost, 211
Winkler, Dr. Johann, 94
Wipp valley, 201
Wiser, Wolfgang, 95
Wilten, 65, 187
Wittenbach, Ulrich, 24
Wittenberg, 6, 18
Wolf Junhans (of Herschwang), 115
Wolfgang (cowherd from Sarn), 19
Wolkenstein, Anton von, 20, 90-3
Wolkenstein, Christoph von, 155, 181, 216-7

282   INDEX

Wolkenstein, Hans von, 94-5
Wolkenstein, Lady Elspet, 92-3, 95-6
Wolkenstein, Sigismund von (Paul/Paulsen), 54, 92-3
Wolkenstein, Wilhelm von, 98
Worms, Edict of, 5, 13, 19
Wurmb, Augustin (from Bixlegg), 34
Wurmbs, Jakob, 203

Zaunried, Jörg (Zaunring), 27, 37, 45, 49, 53, 60-1, 117
Zell, Peter, 198
Ziller valley, 11-2, 31, 39-40, 169, 199, 201, 214, 223, 226
Zimmerman, Margaretha/Paul/Erhard/Jakob/Martin/Wölflin/Wolfgang, 76, 80, 90-1, 175, 180, 243 n.1, 246 nn.14,15
Znaim, 34, 102, 106, 109, 144, 245
Zott, Hans, 10
Zuckenhamer, Hänsl, 21-67
Zwinglian, 20, 42, 102

www.ingramcontent.com/pod-product-compliance
Lightning Source LLC
Chambersburg PA
CBHW051936290426
44110CB00015B/2006